MEN
IN
GREEN
FACES

GENE WENTZ

AND B. ABELL JURUS

St. Martin's Paperbacks

This novel is a work of fiction. All of the events, characters, names and places depicted in this novel are entirely fictitious or are used fictitiously. No representation that any statement made in this novel is true or that any incident in this novel actually occurred is intended or should be inferred by the reader.

MEN IN GREEN FACES

Copyright © 1992 by Gene Wentz and Betty Abell Jurus.

Library of Congress Catalog Card Number: 91-19940

ISBN: 0-312-95052-7

Printed in the United States of America

St. Martin's Press hardcover edition / April 1992
St. Martin's Paperbacks edition / June 1993

10 9 8 7 6 5 4 3

With great respect and deepest gratitude, this novel is dedicated to the men and women of the Armed Forces of the United States, and written for those silent warriors about whom Gene Wentz says, "It was a privilege and an honor to have served alongside the members of SEAL Team."

ACKNOWLEDGMENTS

WE OWE DEEPEST THANKS to our families, especially Bessie and Skip, for their support, patience, trust, and love, while we trekked mountains and beaches, nights, and disappeared to write, days, for twenty months plus. Great appreciation goes to writers Jean Jenkins, Barbara Hartner, and Virginia Fidler, for their invaluable critiques and also to Bill Martinez, Michael Steven Gregory, Mark Clements, and Cheryl Carpenter for their valuable input. Special gratitude goes to early teachers Madeline Tabler, Joan Oppenheimer, and Charles Jerry Hannah, and to the writers of the Santa Barbara and Southern California * San Diego Writers' Conferences for sharing their knowledge. Many, many thanks to an old and dear friend, our most valued, straight-arrow, Beverly Hills agent, Mike Hamilburg, and to senior editor Jared Kieling, for "sitting right up" and taking the risk, and his assistant, Ensley Eikenburg, for help and humor. To author Shane Stevens, a fellow practitioner of the White Art, thank you forever. And to those many others who, although not listed by name, know who they are, we are ever grateful.

Becoming a U.S. Navy SEAL Team member is strictly a personal and voluntary choice. At any time during training, deployment, or in the midst of battle, a SEAL can simply announce that he's had it, doesn't want to be a member of SEAL Team any longer, and he will immediately be returned to the original unit from which he volunteered. During training, especially during Hell Week, more leave than stay. Once Hell Week is completed, few—very damned few—stop being SEALs, active or not . . . for the rest of their lives.

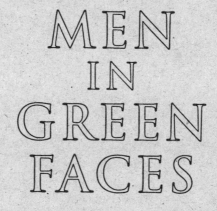

MEN
IN
GREEN
FACES

CHAPTER ONE

THE DEADLIEST MEN IN Vietnam's Mekong Delta were operating . . .

Deep inside the triple-canopied jungle, Brian, at point, held up a clenched fist. The silent stop-look-listen signal passed from point, down the line to Gene, and back to Doc in the rear. The seven SEALs froze, ten feet apart, seeing what wasn't supposed to be there. What wasn't on any map.

Gene, his M-60 aimed wherever he looked, smelled death, looked at death. His chest and throat tightened, adrenaline pumping. One step forward out of the jungle, where he stood invisible in the green shadow, and he'd be in there. The 60 moved very slowly, poised like a cobra.

The SEAL squad had inserted into the jungle hours earlier, after being taken nine miles upriver by boat into enemy territory. From their insertion point into the NVA Secret Zone, they'd patrolled to within two and a half klicks of the mission objective, an NVA Rest and Recovery Center. Progress had been slow. Well trained, all with hard-target combat experience, they'd snaked through dense jungle, weapons off safe, locked and loaded, never disturbing the natural sounds of the environment. The SEALs secured everything metal with green duct tape and made sure they moved quietly.

Now they almost didn't breathe. In there, the jungle was beyond quiet. Totally silent. No birds, snakes, monkeys. Not even the constant insect hum.

To Gene, standing motionless and sweat-soaked in the stifling heat, it looked like the ancient rotting thing had been lifted from a horror film and just inserted in the jungle. A square-shaped structure, like a fort in a western movie, gray with age, sat up on stilts in the center of the fifty-by-fifty clearing. Gunports, high up, looked outward like empty eyes.

No sign of gun barrels or of any kind of life. There were only the walls of thin, rotted tree trunks, tied together with aging rope and rusted wire. Unevenly cut, but sturdy. Dangerous. He breathed out slowly. Probably booby-trapped—both the clearing and that fearful building—from the jungle's edge where they stood, clear through to the far side. The 60 moved again. God, but the place was eerie.

After seven hours in the jungle, he, like the rest of the squad, wore a virtual bodysuit of mud. Sweat dripped into his eyes in spite of the olive-green bandana tied around his head to keep his dark, curly hair off his face and the sweat from washing off the green and black face paint. White-knuckled, he stood his ground and shuddered . . .

Something really bad had gone down here. A lot of people had died. Died real bad. Massacred. He could sense death, feel it. The mud in that clearing—deep, endlessly deep. Year after year of leaves falling, vegetation decaying. Animals dying in there, sinking down into the sludge to join the bodies of men . . . French, Viet Cong, whoever killed, whoever died . . . the men and their weapons . . . all in there, rotting away. God, it stank.

If they went in—no sign of an entrance on the side that he could see—a man on each corner, one at the entrance, two inside, would their squad be the next layer of bones and weapons? In the wet heat, he shivered.

Hand signals, a half-circle followed by the direction to take, came back from Jim: Retreat into the jungle, skirt around the clearing. Avoid. Gene lifted the 60 away, safety off, locked and loaded, as it had been since leaving Seafloat, as it would be until reboarding, whether that was hours or days from now.

The seven SEALs moved as one, disappeared into the returning bird and monkey cries from the trees, and faded into the jungle.

Gene never looked back, but the image of the fort was locked in memory forever. No Patrol Leader's Order could have anticipated a head-on encounter with ancient death. Not when they'd had no intelligence, never dreamed such a monstrosity existed.

Earlier. 1600 hours. . .

Between ops, Gene Michaels, in swim trunks and canvas jungle boots, squatted in the shade beside Lima Platoon's hootch on Seafloat, smoking a cigarette and studying the jungle, as was his habit. The barges that made up Seafloat were anchored midriver on the Son Ku Lon, near Old Nam Cam in the Tran Hung Dao III region, and they were always a target. An added attraction for the NVA and VC was Solid Anchor, the airstrip the Seabees were constructing on the bank next to them.

He kept an eye on the muddy brown river as well, though previous sapper attacks had always come at night. He drew hard on his cigarette as Lt. (jg.) Jim Henshaw came around the corner of their hootch and settled down beside him.

"Gene," he said, "I'm going to run an operation. It's cleared through the platoon's officer in charge. We're going in and eliminate an NVA Rest and Recovery Center. If possible, bring out a hostage for intelligence. You want to be my assistant patrol leader?"

Muscular, tanned, his eyes now as hard as the grin that, tracer-like, flashed and died, Gene looked at the boyish face of his lieutenant. "Sounds like a good op, Jim," he said, his voice low against the cadence of distant thunder over the jungle. "What do you need me to do?" He stood, took a last drag, and flipped the cigarette butt in a high arc off Seafloat into the river.

Jim, too, got to his feet. "Talk to the men, tell them the Warning Order time, set up early chow with the mess hall. And Gene, meet me at the helicopter pad at 1300 hours for a visual recon."

The wall of the hootch was as unyielding as the shoulder Gene leaned against it. "Which men do you want?"

Henshaw named them and left. Gene Michaels went hunting. If the others were drinking, and they usually were, they needed to quit now. And maybe he could avoid running into Willie, who'd want to go, knowing damned well he couldn't, because he wasn't a SEAL. Willie, his best friend, was a photo intelligence specialist and took too many risks as it was, going out with the Kit Carson Scouts. Gene just wanted the southern aristocrat from Tennessee to live long enough to go home and get married as planned.

No such luck. Willie stepped away from the far side of the SEALs' plywood hootch just as Gene rounded the corner.

"Whoa, Gene, I know that look. Y'all are jungle bound. Need a double on the op? Here I stand. At your service, sir."

Gene shook his head. The guy was a redheaded rooster, always ready for combat, but he wouldn't live through a SEAL op, and with him along, neither would the SEALs. "What's the matter, Willie? The Kit Carson Scouts toss your rebel ass out?"

Willie took hold of the chain around his neck and dangled a gold cross at Gene. "Not while I've got this. This is their good-luck charm, and it doesn't go without me attached." He laughed. "Now, if you're smart . . ."

He'd never met a more happy-go-lucky guy than Willie. Though he went out with the Kit Carson Scouts, the KCSs, as a fill-in, he mainly worked with their two combat military advisors, sat in on interrogations. Willie could read aerial photos like most people read road signs. Gene shook his head. "Sorry, friend. We're covered."

Willie's green eyes narrowed. "Doc hates—I say, he hates—to operate. I'll have a word with him."

Gene shook his head. "Not a prayer. Doc's going. He's got no choice. But you, you're going back to The World and get married. That's an op worth experiencing."

"Since you're the only one married in the squad, I bow to your assessment."

"Count your blessings."

"I'll save them for y'all," Willie said.

They clasped each other's shoulders, as close as they ever came to a hug.

"Catch y'all later."

"Right." Gene turned away and didn't look back. Didn't need to. He could feel Willie seeing him off, as always. He operated so often, with his own squad or another, that it was almost a daily ritual.

At 1300, he met Jim at the helo pad down at the far end of Seafloat. The chopper was already warming up. They climbed aboard and took off to inspect the terrain they'd be patrolling into.

Half an hour later, they landed and went directly to the briefing room where Sea Wolf and Mobile SEAL Support Teams, along with the five other members of the SEAL Team squad, were already waiting. Jim walked to the front of the room. Gene secured the door, then dropped into the nearest chair. Double security.

There was a knock on the door. Now, what the hell . . . He opened it to see Willie.

"Flash report," Willie said.

Gene took the sheet of paper. "Okay. Thanks."

Door secured again, Gene scanned the report, then walked it up to Jim.

"Flash report from intel," Jim explained, then relayed the contents. "Information is needed on an NVA advisor, a Colonel Nguyen. It is believed that Colonel Nguyen was previously a double agent, known as Lieutenant Dong—a former Vietnamese SEAL who infiltrated the LDNN program about three years ago, and who disappeared before he could be apprehended."

Shit, Gene thought, a Vietnamese SEAL! No damned wonder nobody can catch him—trained like us, thinks like us, operates like us, knows what we do, how we do it. He'd be dangerous as hell.

"So," Jim went on, "interrogate all POWs concerning the whereabouts and the movements of this individual. The colonel is recruiting throughout the Mekong Delta. Information reports that if he gets any resistance from the local villagers, the villages and indigenous are being eliminated." He looked around the room. "Just keep in mind that we want this guy."

Whole villages and all the villagers? A butcher. Yeah, Gene thought, we want him. Colonel Nguyen. He'd make it a point to remember the name.

"The mission objective," Jim began, "is a North Vietnamese Rest and Recovery Center. We're going in to collect information, take a hostage, search and destroy the rest."

Gene watched the helo crews and the boat people throw quick glances at one another. The five other SEALs, sprawled in their chairs, were still, focused on Jim. No mission was ever the same. They needed to know exactly who would be doing what, and what they'd be carrying.

"Okay," Jim said. "We take no water, no food. Brian, you're

point man. Take a Stoner with eight hundred rounds of ammo, a nine-millimeter with a Hush Puppy, two magazines of fourteen rounds each. 'X' the nose of the bullets. One in the chamber. Four grenades—two fragmentation and two concussion—one claymore mine with a thirty-second delay fuse, two pop flares—one red, one green. Two smokes—one green, one violet. Pick up an area map at the platoon leader's office. You'll also need a Lensatic compass and a flashlight with green lens."

From the back of the room, Gene saw the seaman nod. Brian Norwood usually drew point position because, at five foot three, 135 pounds, he was the smallest man in the squad, able to go into tight places in heavy brush and find them a path through the jungle—their eyes and ears up front. Good at spotting booby traps, good at navigation. And the Hush Puppy, with two magazines plus one round in the chamber, would give him the capability of fifteen silent kills.

Jim told each man what to take, following the same order they would patrol in. He named himself next. "I'll be the PL. I'll be carrying a Stoner, eight hundred rounds, two LAAWS rockets, Hush Puppy with two magazines, two smokes—one red, one green—and two pop flares, map, compass, and flashlight with red lens."

Gene watched Jim take a careful drag of his cigarette. The ash was about three-quarters of an inch long. Maybe the PL would, one day, be able to smoke one to the end without the ash dropping off.

"Roland, you're radioman. M-16, four grenades—two fragmentation, two white phosphorus—four pop flares—two red, two green—an extra battery for the PRC-77 radio, ten pounds of C-4 in two five-block charges with five-minute delay fuses."

Stretching out his legs, he glanced over. Garson, the second-class radioman, was a good communications specialist. Lousy poker player, though. His face gave him away every time. His favorite phrase fit any and all situations: Everything's all fucked up. Made Gene laugh, so it became a private joke between them, and Roland muttered it each time they met. It was the way Roland said it.

Clearing his throat, Jim went on. "Assistant PL and automatic weapons man is Gene. Take eight hundred rounds for your M-60 and a few grenades, map and compass, flashlight with green lens." He took a careful puff and the ash fell off.

Gene kept a straight face and nodded that he understood. Jim ground the cigarette out.

"Grenadier is Alex. XM-203, four hundred rounds of 5.56 ammo, thirty rounds of 40 Mike-Mike, two claymores, twenty rounds of high explosive, five rounds of white phosphorus, and five fléchettes."

Third Class Alex Stochek was their real loner. Strange, silent guy. Woke up with a hard-on every morning. Must be tough on his women, Gene decided. The only one of the squad with a full beard, he was hot with the XM-203, an over-and-under weapon with an M-16 on top and a grenade launcher underneath, but the fléchette seemed somehow more evil. Its pattern was like a shotgun's, only each load was a cluster of barbed darts about half an inch long. Ugly. Strange guy. Yearned to make a knife kill. Really strange.

"Stoner man, Cruz Bertino. Take the Stoner, eight hundred rounds, four grenades, two LAAWS rockets, two claymores—one with a thirty-second delay fuse, one with a one-minute delay—and two pop flares—one red, one green," Jim continued.

Cruz, the original cumshaw man. First words out of his mouth, most times, were "You owe . . ." Half the time they called him You-O, and if Gene remembered correctly, Jim owed Cruz first choice of his next box of cookies from The World—back home—in exchange for the case of Pepsi You-O produced out of nowhere two nights past.

"Rear security is Doc Murphy. M-16, six hundred rounds, medical kit to include emergency surgery kit, chloroform pack, two hand grenades, and two five-pound charges of C-4 with five-minute delay fuses."

Gene's grin flashed. The second-class corpsman hated operations where enemy contact was likely. Doc was a SEAL but hadn't gone through training. He'd had Basic Land Warfare, SEAL Basic Indoctrination, and diving school. He hadn't gone through Hell Week. Assigned to SEAL Team's Lima Platoon, he had no choice over going. He constantly protested, "Goddammit, I'm not a SEAL. I'm a corpsman. You can count on me to treat you, but don't count on me for battle." He'd fire his weapon, but as soon as somebody got wounded, he'd quit firing to care for the man. He hated to operate. Just despised it, because he wasn't a SEAL. Still, if Gene ever had to operate with just himself and one other man, Doc would be the other.

Jim turned his attention to the Sea Wolf crews, the two pilots, two copilots, and four gunners who would man the two helicopter gunships. "We need two helos. Fully loaded rocket pods, two M-60s on each gunship, with as much ammo as you can carry."

Hottest pilots in the world, Gene thought. They'd go anywhere, do anything, to get the SEALs out alive.

He watched Jim pace, glance down at the paper in his hand, then look at the boat personnel, the eight men from Mobile SEAL Support Team unit assigned to Lima Platoon. "We need two MSSCs, Medium SEAL Support Crafts. I want two .50-calibers with five thousand rounds each on each boat, as well as two M-60s with five thousand rounds, per weapon, per boat."

"Uniforms." Jim announced the second half of the briefing, as was SOP—standard operating procedure—for the Warning Order. "Everyone in the patrol will have cami tops, pants—Levi's 501s or cami bottoms—jungle boots, insect repellent, first-aid kits, UDT SEAL life jackets, knife, UDT emergency flare, and green and black face paint."

Behind them, Gene stood up and stretched. UDT, he thought. Underwater Demolition Team. Frogmen, they were called, and they were good at what they did. Had some aboard Seafloat, but in spite of what people thought, UDT people weren't SEALs, and SEALs sure as hell weren't UDT. The UDTs hadn't had the massive amounts of advanced training SEALs got.

"Inspections are set at 1530 hours, ready for patrol. Help each other out. Jump up and down and make sure nothing rattles, and that everyone has all the equipment and ammo brought up. Patrol Leader's Order is at 1600 hours," Jim finished. "Eat early. See you at 1600. In uniform. Ready to go."

Gene unlocked the door, stepped out onto Seafloat's deck and into steaming heat. The rest of the details he and Jim had worked out for the op would come later, during the PLO. It was his time now. He needed it to stay alive, stay sane . . . go quiet and read from his little pocket Bible. At least he still had his faith, but he'd given up a long time ago his high school dream of becoming a missionary. Becoming a SEAL had changed him too much. Now the jungle and the enemy were waiting . . . and so was he.

The Viet Cong, partly because of Gene Michaels, came to believe the Navy SEALs could fly, could breathe underwater, and could not be killed. Other military people who encountered them believed they were individually and collectively crazy. Nobody, not even other Special Forces, messed with the SEALs, one of the deadliest and most elite intelligence-combat entities in the world, a status shared only by Britain's Special Air Services.

The SEALs of Lima Platoon, legendary for their fierceness in combat, were base-camped in midriver on Seafloat, one of the hottest AOs—areas of operation—in Vietnam. Lima numbered fourteen SEALs, divided into two seven-man squads. Though assigned to Lima's first squad, Gene operated not only with both squads but with other squads on Seafloat and with the Kit Carson Scouts, the Montagnards, and any other unit that wanted him and his 60. They all did. He was the most lethal of all the SEALs, and he loved to operate.

The men swore his big M-60 sang in combat, with a firing rhythm that was his alone. SEALs who'd operated with him insisted they'd recognize the *da-da-da, da-da-da, dut, dut, da-da-da, da-da-da, dut, dut* rapid-fire music of his 60 forever after.

He stood six feet tall, weighed two hundred pounds. When his laughter died and he went off alone, his features icy, his eyes gone from brown to black, not even Willie dared approach. But the squads considered Gene their lucky element. No SEAL on patrol with him had ever died. Nor had any ever been seriously wounded or captured.

Gene had caught some shrapnel, and he carried flecks of it still, inside his left wrist and arm. He refused to report such minor injuries, knowing a report would cause a Purple Heart to be forthcoming. Having seen the savage wounds others sustained, he had his own ideas about when a Purple Heart was called for.

Carrying a pack of Marlboro cigarettes in the left pocket of his cami shirt, and in the right pocket a small Bible, read before and after every mission, he ignored his squad's comments about luck, the kidding about his praying. He just counted, like beads on a rosary, the number of times he should have been dead—they should all have been dead—and was silent.

CHAPTER TWO

BY 1600 HOURS, THE ten-by-twenty-foot briefing room on Seafloat had been secured and the Patrol Leader's Order was under way. Tarps, rolled down over the three-foot-wide screened windows, muffled the voices inside. Outside, two armed SEALs stood security on opposite corners of the building, able from their positions to take all four sides of the structure under fire. Only those involved were allowed to know anything about the upcoming operation.

Inside, the Sea Wolf and Mobile SEAL Support Team crews, along with six of one of Lima Platoon's seven-man SEAL squads, settled into green or gray metal folding chairs. The SEALs lounged in them, some tilted back against the plywood walls. They looked completely relaxed. Gene Michaels, at the rear, had his head propped on one hand, his other arm across the back of an empty chair, his long legs stretched out in front of him, and his M-60 slung, hanging at his side, but his concentration was total, focused on the seventh SEAL, Jim Henshaw, patrol leader for this operation.

Nobody took notes. Everything pertaining to the operation, their parts and the other men's parts, had to be committed to memory. Except for the sound of Jim's voice and an occasional shift in someone's position, the room was silent.

Jim paced in front of the blackboard and situation map, both permanently attached to the wall behind him. The situation map showed all past operations run in any particular area; the locations were marked by colored pins. Red meant heavy enemy contact at that coordinate. Yellow signified light contact. Green, no contact. There were very few green pins among the fields of red and yellow.

Gene, scanning the map, focused on a particular green pin, thought of Doc, and couldn't help but grin. That op had been a honey.

They'd inserted in early afternoon, and the seven of them were about an hour into the jungle with another hour and a half to their objective, a tiny Viet Cong village. Intelligence had it that the village hosted an NVA encampment. The SEAL squad headed in to check the situation out. If the NVA had indeed moved in, the SEALs would call in the coordinates, their helo gunships would bear down, and the whole area would disappear.

As always, Gene remembered the heat. Patrolling through dense foliage beneath the three ascending heights of trees, the tallest hidden from sight by the two levels below, they'd sweltered in the dim light under the triple-canopy jungle. The heat joined with the deep, stinking mud and the insects to make the squad truly miserable. None more so than Doc, walking rear security, whose face made plain that he was one unhappy corpsman. He purely hated to operate.

The Mekong Delta ran water everywhere in the form of rivers, streams, creeks, and canals. Shit ditches, the SEALs called them, due to the people's habit of using them as toilets. Nobody wanted to fall into one. Not even the villagers. And especially not Doc, who saw them as writhing with bacteria, fungus, and God knew what else. And here they were, Gene thought, with a narrow canal to cross and no bridge.

Jim had signaled that the squad should improvise a monkey bridge. As silently as possible, they foraged for dead and fallen palm branches and layered them across. With their boots caked with mud, they crossed one at a time.

Gene remembered Brian, on point as usual, walking carefully out on the narrow monkey bridge, the branches giving slightly under his weight. Jim crossed next, followed by Roland. They immediately stood security for the rest.

Carrying the 60, and loaded with ammo belts, Gene had

weighed the most. He stepped on the bridge and felt it bend under him, but it held. The fronds were slippery, but his balance was good. Once he was back on solid ground, he sighed with relief and took his security position.

When Cruz and Alex were across, Doc started. By then, the monkey bridge bore a thick layer of mud. Midway, Gene saw Doc skid. At the moment his feet went out from under him, he yelled, "Oh, no!" and landing astraddle the spiky fronds, let out a Tarzan shriek that must have echoed across the entire Mekong Delta. Gene couldn't believe his eyes or his ears. Teetering out there on the branches over the shit ditch, Doc was inventing new words at the top of his lungs between howls of pain and fury.

Gene thought about going to help him, but didn't dare. Doc was having such a fit that he'd probably shoot the first person who went near him. Biting his lip and trying to keep a straight face, Gene glanced at Cruz, who caught Jim's eye, who looked at Brian and Roland, who stared first at Doc, then Gene. Gene shook with silent laughter. Tears came to his eyes. When he saw Alex struggling not to laugh, and Alex saw him, it was too much. The entire squad lost control. Tears streamed down green and black faces. They roared. Arms around their stomachs, holding their sides, rolling on the ground, they howled, while Doc called them every SEAL and Vietnamese name he could come up with.

With their location completely blown, Jim aborted the mission. When they could stand up, six recrossed the monkey bridge to head back to Seafloat. Doc refused. He waded. Dripping wet, testicles swelling, he waddled along at rear security, hissing unprintable things with every step. Gene couldn't remember ever laughing so hard and so long. The 60 and its ammo had weighed a little less on the way back from that op . . .

Gene looked away from the no-contact green pin just in time to catch Brian grin at him and shake his head. He knew their point man had also been remembering Doc and the monkey bridge.

"Okay," Jim said, and took a deep breath, "let's get on with it. Patrol Leader's Order."

Gene straightened slightly in his chair and prepared to listen to the tactics he and Jim had worked out. Under the layers of bandoliered ammunition, he flexed his shoulder muscles and the patrol leader began.

"*Situation:* As indicated in the Warning Order. Our target is an R&R Center for approximately ninety NVA officers who have been released from hospitals and are being . . . are getting ready to take command of enemy forces throughout the Mekong Delta.

"*Enemy forces:* Intelligence reports there are a minimum of three companies of NVA, constantly on patrol around the NVA officers' R&R Center.

"*Weather:* Tonight should be overcast, possible chance of rain. Sunrise at 0530. Sunset at 2050. The tide will be going out during extraction. High tide at 0130.

"*Terrain:* Basically a triple canopy, as indicated by the visual reconnaissance that took place earlier today. If by any chance the weather clears up, there'll be very little light coming in due to the triple canopy.

"*Identification of the enemy forces:* Not known, other than the fact that they're NVA, who are used to protect the R&R Center.

"*Enemy strength:* Seven hundred fifty to a thousand enemy forces."

Seven of us, Gene thought again. The hard grin flashed. Good odds.

"They are not based at the R&R Center. They have company camps set up in different locations around its perimeter, ranging from five hundred to a thousand meters from the R&R Center."

"*Friendly forces.*" Jim looked up. "There are no friendly forces."

There never were. Gene adjusted the position of the 60. Before they ever went into an area, they made sure no other operations were going down. When the SEALs operated off the Float, the area they went into became a free kill zone. Anybody they encountered was considered the enemy and therefore a target.

"*Mission of the next higher unit,*" Jim continued. "Again, there are no other operations taking place in the AO.

"*Location and planned action of units on the right and left:* Again, there are no other operations within the AO.

"*Fire support available for the patrol:* We have two Sea Wolves, which we'll be using for air support, and they can be called upon for emergency extraction. We have two MSSC units."

The SEALs looked at the Sea Wolf and MSSC personnel, studying them, watching their expressions, making sure they understood, would be ready.

"*Mission and routes of other patrols:* Not applicable. We are the only friendly forces within the Secret Zone.

"*Attachments and detachments:* None, other than the Sea Wolves, who will remain on Seafloat up until the time they are called by radio to bear fire support, and our MSSC vehicles, which, after insertion, will be standing by on the Son Ku Lon river until the time the extraction is called for and/or emergency extraction is necessary.

"Our mission this evening . . ."

Gene focused intently on Jim. Here it came.

". . . is to infiltrate the R&R Center, pulling out or abducting one of the highest ranking officers, who will be returned to Seafloat for interrogation and then released to the V Corps Interrogation Center. The rest of the R&R Center will be destroyed. We will take no other prisoners."

Gene didn't move. "No other prisoners" translated instantly to an image of explosions, screams, total annihilation.

"*Area or location:* This is going to take place approximately 11.4 miles up the Dam Doi River, in the northern section of the Secret Zone. Coordinates of our target are 68745832. MSSC will take us to the river just west of the Dam Doi, approximately 9.4 miles in, to our insertion point at 68745832.

"*Execute, concept, plans, objective area:* We are going to patrol into the southwest side of the R&R Center. Insertion coordinates are 83783761 for primary. We will take compass bearing, thirty-five degrees magnetic. We will be patrolling about four thousand meters to the objective site with the Dam Doi River to our right."

Jim paused and looked up for a moment, then continued. "If we can't get in with compass bearing, we will connect with the Dam Doi River and take it up to the objective site. Intelligence reports three guards inside the compound. Once the objective is in visual sight, we will stop the patrol, and that location will be our primary rally point if anything should happen before completion of the operation. If nothing does happen, prior to the charges going off, all members will rally back to that location."

Gene made quick eye contact with the others in the squad.

Everybody understood. Especially Doc. He looked ready to bite the barrel of his weapon in half.

"There are two roving guards patrolling the east and west sides of the compound." Jim tapped the blackboard. "Intelligence reports also reveal that there is a heavy-machine-gun emplacement at the south end of the compound, just inside the open area and backed in against the trees of the jungle. Here. The diagram on the board shows the locations."

The chalked-on diagram stood out on the green board, white and solid. Gene studied it, listening to Jim.

"Brian and I will eliminate the two roving guards using our Hush Puppies." He looked at the rear of the briefing room. "Gene, can you take out the gun emplacement? Silently?"

All eyes focused on Gene. Knife kill. From the back of the room, he answered with one word, "Yes," and realized his hand had found the hilt of his bowie knife. He moved it back to the 60. The men looked back at Jim—except for Alex, who was pointing to himself and mouthing "Me." Nobody could figure what went on in his head, Gene thought. Strange, weird guy. He wanted the kill.

"Prior to Brian and myself eliminating the two sentries," Jim continued, "I will be leaving the two LAAWS rockets with Roland, and Roland will give Brian ten pounds of C-4 explosives with five-minute delay fuses on them."

As Jim named names, Gene, with the rest of the men in the room, studied each man's face to make sure he had no hesitations, no unanswered questions. Mistakes were almost always fatal.

Jim paced, pointing out locations on the board. "Roland, Alex, Cruz, and Doc will set security for Gene taking out the heavy-machine-gun emplacement, and take up positions ten to fifteen feet apart on both sides of the gun emplacement so, if need be, we can take the entire compound under fire in support of Brian and myself. Roland and Alex will be on the left side of the machine-gun emplacement, and Cruz and Doc on the right side. I suggest fifteen-foot intervals, but maintain sight of each other."

He cleared his throat and went on. "Brian and myself will each place five pounds of C-4 approximately two feet in on the underneath side on each corner of the main structure housing the ninety officers. All three buildings are on stilts, about three feet off the ground. Brian will be on the west side and I'll be on the east side, which will put me between the structure housing the ninety and the NVA doctors' hootch. There are five doctors. The number of personnel sleeping inside the security hootch is unknown. I will be looking inside the officers' quarters to see about the feasibility of bringing one of them out prisoner.

"While I'm looking in, if at any time the op is compromised, Brian and I will hit the deck, Gene and the other security will take all buildings under fire, firing into them at a three-foot level and up, which will enable Brian and me to crawl back out and head into your location.

"Gene, if the shit hits the fan, I want you to take the officers' quarters under fire. Primarily I want you to take the main structure under fire."

The scenario ran like a movie through Gene's mind.

"Alex, if the shit does hit the fan, I want you to drop 40 Mike-Mike into the security building. It's the closest building to our security element's location. And then everyone will be raking the buildings at the three-foot level. *Everybody.*"

Jim cleared his throat again, smoothed his headband on both sides, then continued. "If everything goes to plan, and we can take out a prisoner of war, I will bring him out, placing him on the ground. Then Brian and I will pull the fuses on the C-4 charges. I'll pick up the POW and move into your location.

"Once the hostage is captured, Cruz will be responsible for carrying the POW to the extraction point. If we should take casualties, Doc will render emergency treatment on location and, if need be, Doc will use the fireman's carry to get the wounded man out. If we take more than one casualty, the nearest man will be responsible for carrying him out to a safe location where Doc can render first aid.

"Again, when Brian and I, with the hostage, get back, we will all come on line, and at the time the C-4 is detonated, Brian, Cruz, Doc, and myself will fire the LAAWS rockets. Two into the center of the main structure housing the ninety officers, one into the doctors' hootch, and one into the security hootch. Along with, if need be, 40 Mike-Mike, should any building remain standing.

"At that time, we'll get back into patrol formation and head due south for approximately five hundred yards."

With the whole world coming after us, thought Gene.

"We will swim across the Dam Doi River to the far bank, setting up security for the crossing, and patrol down the east bank to our extraction point."

Gene grinned. Doc's sour expression left no question about what he thought of getting into the river water.

"*Time of departure:* 1700 hours. We intend to return to Seafloat at approximately 0600 to 0700 hours.

"*Alternate route,* if need be, will be straight down the Dam Doi River."

God help us if we have to go alternate. Gene swallowed. They'd be eleven long miles in, and all of it enemy territory.

"*Organization of movement:* As stated in the Warning Order.

"*Chain of command . . .*" If they were, one by one, killed or wounded, Gene thought. Would God, the element the other men called luck, keep them safe? "Myself," Jim said, "patrol leader. Gene, assistant patrol leader. Brian will be third in the chain of command. Cruz, fourth. Alex, fifth. Roland, sixth. Doc is seventh in the chain of command."

If it came down to Doc, they were all dead. Doc would die too because he'd never leave them, even if the last man was seconds from dying, and they all knew it. That's why he was seventh. Gene stroked the 60. The enemy would never take and torture Doc, then kill him. Not if he still breathed. Doc knew too much. He'd pop the pill and suicide before sure capture, just like they would. They all had a pill.

"*Action in danger areas.*" Jim illustrated with hand signals as he spoke. "A hand across the throat indicates danger area after a halt sign has been given. Gene will take up the left flank. Alex will take up the right flank. We will send Brian across. He will search up to fifteen meters on the other side of the danger area, whether it be the river or an open area."

Scary, Gene knew from experience. Damned scary. He looked at Brian. The expression on his face didn't change.

"Brian will come back out, and if it's all clear, will give the come-forward sign. I'll go over. Once I'm halfway across, Roland starts across. Then I want Cruz to come across, and then Doc will come. Once you, Doc and Cruz, are across, you will pick up our left and right flanks to protect Alex's and Gene's crossing. We'll stay in that position for about five minutes; stop, look, listen, to see if anyone detected our crossing of the danger area. This order will be consistent—SOP—throughout this operation.

"*Actions on enemy contact:* The squad is broken down into two sections, if need be, for fire and maneuver."

Maneuver, Gene noted. His section.

"The first element will consist of Brian, myself, and the radioman, Roland. The second element will be Gene, Alex, Cruz, and Doc. We want to avoid contact if at all possible, but if we have to engage in combat, we will use fire and maneuver, in which we'll all bring fire to bear on the enemy to gain fire superiority. Once fire superiority is achieved, the first element will move in a direction given at that time, ten to fifteen yards back, while the second element maintains fire superiority. Once we have moved back ten to fifteen yards, we will pick up fire and Gene will move his element back ten to fifteen yards beyond our position.

"If need be, we will set up our claymores."

Gene's fingers tightened on the 60. The whole world would be coming after them, all right.

"We have our 40 Mike-Mike and grenades to help break contact as well. If we all maintain our personal discipline throughout our patrol, we should be able to avoid any contact."

Personal discipline, Gene thought. The bottom line of training. If you're shot, make no sound, die silent. If you're terrified, do your job, stay silent. Controlled breathing, controlled thoughts, controlled emotion. Do it, make no sound, execute the plan, become a machine to keep yourself and the other SEALs alive and achieve the mission objective.

"If a secondary target should arise, we will take the same actions as at the danger area, bringing up Gene and Alex to the flanks of the objective, and eliminate the secondary target. Silently, if possible. If this cannot be done silently, we will avoid the contact. The elimination of the ninety officers, and the abduction of one, is of high priority."

Very high priority, Gene thought. Good officers were damned hard to replace, that level of intelligence hard to get. He shifted on the hard metal chair. His bandoliered ammo was uncomfortable to lean against over a long period.

"If we encounter any patrol as we draw near the objective, I will signal by putting both hands out from my sides, waving you into the jungle, on line, as you are, allowing the enemy patrol to pass. We will not take them under fire unless we've been compromised. If we are compromised at any time on this operation, prior to getting to our objective, we will abort the mission."

Jim continued to pace. "If we make contact on either flank, use fire and maneuver. If we make contact head-on, use the Australian peel-off: Point will open up, fully automatic. Once his rounds are out, he runs down the side of the patrol and the next man opens up, fully automatic, straight in front. The point man goes to the rear of the patrol as I open up. When my magazine is empty, the next man opens up, fully automatic, then he goes to the back of the patrol. So it keeps leapfrogging backward in line. While everyone else is firing, the man at the end of the line is reloading his weapon."

Gene grinned. Shit-hot, that tactic.

"*Rally points and acts at rally points* will be determined in the field as the patrol is en route to and from the objective. If we are in a file formation, everyone will maintain their fields of fire. If we are called in on a circular formation, I will place each man personally into a location with your backs toward the center of the circle where myself and Roland, with the radio, will be located. This will enable us to have a 360-degree field of fire.

"MSSC people, you've been given our insertion coordinates, 9.4 miles up the river. Once we're off the boats, we want you to go back downriver and bank close to the mouth of the Dam Doi River, on the Son Ku Lon river.

"Sea Wolves will remain on Seafloat and be ready to cover our extraction if necessary and/or be in support of emergency extraction.

"We will maintain radio silence during the entire operation. Our primary frequency is 3570. Secondary is 4085. Our call sign is Tobacco Road. The boats' call sign is Rolling Papers.

"*Passwords:* If at any time the patrol is broken up, or we send out a search element to check out a particular area, to avoid opening up on our own people, believing that they may be the enemy, our passwords will be Bloody Mary. The stationary group will initiate when they hear the movement coming in by challenging with 'Bloody.' The returning party will reply 'Mary.' The challenge will be given two times. If we do not get the proper response or reply, we will take those individuals under fire."

Gene watched Jim rub both sides of his olive-green headband. He was getting ready to go.

"*Emergency signals:* During the patrol, we will maintain radio contact by using the squelch method. We will initiate contact by three squelches on the radio. If you read loud and clear, you reply with two squelches. This will be done every hour on the hour. If we've lost communications, and we're ready for extraction, we will send up two green pop flares. After five minutes, if we're too far away for you to see the green flares, we will continue to patrol south until we make radio contact or the flares are visible to you."

Gene studied Roland's face. A damned fine radioman. The MSSC people looked like they had no problem, like they understood. They'd better.

"As the boat moves up the Dam Doi River to our extraction location, we will be able to make radio contact and bring you in on our location by using a series of short flashes of a red-lensed flashlight and voice communications. If it's an emergency extraction, we will send up two red pop flares. If you see the red pop flares, scramble the Sea Wolves."

Crazy, hot pilots. Gene studied them. Really awesome to watch.

"Come up the Dam Doi on step. Full bore, opened up. When you're close enough to our location, and we make radio contact, we will direct you into our location.

"If emergency extraction is required, we will need all guns bearing on location, as directed by radio communication. By that time, Sea Wolves should be overhead, and we will direct rocket fire into the target area."

Almost finished now. Jim adjusted his headband again. Gene leaned slightly forward.

"Once more," Jim said, "I want to state that our primary objective is the elimination of the officers' R&R Center. This will have a direct impact on enemy operations throughout the Mekong Delta. We will avoid contact at all costs which could jeopardize this operation.

"Safety is paramount," he said, pronouncing each word distinctly and with emphasis. "If we don't get them today, we can still get them tomorrow.

"*Rehearsals:* We will go over the blackboard again, showing the locations where everybody will be, as it was stated earlier in this briefing. Are there any questions?"

During the long pause, Gene had watched the men shake their heads in answer to Jim. No questions. They'd been ready to go. Bulky with ammunition and weaponry, faces, hands, arms, necks, every inch of exposed skin, covered with green and black face paint, everything taped down, the squad had risen to study the blackboard and situation map.

From the moment that they'd left the briefing room to board the boats transporting them upriver, they had been operating off safe, locked and loaded. Now, hours later, out in the jungle, the eerie fort relegated to future nightmares, Gene concerned himself only with achieving the objective, the R&R Center, without dying along the way.

CHAPTER THREE

A SEAL SQUAD ON patrol moves in silence, at the speed of its slowest man. Carrying his heavy 60, bowie knife strapped low on his right hip, and with fifty-six pounds of bandoliered ammo body-fitted around his hips and crisscrossing his chest, Gene set the pace, glad to leave the fort behind.

The wet heat, even in the deepening green shadows of the jungle, maintained its intensity. Drenched with sweat, Gene slogged through mud a foot deep, making sure he didn't trip or get a boot caught among the roots that snaked out from the trees. Automatically he sorted out the sounds of the jungle, listening for those of NVA or VC patrols. A single metallic click, and they had a target, or were one. Instantly the squad would fire, tearing up the jungle and any other living thing within range.

Their wagons were circled even when they walked one behind the other, Gene thought. At point, Brian's field of fire was 180 degrees, from side to side. Behind him, Jim took the field of fire to the left. The radioman, Roland, aimed right, Gene left, Alex Stochek right, Cruz Bertino left, and Doc Murphy secured the 180 degrees at their rear. Together, they could pour five thousand rounds a minute into their kill zone. Establishing immediate fire superiority was crucial. Failure meant they died, unless they broke contact with the enemy fast. The last thing they wanted was any unexpected contact with the enemy. A sudden firefight would abort the mission.

Gene, who hated snakes and creepy-crawlies, kept an eye out for signs of the enemy—the outline of a hidden shoulder, a glimpse of a gun barrel—as well as bushes covered with the fiery ants called *dau-dits*. Drawn by body heat, they dropped like mist to the man or animal below. A *dau-dit* attack, with its instant welts and excruciating pain, would stop the squad on the spot. He had gone into a shit ditch, ammo and all, the time they got him.

He blinked, clearing sweat from his eyes, watching for movement, for trip-wired booby traps on the ground, for grenades, and for the bamboo vipers that hung from branches about head height. They called the vipers two-steps because you were dead before you could take the third step. The rest of the patrol was doing the same.

Freeze. Brian, at point, signaled. He had run into impenetrable brush and would have to search for a way through. He faded into the tangled dark greenery and disappeared.

In the deep shadows, Gene, like the rest, maintained position, waiting. They were well inside a Secret Zone, places no American had ever entered. The NVA and Viet Cong considered them secure. They were not far now from the NVA R&R compound. All through the Secret Zone, Charlie patrolled in force. Had to avoid him, get to the objective. Afterward, they'd *didi-mau* to the Dam Doi River for extraction.

Ten feet ahead, the radioman, Roland Garson, signaled *forward.* Gene passed the signal to Alex Stochek, ten feet behind him, and moved out, still thinking taking a hostage would be dangerous. He'd rather KISS—Keep it simple, stupid—just eliminate the ninety officers, plus the doctors, plus their security people.

He stepped over and around tree roots, weaved under and between low-hanging vines and branches, ignored the eight-inch-deep sucking mud, and trudged on. The air hummed with insect sound. Eerie, that fort, that dead-quiet clearing. Movement caught his attention. Gold butterflies just covering that bush ahead . . . like little bits of sunlight fluttering away. They were making good time in spite of the damned mud and roots. Just a couple of miles more.

Ahead, Roland's fist was in the air: Halt. He cupped his ear: Listen.

Gene froze, signaled back to Alex, and listened. Soft voices. Somebody out there . . . over there. He pointed: There! Roland looked back. Gene signaled: There. Roland gave the thumb-up I-understand signal and turned away to signal Jim, ahead of him.

Jim, Gene knew, would send Brian out to search and identify while the silent squad maintained their stop, look, listen position exactly where they were. For a second, a series of images flashed through his mind, triggered by the yellow butterflies: a golden sunset he'd swum into, back in The World, during SEAL Team training on Coronado's Silver Strand. San Diego's skyline was across the harbor, golden too, at sunset, as gold as the lining of Tommy Blade's blue and gold instructor shirt during Hell Week, and—

Signal from Jim: Retreat.

The seven moved back and away, deeper into the jungle. Jim silently pointed them into position. Gene watched the PL motion the squad members to his position, one by one, while the rest set security, relaying Brian's report and what the tactics would be. There was no debate. "SEALs," Tommy Blade had stressed, "don't argue tactics."

"B-40 rocket team," Jim whispered when Gene moved up. "Three VC, setting up a night ambush on the riverbank two hundred yards out on our right flank." He shifted the position of his Stoner and smoothed his green bandana, first on one side, then the other.

Gene waited, then leaned in again, his cheek against Jim's to hear the next barely audible words.

"We'll sneak up behind them. SOP. You and Alex on flank; Brian and me, center front with the Hush Puppies. Roland, Cruz, and Doc will maintain rear security. Soon as we eliminate them, you'll all guard our backs while we conceal the bodies."

Gene nodded, moved back to his position, watched Jim signal Alex up.

They moved out at twilight, barely able to see each other. But then, he thought, they didn't need to. The positions they were taking were SOP. Each knew where the others would be, what they'd be doing. Moving left to the flank, peering through the dimness, he spotted the B-40 ambush team. Joe Shit, the ragman

. . . VC. The three Viet Cong, scrawny, wearing dingy black pajamas, barefoot and hatless, squatted side by side, looking out through a screen of bushes at the river. Still talking, the *dau-mau-mee*, the motherfuckers.

One slow and careful step at a time, he moved toward a thicker area of trees and brush ahead and to the left. Once set, he aimed the 60 to position the three VC directly in the center of his kill zone. No matter what happened now, the B-40 team was dead.

Through the concealing foliage, he watched Jim and Brian slowly moving closer and closer behind the three VC to get clear shots. A branch cracked. Adrenaline sparked through his body like an electrical charge. The right VC's head began to turn. The Hush Puppies coughed softly, simultaneously. Two heads exploded. With two bodies in spasm beside him, the third VC's eyes were wide with shock as he spun around. A third round killed him.

Gene doubted the VC saw the source of his death, it came so fast. And now Brian and Jim walked to the bodies. The Hush Puppies coughed three times more, making sure. SOP. He turned his back then, watching outward, but hearing the sounds of the bodies and the rocket launcher being dragged away and covered with mud and brush.

Had to eliminate them, he thought, straining to see through the gathering darkness. Could have blocked the squad's extraction, blown up the two MSSC gunboats coming to take them back down the river. Once the squad hit the R&R Center, everything in the area would be coming after them. God, it was getting dark. The black of night was like no other black, in the jungle.

Silently the squad re-formed and moved forward, each SEAL with his hand on the life-jacket-covered shoulder of the man in front of him. There was no other way. Gene could barely see anything and knew nobody else could either. They stopped. The pale tinted glow of Brian's green-lensed flashlight moved against the map in his hand, then went out. They continued, one careful step at a time. Pause. Stop, look, listen. Go again.

At point, Brian held a long, pliant twig before him, checking out anything that bent it. Things like wires to booby traps. The rest of the squad had better catch anything he might miss. Gene moved with extreme caution, covered with mud, stinking with mud, the smell of his insect repellent and sweat masked by mud. Only the 60 was halfway clean.

It took the next hour to travel three hundred yards. Finally they got past the deepest mire to easier footing and were able to set a faster pace. When they heard the sound of running water, the squad stopped to locate the tiny stream. Gene rinsed caked mud from the bandoliered ammo for his 60. The water ran cool over his hands. They moved on.

Two and a half hours before dawn, they reached their objective—the NVA R&R Center.

Gene crept forward, moving in on his hard target, the lone NVA soldier manning the compound's machine-gun emplacement. Backed up to the jungle, the gunner could take the entire R&R Center under fire.

Invisible on his left, but close behind, were Alex and Roland. On his right, Cruz and Doc set security. Somewhere in the dark, near the officers' quarters, Brian and Jim counted the minutes allotted for him to eliminate the machine gunner. The final moments in the two roving NVA guards' lives were being measured out at the guards' own pace, each step they took bringing them nearer to the two waiting SEALs.

Gene inched forward, barely disturbing the foliage concealing him. He was a moving shadow among the flickering shadows set in motion by the small campfire in the clearing's center. The gunner was a stupid bastard, looking at firelight. His night vision was destroyed. He sat dreaming, not hearing. The fire crackled.

In the dark before dawn, Gene crept forward, moving closer and closer to the gunner, who was now stretching his arms and yawning. Just a little time left until the Hush Puppies would cough and the roving sentries would be corpses. Jim and Brian knew that if, in taking out the sentries, they didn't draw fire, he had been successful in taking out his own hard target.

One ever-so-careful step at a time, he moved forward, barely disturbing the stems and stalks that concealed him. He was going through mud, weeds, reeds. Stiff stalks brushed against his body. He came in low, ghosting through them, breathing their green, dank, thick smell. Smooth, silent, easy. The target stank of sweat.

Two body lengths away.

The bowie, with its long, dark, razor-sharp blade, was out. The hilt was familiar, comforting, solid, in his palm. Closer . . . closer. Flex the body. Smooth movement. Think black. Think invisible. Think earth. Silent. Breathe quiet, slow. Don't look at target's head . . . he'll feel your eyes . . . just the shoulders leaning against the earthen barricade. Closer. Another inch . . . another. Could touch him now. Closer . . . close enough to hug. Silent . . . don't breathe. Blade a silhouette against the firelight . . .

Go!

Adrenaline shooting—a purple haze. Left hand clamped hard over the mouth. Violent motion pulling head back . . . hard. Quick, fierce slice across the throat, forearm across the severed carotid artery . . . silence the gurgling, bubbling air from the windpipe. Body spasming. Hold. Blood pouring. Hold. Quiet, heavy. Lift the body over the side, set it down in the inky, jungle blackness. No time to hide it. Slide over and into the emplacement. Breathe. Wipe knife on pants, sheathe it. Breathe . . . swallow. *Stop, look, listen.*

Nobody woke.

Nobody heard.

Satisfied, Gene extended his arms, swept them forward, signaling to the four behind him: Come up on line. He pulled on the 60's sling, brought it around from his back to its firing position at his side, and scanned the compound, the 60 tracking with his eyes. He checked the NVA's heavy machine gun, making sure it was off safe, locked and loaded, like the 60. Cruz, Doc, Alex, and Roland were moving up to flank him. He couldn't see or hear them, but he knew.

He glanced left and right. Good. There they were now, two on each side of him, about fifteen feet apart.

He studied the rectangular building housing the ninety sleeping officers. Entrances were on both ends. Brian and Jim were up there, each going toward a doorway, Jim to go in, bring the nearest officer out. Top ranks always got beds next to the doors.

He shivered. Hard to swallow. One unnatural noise, and all hell could break loose. His hands and arms were sticky with blood. Hard to hold the NVA gun easy. Breathe slow. Slow. His breath shuddered in his throat, almost a sob. He sucked in air that smelled of blood, urine, excrement from the dead gunner, who lay like debris, a shadowy heap. Still. *Look, listen.* A soft sound. He stiffened. So dark, so hard to be sure, even with the light from the dying campfire. Nothing. Another sound, a scrape. The NVA guards dying? He froze. A quick, deep intake of air . . . let it out, soft. Hold it . . .

He glanced left. Roland, his head tipped toward the silent radio on his shoulder and his M-16 in firing position, was probably thinking, Everything's all fucked up, even though it wasn't. Not yet anyway. Alex, his 40 Mike-Mike aimed straight ahead, flicked a look toward him, then away, and Gene knew what the look meant. Resentment over not getting to make the knife kill. The squad's security elements seldom made close-quarter kills, and Alex was security element.

Slight sound again. Natural sound. Branches moving in the trees. Gene stared ahead, saw Brian and Jim carefully set the sentries' bodies under the corners of the officers' hootch, then bend to attach the twenty pounds of C-4 on the underside of the stilted building, placing five pounds under each of its corners, about two feet in. Jim disappeared inside.

Gene tensed, finger on the trigger, cast a quick look to his right, where Cruz and Doc, weapons ready, now leaned slightly forward, then concentrated on the entrance Jim had used. The seconds went by at a glacial pace before he reappeared with a chloroformed hostage slung over his shoulder. The prisoner wore only briefs. His bare skin gleamed pale in the light from the campfire.

Jim set him down on the ground next to the dead sentry. He straightened, brought his fists together, then apart, signaling *pull* to Brian. At opposite ends of the hootch, in unison, they pulled first the rear, then the front delay fuses on the C-4. They now had five minutes to get back. Gene, muscles rock-hard with tension, watched Jim hoist the prisoner to his shoulder and start across the compound toward their position. Brian was right behind, covering their rear.

As soon as they came on line, Cruz took charge of the POW, and the LAAWS rockets were distributed. Moments later, Gene jumped as the C-4 went off, high-order, and clamped down on the trigger of the machine gun. The night exploded into a fiery hell as the LAAWS—two into the center of the officers' hootch, one each for the doctors' hootch and the security hootch—along with Gene's NVA machine gun and the squad's firepower, combined with the C-4 detonations. The wooden hootches disintegrated, blown to splinters, bodies to bloody fragments, pieces flying everywhere. The jungle trembled, shaken with sound and concussion.

Gene grabbed his 60 and leapt out of the gun emplacement as Cruz threw the POW over his shoulder and the squad, automatically dropping into file formation, outright booked, running for their lives toward the Dam Doi and their extraction point. He could hear NVA troop movement coming in from the jungle around the R&R Center. A deaf man could hear them. And he knew what they'd find—the area leveled, on fire, smoldering, pieces of bodies all over the place, and the dead machine gunner. That's where they'd pick up the squad's tracks, start coming, start reconning by fire to get them to shoot back and give their location away.

They slowed, still moving fast, just short of running, Brian up front, leading the way. Cruz applied more chloroform to the POW slung over his shoulder. Had to keep him out. Bullets snicked through the air, thunked into jungle trees. The enemy was closing in faster than they had expected.

They paused just long enough for Alex and Doc to place claymores with fifteen-second delay fuses, then rushed on in the waning night. Sweat poured down Gene's face, stung his eyes. Branches, vines, bushes, grabbed at his body, at the 60. Mud sucked at his boots, unseen roots tried to entangle his feet. Behind him, claymores detonated with a brilliant flash, followed by yells and screams. The sounds of fear, horror, pain, agony, and mass confusion covered the sound of the SEALs' movement, and his own gasps for breath.

The thirty-second delay claymore went down and they moved out again. Get 'em down and move, get 'em down and move. Have to break contact with the enemy coming in. Go, go, go. As if in answer to his silent plea, they ran. Too close, the enemy was too close. Another explosion, another flash of a claymore going.

Screams, yelling behind them. A little more distant now, but still too close, way too fucking close. They had to have support to get out, had to get to the Dam Doi to use that help coming. Please God, no enemy in front between them, the river, and extraction.

NVA and Viet Cong were everywhere, all around them, coming in on them fast. Coming to kill them. Brian dodged, ducked, found them a path, a way through, kept moving. He was lit up for a split second by a claymore going off; all of them were caught in frantic motion by the strobe-like flash. They had to get to the river to get out, but might never have time to cross it.

Gene gulped air, his throat burning, hearing the yells behind them. The enemy was still coming—God, how many of them? 750 to 1,000 reported—but they hesitated with each explosion. Men hurt, screaming, dead, slowed them down for precious moments. Eight hundred pellets from each exploding, devastating claymore, and just as their pursuers got past one, another would go off.

Wordless, he ran on. The explosions were farther and farther behind them. Then Alex had set his last claymore.

And Gene realized they'd reached the Dam Doi.

Automatically the squad's security element went SOP. Cruz, hostage over his shoulder, swung with Gene, Doc, and Alex to face the enemy's approach, whether from flank or rear. Behind them, Brian went into the river and, midway, swam, then waded out on the east bank. He disappeared into the jungle's edge, ran a quick check, and reappeared to wave them across before moving back into the trees to set security for their crossing.

When Jim got about five feet into the river, Roland went in. After him went Doc, who, upon reaching the east bank, immediately set security on their left flank. Cruz followed, taking the longest to cross, the limp body of the POW over his shoulder. When he had to swim, he turned almost on his back with the hostage faceup, across his chest, having reached over the officer's right shoulder and under his left arm to clamp the unconscious body to his own. Side-stroking with his left arm, he crossed the river, his Stoner hanging by its sling underwater. Alex waded in behind him.

On the west bank, his back to the river, for those last few moments, Gene and his 60 stood rear security alone, facing the jungle. Sure death if he didn't cross damn quick. He could hear Alex in the water behind him, heard the normal jungle sounds being disturbed somewhere in front, heard his own breathing.

He held his ground for the last few endless seconds until the splashing behind him stopped and he knew Alex had made it to shore. He spun then and hit the water, wading in as fast as the current would allow, then swimming with the 60 slung on his back.

The smell of the muddy river filled his nostrils. As his powerful strokes brought him closer and closer to the east bank, he was thankful he'd used so much of the 60's ammo, or its weight would have pulled him down and he would have had to walk across underwater.

Wading out of the river, he tipped the 60 up, then down, to drain water out of its bore and chamber.

Gene reached shore, and the squad broke into the jungle just as the enemy hit the west bank and started firing. The SEALs returned fire, gaining fire superiority just long enough to keep the enemy from crossing the river, and long enough to run deeper into the jungle. Back in file formation, they moved south as fast as they could, leaving the enemy firing at where they'd just been.

In front of him, Roland called in on the radio. "Scramble everything! Wolves! Wolves! Emergency extraction! Get those boats up here! Scramble everything! Boats! Wolves!"

Bullets smacked trees. The enemy paralleled them. Some were beginning to cross the river, others were moving south without knowing where the SEALs were but guessing they'd head downriver. Jim and Roland were like Siamese twins in front of him, Jim feeding Roland information in short bursts, Roland calling it in.

Charlie was coming, but so were the SEALs' gunboats and the Sea Wolf gunships. Gene could hear the boats' diesel engines under the sound of the choppers. He saw them now, in breaking dawn, the boats coming in on step, fast, with the Wolves full bore behind them.

Running in front of Gene, Roland called in, "Charlie on the west bank, attempting to take us under fire," and relayed the boat's reply to Jim. "We've taken rocket hits, we have casualties, coming in." Jim yelling to Roland, "Tell the boats and choppers to take the west bank under fire and rocket attack. Our location is east bank. All direct firepower into the west bank." They ran.

Above, the Wolves fired. The MSSCs turned and pulled into the bank at the squad's location. Gene went into the first gunboat and added his 60's firepower to theirs. The 60 jerked in his hands, laying down the deafening, rock-steady rhythm so familiar, so comforting to him now.

The jungle was a nightmare Fourth of July gone mad, with Gene's 60, the Stoners, the grenade launcher, both boats' 60s and

.50-calibers, and the Wolves' rockets. They threw everything they had at their attackers, to gain fire superiority long enough to escape. The boats wheeled, headed down the river on step, with the SEALs firing, screaming now, finally released from the enforced silence of patrol. They screamed and yelled themselves hoarse at the people shooting at them, until they made it far enough down the Dam Doi that enemy contact was broken.

"We have a kill zone about five hundred meters ahead," the boat personnel relayed. "That's where we got hit."

"All reload," Jim ordered. "We're going back through the B-40 kill zone that got the boats on the way up."

Gene, checking his 60 and its ammo, could hear Tommy Blade's instructions during training. "Always save enough ammunition to get yourself home." Gene always had, and he'd always needed it.

Beside him, Jim, his young boy's face tense under green and black streaks of face paint, pushed at his headband and relayed instructions to Roland. "Tell the copters to break contact and cover our extraction through the B-40 team, approximately three hundred feet in front of the boat, on the east bank. We'll direct fire as they come overhead for their rocket strikes."

Less then a minute later, closing on the B-40 kill zone, both boats and the SEAL squad opened up.

Furious, raging, Gene stood—he always stood to fire—entirely gone into the purple haze of firefight.

The Wolves roared over his head, low level, and launched their rockets into the enemy ambush team's location. The explosions were deafening. Still firing as they passed the kill zone, Gene heard a secondary explosion that told him the B-40 team was hit. Then a second blast was caused by their own B-40 rockets going off.

Doc was working at Gene's feet, weapon slung on his back, trying to stop the bleeding gut wound of one of the boat crew on the deck beside him.

Somewhere behind him, Gene heard a moaning, crying, hurt-so-bad sound that wasn't him, wasn't any one of the SEALs. Now, with the other SEALs setting security, he knelt to take Doc's place, render what aid he could to the bleeding crewman, releasing Doc to go to a second man who had arm and shoulder wounds. He worked quickly, efficiently, knowing from training what needed to be done to keep the crewman alive until they reached Seafloat. "It's gonna be okay. You're gonna be okay," he repeated, trying to counter the fear in the man's eyes, even as he worked to staunch the bleeding and ease the pain. He stayed with him until Doc returned. Then he stood again.

He was still standing when they reached, dear God, finally, Seafloat. Standing with his 60 off safe, locked and loaded. Standing until the wounded were lifted into the medical team's care, then moving, blood-encrusted, mud-covered, unseeing, adrenaline still pumping, through and away from the doctors, from Willie, from everyone.

Alone, he put the 60 on safe at last and went to the edge of Seafloat's deck. There he pulled the little Bible from his pocket, the eerie fort, the jungle, the B-40 rocket teams, the explosions, the machine gunner at the R&R Center, the screams, replaying in his mind. He bent his head, closed his eyes, and prayed, before going to eat and then break down his 60, clean it, and get it ready to sing again.

CHAPTER FOUR

GENE TUCKED HIS BIBLE back in his shirt pocket and headed for Lima's hootch. Inside, he grabbed a PBR, a Pabst Blue Ribbon beer, opened it, and took a long swallow. They'd had nothing to eat or drink since leaving Seafloat the day before, and he could feel his adrenaline still pumping. He was uptight, energized, jumpy. The beer would help.

Crisp and sharp, it slid cold down his throat like July lemonade with about as much effect. Two more long chugs finished the can. He tossed it, lay the big 60 on his upper bunk, stripped off his gear and what was left of his ammo, then went to join the rest of the squad.

Inside, the chow hall reverberated with the clatter of breakfast trays and utensils, mixed with the usual talking, yelling, and laughter. Gene went through the food line and to the table where the squad sat. They'd saved a place for him between Roland and Cruz, who were, he saw, stuffing their faces. So were the rest, and so would he, the second he had fork in hand. His stomach felt empty enough to echo.

"Man, we were lucky," Roland was saying. "We should all be dead, as outnumbered as we were. Pure dumb luck."

"And damned good planning," Cruz put in. "Nobody in the squad even so much as scratched."

"You men were great. Just outstanding," Jim said. "I'm really proud of you."

Gene washed down a forkful of hotcakes with milk. "You're damned good operators," he said. "A shit-hot op, thanks to everybody doing what was needed and doing it right."

"Needed, by God. Ever see a place go up like that?" Brian shook his head. "High-order. I mean, it went up really high-order. Nothing left but splinters."

"If they'd had forces between us and extraction at the river," Roland said, poised to take another mouthful of scrambled eggs, "everything would have been all fucked up. We'd never have made it out alive. Really lucky."

"No shit, Sherlock," Cruz said. "Purely luck."

Doc glanced at him. "Can say that again, You-O. Anything could have gone haywire." Doc wiped milk off his upper lip. "The dau-dit bastards could have woke up, turned us to Swiss cheese. Lucky as hell they didn't."

"Had our lucky element here"—Roland nodded toward Gene—"riding his 60. Nobody's ever got killed operating with him. Right?"

Gene looked up. He didn't like that. "What you guys need to realize is, it wasn't just luck. Somebody up there was watching over us."

Down the table, Alex took another bite of toast, listening but saying nothing. Sometimes, Gene thought, it was like Alex had them all stuck on little specimen pins, the way he sat back and observed.

"Maybe so," Doc said, "but did it have to be such a dick-dragger? Bad enough to have to operate in the first place, but it seems like every time I go out, when you're there, it turns into a fuckin' dick-dragger and I get the shit scared out of me. Takes three days just to stop shakin'."

Laughter drowned out his last words.

Jim stood. "Good job. Good op. Every one of you, just hot. The best plan isn't worth a damn unless it's executed properly. You men can really execute."

They left the chow hall and walked in a loose group back to the hootch, where they picked up a case of beer and then their weapons from atop their bunks. Outside, they regrouped around the cleaning table. Methodically they began taking the guns apart to clean and repair, stopping frequently for long swallows of beer.

"Op like that, you begin to understand why they put us through the training they did. Like the mud flats," Gene said, unscrewing both ends of the 60's gas port. "Remember the mud flats?"

"Remember?" Roland's eyebrows lifted. "Ain't no forgetting SEAL training. Thought I'd died and gone to heaven once I made it through Hell Week and Land Warfare Phase on San Clemente Island. Even this forsaken place ain't as bad as that was." His voice went mournful. "Everything was all fucked up. The whole time."

Gene laughed. Couldn't help it. He released the feed tray cover and took it off.

"Time's now. Still can't believe we survived that extraction," Brian said. "They were right on us, every second."

"Never so glad to hear claymores go off, buy us some minutes." Jim reached for a cleaning rod. "Never so glad to see the boats and Sea Wolves coming in on step. Hoo-Ya!"

"Hoo-Ya!" the rest chorused, thrown instantly back to the response learned in training by all SEALs.

"Crewmen on the boat caught it, though." Gene frowned, remembering. "Wonder how they're doing." He set down the nickel that he put behind the buffer assembly. The nickel was one of the modifications on the 60 he'd done. Gave a faster rate of fire, but there were some side effects. The firing pin could break, or the operating rod might not be able to withstand the force of the impact being put on it during firing, so there was always the possibility of fractures or cracks, or the rod breaking, leaving him with a useless weapon.

"Poor bastards," Doc said. "We sure were lucky."

"Hey," Brian interjected. "What did you think of that old fort?"

"Helluva shock to see that thing, whatever it was, way out there in the jungle." Doc shook his head. "Just a helluva shock."

"Eerie," Gene said, visualizing it again. "Really eerie." Holding the operating rod up, he looked it over, shook his head, and deep-sixed it in the Son Ku Lon. SOP if they'd had heavy contact on an op. They had. He'd never had an operating rod break during an actual combat situation and never intended to. A new one went in before every op. "I could feel it," he added.

"Felt it. Yes." Brian reached for the gun oil. "Couldn't believe my eyes when I saw that place. Not the time to be on point. Scary. Just like I'd walked into . . . what do they call those places where . . . like cemetery houses . . ."

"Mausoleums?" Roland looked at Brian, across the table from him. He was cleaning his Stoner. "Ain't there some in the cemetery in Queens?"

Gene listened while he worked with the 60, cleaning the baked-on carbon, first with a scribe, then with a steel brush and gun solvent. Brian and Roland were tight, both being from New York City. They constantly compared their neighborhoods back there. The minute they'd discovered they both liked to eat at Orloff's Deli across from Lincoln Center, and that they both loved to play with the windup toys at the little shop down the street, they were friends.

"No, man," Brian said. "Tomb. Tomb is what I mean. That place was worse than a tomb. No . . . catacomb, like in Rome. I mean, you just knew the bodies, the weapons, everything was still in there in the clearing under all that gray gunk."

They hadn't been able to even think about the fort until now, Gene mused. A result of training. In enemy territory, they just blocked that kind of thing out. Had to keep the mind on the op and survival, and nothing else.

Roland used his wrist to shove a lock of his black hair back off his forehead. "One peek through the brush and I knew everything was all fucked up in that place. Relieved to get away from it."

"Dead," Gene said. "Never been near a place so dead."

Jim, standing next to Roland, echoed Gene. "Dead is the word, all right. Extraordinary, to encounter something like that. Undoubtedly French. Totally unexpected. No reason to go in. Not a sign of life anywhere."

Cruz ran a cleaning rod down the barrel of his Stoner before glancing at Jim, on his left. "Wonder what was in there."

Doc looked across the table at him. "Boom-boom, you're dead, is what was in there. Booby-trapped from end to end. I'd bet on it. Didn't want to put one toe in that clearing. There weren't even creepy-crawlies, and if critters won't go in, men sure as hell have no business hanging around."

"You noticed that too?" Gene asked, reassembling the 60. "Not a breath of air moved. Nothing."

Everybody nodded, remembering. Except Alex, working on his grenade launcher, Gene noticed. What the hell went on in his head? He often wondered, especially when Alex, so quiet, so serious all the time, would break his self-imposed reserve to volunteer to make a knife kill. Gene shook his head. Very strange guy. Candidate to be a Charles Manson once back in The World.

"All I've got to say," said Cruz, "is that we don't deserve to be alive after an op like that one. But, God, it was hot. Ka-boom!"

"Hoo-Ya!" they yelled.

It took a little more time to get the bowie knife clean. Gene offered another silent prayer of thanks as he wiped rust-inhibiting lubricant on the eleven-inch blade. If the NVA machine gunner hadn't been lost in thought, watching the campfire . . . if he'd heard, turned around . . . He wet his arm, ran the blade over it. It shaved. It was sharp enough.

With the 60 and the bowie cleaned, he turned his attention to his personal gear. Unscrewing the CO-2 cylinder from his UDT life jacket, he washed out the activating device, then the jacket itself, before screwing the cylinder back in. He hung the jacket, dripping wet, on the little post at the corner of his top bunk, and the 60 from the sling on his bed frame, ready.

Weapons and gear taken care of, he finally stripped off his wet, stinking clothes and dropped them on the floor. The Kit Carson Scouts' women, the hootch maids, came daily to clean the place up and wash their clothes. Naked, he went back out to the fifty-five-gallon drum sitting next to the cleaning table between the hootches. The drum was always full of rainwater. They used it more often than the showers farther away on Seafloat.

No hot water anyway, Gene thought, using a pith helmet to pour water over his head and body before soaping down. So what was the difference?

Face and body clean of paint, mud, and dried blood, he returned to the hootch, dried off, pulled on a pair of shorts, and strapped the bowie back on. Between ops, it came in handy to cut wire, open crates, whatever he needed it for.

In shorts and shower shoes, he leaned against his rack. What he never wore—what no SEAL wore—was underwear. Another lesson from training. Wet sand in your shorts and you'd be rubbed bloody-raw. During training they were always wet and always sandy.

He looked around. The rest of the squad were either dressed and waiting or finishing getting dressed. And they were still talking about how amazing it was that they had lived through it all.

"Debriefing in five minutes," Jim called as he went out the door.

Gene settled in the same chair at the rear, by the door, that he'd used for the Warning Order and Patrol Leader's Order the previous day. He preferred his back to the wall and the exit handy. Now he began to feel fatigue. None of them had had any sleep for about thirty hours, and the op had, as Doc put it, been a real dick-dragger. Fear didn't set in until they were safely back. Couldn't even think about being afraid out there. Too busy trying to stay alive.

But once back and safe, fear took hold. Shook him to his very soul. Everything he couldn't allow himself to feel during an op, he felt when he got back. Then he tried to drown the fear and blot out the memories with booze. They all did. Sometimes it worked for a while.

Jim walked to the front of the room.

Gene closed the door and settled back. The debriefing, as always, would be very orderly. Basically they'd be going over what had happened from insertion to extraction.

"Everything went to tactic," Jim began. "The first thing is that the wounded MSSC crewmen are doing okay. They will recover, according to the medical people. The second thing is that the captured NVA officer has been released to V Corps for interrogation. Good job bringing him out, Cruz. Now, let's get on with it."

It wouldn't last too long, Gene knew, because they'd had a hard target. They'd gone out to destroy, not to gather intelligence, though taking one NVA officer hostage should provide some.

He listened as each individual discussed what he'd seen during his portion of the op, and then the usual questions were asked: Had they picked up another man? Had anyone been able to catch the identifying marks on enemy uniforms, so they might identify exactly which NVA force or forces were in the area? Had anyone found any defecation? If so, a sample brought back could be analyzed to learn what the enemy's main food staple was. Had anyone seen any of the NVA coming in on them?

Gene knew beforehand the answers would all be no, except for the last, when they'd seen the enemy across the river. Once the R&R Center blew, they'd outright booked, and the enemy never caught up with them. Thank God.

Jim continued with the debriefing, and Gene listened intently in spite of increasing weariness, as did the rest.

"Did anything go wrong?" Jim took his time looking around the room.

No, again. It was a successful op. If there'd been a breakdown, Gene knew Jim would ask if the op hadn't been covered well enough in the PLO, why there'd been confusion out there, and what they could have done to prevent an adverse situation. So the debriefing was relatively simple because they achieved all they'd set out to do, plus taking out a B-40 team on the way into the objective.

They'd actually had two ops, is what it boiled down to, he thought, yawning and shifting in the metal chair. The R&R Center and, coming out, the B-40 rocket team.

"We'll be sending a Vietnamese SEAL out to one of the local villages around the R&R Center, to listen and bring intelligence reports back," Jim said. "In three or four days, we'll have the total numbers of enemy killed in action and wounded in action." He rubbed the back of his neck. "That's it. Good job."

Amid the screeching of chairs being shoved back as the men stood, Gene rose and opened the door. Time to get some sleep.

Back in the hootch, he unstrapped the bowie, hung it on the bedpost, kicked off his shower shoes, and vaulted into the top bunk above Brian's. Lying on his back, mosquito netting pulled down around him, he ached to be standing at the edge of the pines in the Laguna Mountains, east of San Diego, looking out over the endless, golden sweep of desert below. The space of it . . . hawks freewheeling above . . .

He fell asleep to the sound of the droning fans and the voices of Brian and Roland talking about Manhattan.

He woke, with no recollection of dreaming, at 1750 hours, in time for evening chow. The hootch was comparatively quiet. Four SEALs from Delta Platoon were playing poker on a bunk at the other end. Alex and Roland were still asleep. Nobody would bother them. Nobody ever disturbed anyone sleeping without damned good reason. First, it was a courtesy. Second, you could get hurt waking somebody.

Standing at the side of the bunks, he put on insect repellent, swim trunks, his blue and gold SEAL T-shirt, the bowie, and the dry pair of his two sets of canvas jungle boots. He went then to take care of another one of his jobs . . . that of Lima's intelligence petty officer.

He opened the door of the Naval Intelligence logistics officer's hootch, and found NILO Lt. Jonathon Blake still at his desk. A good man, Johnny Blake, but very serious. He respected the SEALs, loved to associate with them. Johnny's responsibility lay in receiving and disseminating intelligence reports from all investigations or intel sources.

Gene liked the fact that Johnny worked well with all the U.S. military as well as the South Vietnamese military. Not an easy job. Too, Johnny would often clear the SEALs' AOs with both the foreign and domestic military commands, and with local and province-level political personnel. When the SEALs inserted, their area of operation became a free kill zone. Damned important that no friendly forces be in there. Whoever they contacted out there died. Johnny made sure no friendlies were around.

"Well, hello, Gene," he said, half standing and extending his hand. "Congratulations. I was glad to hear everyone returned safely, and with a POW. Any intelligence from an NVA officer is useful. What can I do for you?"

"Anything further come in on the NVA advisor, Colonel Nguyen, since the flash report?"

Johnny smoothed his brown, carefully brushed hair. The gold of the Annapolis class ring on his left hand glinted. "Nothing since then. Sorry. You have a special interest?"

"No," Gene replied. "Just doing my job. But this damned colonel, the flash said, wipes out entire villages—people, hootches, everything—in his forced recruitment campaigns. Personally, no special interest. Professionally, yes. Terrorist tactics work. He has to be stopped. We want the bastard bad."

With a sigh, Johnny straightened an already orderly stack of papers at the left front of his desk before looking up, his brown eyes tired. "It's true. His tactics do work. Too well. But no, we don't have further intelligence on the colonel."

"If any comes in, let me know right away, if you would." Gene started out the door, then turned back. "By the way, you have any intel on tonight's movie?"

Johnny smiled his broad smile. "Word is that it's *Bullitt* with Steve McQueen."

"Hoo-Ya! It finally came in?"

"Rumor has it."

"Rumor had it before."

"True. Hope and such springs eternal."

"Yeah. Well, thanks, Johnny."

A few minutes later, standing in line at the chow hall, Gene noticed two things: Willie's waved invitation to join him at the table, and Freddy Fanther, third man in line in front of him. He nodded an okay to Willie, then glared at the back of Fanther's head. Goddamned slipknot. What an asshole. Alligator mouth and parakeet ass. Delta Platoon's pretty boy. Talked all the time about how his looks were going to make him millions. He'd be the new Marlboro man. The asshole was a skate as well. Any work to be done, he found a way to skate out of it. Never volunteered for possible heavy-contact ops. Had to protect his face.

On the way to join Willie, he saw Fanther settle down at a table near the door. No Marlboro man had *that* many freckles. More than a kid with chicken pox. Not only that, Fanther might be a decent operator when he did decide to go, but he didn't like the way Fanther used his weapon. Something about the way he handled that 40 Mike-Mike . . .

"Rumor has it, my friend," Willie said as Gene sat down, "that *Bullitt* has come in at last."

Gene grinned. "So I heard."

"Who told y'all?"

"Johnny Blake, over at NILO."

"I told Johnny."

"Well, hell, Willie, who told you?"

"Half a dozen gentlemen."

Gene laughed. "So what else have you heard?" He waited while

Willie forked up a bite of steak, chewed, and swallowed. A southern gentleman never talked with food in his mouth.

"Heard y'all had a real testicle-cruncher of an op. Not like going after the B-40s on the Mighty Mo."

Willie loved to talk about the Mo. Particularly about that trip.

"Well," Willie was saying, "with the B-40 rocket teams, up in the Secret Zone on the Dam Doi . . . there surely was no way to go up the river safely. And, as y'all knew, we had to go up to recon, so—"

"So *we* went up. Inserted. Made contact and killed those three armed VC. God, I never will forget the one." Gene shook his head in disbelief. "Kept getting up after being shot. Must have been so loaded with whatever he was on. I don't know how many times he got shot, and still he ran off. Finally followed his blood trail and used the 60 to take him out. God."

"And then, Lordy, in comes the Mighty Mo to extract you." Willie laughed. "What a sight that lady is."

"One look at her"—Gene laughed—"and any enemy with the brain of a gnat knows to stay low."

"Only mike boat I've seen that carries that kind of firepower. Armored like a battleship. A fortress. Painted black. Never saw one painted black before. Have you?"

Gene shook his head. "Only the Mo."

"Only the Mighty Mo's crew would do what they did either." Willie grinned. "I sure do wish I could have seen that."

"Heard it, you mean." Gene rubbed his left shoulder, which was still sore from the weight of ammo and the 60, then swallowed the last of his milk. "I'll never forget heading back down the Dam Doi, with those loudspeakers just blaring, 'I Want to Hold Your Hand' by the Beatles. I yelled, 'What the hell you trying to do? Draw fire?' "

Their laughter turned heads.

"Worked too," Willie said.

"Sure did. The first time she drew fire, the Mo returned it. The 105 cannon with fléchettes. Awesome. You should have seen it. Blew a fifty-foot path right through the tree line. Good-bye, B-40 rocket team. Played that song full volume all the way back to Seafloat.

"One of the things I most want to do before I leave here is go out on the Mighty Mo."

"With music?" Gene asked.

They walked out together still chuckling and went their separate ways. Willie to NILO, Gene back to the hootch housing both Lima and Delta platoons.

"Going out tomorrow," Jim told him when he stopped on the way to his rack to get a PBR, "with Delta. On a recon."

"Oh, yeah? Whose squad?"

"Walker's."

"Yeah? Okay. Sure." Gene allowed himself a small smile, watching Jim walk away. Had been a while since he and Delta's big man, Marc Kenau, operated together. He vaulted up on his rack, opened a can of beer, and stretched out. Kenau meant War Eagle. It fit. Eagle was big. Six one, 210 pounds. An archery champion. Hot-tempered. Man, was he hot-tempered. Fight, right now.

He took a long swallow of beer. And if Kenau got drunk, he was dangerous. Took five or six SEALs to bring him down. They'd been . . . still were . . . like brothers. Taught hand-to-hand combat together back at SEAL Team.

Grinning, he heard Eagle yell out "Hoo-Ya!" down at the end of the hootch, having just won a poker pot. Nobody else called him Eagle. He'd bet there was a lot more to Marc Kenau than that warped sense of humor of his, which was about all the rest got to see. Unless he was drunk, of course.

He turned on his side, propped himself up on an elbow, and had another swig of beer. The only man he feared in a fight was the Eagle. The only man Eagle feared was him. The rest feared them both. Yeah. Be good to operate with the Eagle again. But now . . .

Finished with the beer, he lofted the empty into the garbage can, then braced his pillow against the wall at the head of his bed and leaned back against it while he took out pen and paper. *Dear Karen,* he began, and stopped. It was hard to write home when the only thing he'd done was take people's lives. He couldn't tell her what he really did, with her alone and pregnant with their baby.

He took a deep breath. *I thank you for the letters. I love you,* he wrote, *and I miss you so much. I'm counting the days until I can hold you again.* He blinked and changed the subject. *It's hot here. Mosquitoes everywhere. The repellent we use helps a lot. If you can, please mail me a CARE package with some chocolate chip cookies and as many cans of tuna fish as you can send. I'd really appreciate it.*

He paused to think what to say next. *Thank the church members for their prayers and tell them they're in mine, every day. And so are you and our baby. How are you feeling? I hope, okay. I wish I could be there too, to rub your back and hold you when you're tired. Some of the men here are playing their radios and tapes and I just heard that song we danced to the last time I was home. The one I never remember the name of. I love you. You are the sunshine of my life and the rainbow of my dreams.*

He swallowed. There wasn't anything more he could really say. *Your loving husband, Gene. P.S. Pray for me.*

For a few minutes after sealing the envelope, he let himself remember how her body felt under his hands, her lips against his, the silk of her hair sliding through his fingers, the way her eyes shone when she smiled at him. His eyes stung. He slammed memory's door shut.

Dropping lightly to the floor, he let the letter fall into the outgoing mail sack.

The hootch was alive with most of its twenty-eight resident SEALs trying to be heard over a dozen radios turned to different stations. People in card games yelled their bets over the pounding beat of rock, the horns of jazz bands. Others argued, laughed, kidded each other against wailing voices and steel guitars competing with the classical music Marc Kenau had on. He opened another PBR. A couple more minutes and the movie would start.

Outside, between the SEALs' hootches, the projector was being set up. It faced a sheet hung on a line across the center of the walkway. Chairs sat in rows on both sides of the sheet. Since the film showed through, it didn't matter which side people sat on, but he wanted to sit on a chair, not on the cleaning table or an ammo box. Especially if *Bullitt* really had come in at last.

"*The Bride of Frankenstein!* Who was the fucking asshole who started that fucking rumor?"

Gene grinned. Sounded like You-O was disappointed. The film

46

was half through when Willie tapped him on the shoulder and called him aside.

"A new Kit Carson Scout just arrived," he said. "Name's Tong. He's seen Colonel Nguyen. I'm on my way over to the KCS camp for the interrogation. You want to come along?"

Five minutes later, bowie strapped on, carrying his 60, Gene followed Willie through the Kit Carson Scout camp. They'd taken a boat, a Whaler, from Seafloat to the riverbank. The camp, smoky with cooking fires, teemed with the KCSs and their families. All around them, people milled amid yelling children playing and chasing each other before settling for the night.

Inside a small, guarded hootch, Sean Browning, SEAL military advisor on his third tour, and three KCSs, one of them an interpreter, waited. The oldest KCS was Truk, the camp's chief, one of the few that Gene trusted. Truk was in his early fifties. He'd been there the longest of all. They acknowledged each other's presence with a nod.

Tong, responding to questions, began to tell his story.

Two days earlier, Colonel Nguyen had come into Tong's village around 1600 hours with about sixty armed NVA soldiers. They'd rounded up every man, woman, and child.

"How many in the village?" Gene asked the interpreter.

Tong, small and wiry, listened to the question and replied. "About thirty men, ages from twelve to seventy, the eldest being the village chief."

It seemed the chief gave some flak to the colonel. As Nguyen pulled out, he put out the word that every man would pick up a rifle and become VC, and that their taxes were being raised. The chief objected.

Tong became agitated, but continued. Gene concentrated, listening to the translation.

"The colonel, angry, singled out the chief's family, ordering the chief and his wife to be held by NVA soldiers. Colonel Nguyen hit the chief with his handgun, splitting his face open. He then kicked the chief's wife in the stomach. When she doubled over, he took a machete and, while she tried to catch her breath, decapitated her. By then, the chief was crying. The colonel blew his head off."

The villagers, according to Tong, were told Nguyen would be back in five days. If the villagers refused to become VC or resisted in any fashion, he warned he would destroy the village and kill everyone.

Tong said he was the son of the village chief and had seen his parents killed. He had run, he admitted, and even as his eyes filled with tears, his voice got louder, the words tumbling out.

"What's he saying?" Gene asked Willie.

"Saying he wants to fight now," Willie answered, "but not the South Vietnamese or the U.S. He's saying he wants to kill NVA and VC." Willie stopped to listen further to the rapid-fire translation. "He's afraid for his own family. He has a wife and two little girls, two and a half and four, who are still in the village. He wanted to return right away and get them, but he was torn between going back alone and wanting revenge for the way his parents were hacked down and shot in front of him."

"All right." For a few seconds longer, Gene watched Tong trying to regain his composure. "Have him kept under guard, Willie, until I can check out his information. Talk some more with him. Try and convince him to guide us back to his village. Tell him we'll pull his family out and set them up in the KCS camp. Tell him we'll house and clothe them and see they have medical treatment. If he'll guide us in. I'm heading back now."

"Will do," Willie said. "I'll see y'all later."

If Tong's story checked out, Gene thought, then finally they'd know where Colonel Nguyen would be, and when he'd be there. They had three days to put an op together.

As soon as he reached Seafloat, he went straight to the NILO hootch, also Johnny's living quarters, and gave him the information. "I need intel on the colonel, no matter what or how little you get. If there's any truth in Tong's story, it's the opportunity we've been looking for. We only have three days."

Leaving Johnny to return to the western novel he'd been reading, Gene set out to find Jim. Nothing could be done until the intel came in.

Just outside their hootch, he ran into his lieutenant.

Jim's brown eyes lit up when he heard Tong's story, and he rubbed a nonexistent headband. "Maybe," he said, "we can get him."

"One of the most wanted men in the Mekong Delta, and he's going to walk right into our hands."

Jim considered it. "The asshole's ours."

So, Gene thought, just before falling asleep that night, Colonel Nguyen has three days left until capture. His ancestors wouldn't have long to wait for him after that.

CHAPTER FIVE

THE RECON OP BEGAN before lunch with Delta's PL, Devin Walker, giving the Warning Order. That's when Gene's and Marc's squads, Lima and Delta, learned they'd be inserting on the Mighty Mo. Gene could feel the strange combination of reassurance and concern among the SEALs in the room. Reassurance, because they all felt safe on the Mighty Mo. She carried four .50-caliber machine guns, four M-60s, two Honeywell grenade launchers, an 81mm mortar, and a 105mm cannon. Plus, she'd have the combined firepower of fourteen SEALs within her black, armor-plated interior. Concern, because any op that called for using her brought with it the possibility of very heavy contact.

Knowing it was a recon op didn't help much. He remembered, very damned well, the crew of the Mo reconning by playing the Beatles' music over their loudspeakers. Arrogant, crazy bastards. But it worked. Couldn't argue with tactics that succeeded.

He threw a final length of ammo belt over the ones already crossing his shoulders, caught the ends, pulled them across his chest, broke off the excess length, and snapped the two ends together. However, he reminded himself, body-fitting more ammo belts around his hips, Delta was running this op. Devin Walker was patrol leader, with Jim acting as Devin's APL . . . unless the squads split up after insertion. In that case Dev would remain

Delta's PL, but Jim would be PL for Lima. They wouldn't be splitting while aboard the Mighty Mo.

He checked the bowie, making sure it was secure in its sheath, and flexed his shoulders under the belts of ammo. Good fit. He patted the grenades, made sure the Bible and cigarettes were in their pockets on his cami shirt, and ensured the compass was readily available. Finally he jumped up and down, making sure nothing rattled. Everything that could make noise was taped. Satisfied, he gave one last tug on his headband and picked up the big M-60 with about 150 rounds loaded and on safe. In green face and full combat gear, he left the hootch and joined the rest of Delta's and Lima's SEALs to go hear Devin's Patrol Leader's Order.

Devin stood, one hand on his hip, the other holding the PLO form, looking down at them. "Now, intelligence reports show heavy enemy movements," he said, "in our area of operation."

The Naval Academy grad had a voice like a bullfrog. Really deep. Gene liked to listen to him talk. Dev looked down on people even when they were standing. At six foot five, there weren't many who could look him in the eye. A good operator too. Admirable poker player, good drinking capacity, but Dev couldn't match him drink for drink. He'd tried. Passed out. Not an ounce of Dev's 225 pounds was fat either. Clean-shaven, with dirty-blond hair and brown eyes, he looked, in Gene's opinion, like an Old West gunfighter, only dressed wrong.

What really got all the SEALs' respect was Dev's deviousness in getting what he wanted, and what they wanted. He ran good ops.

"Now," he said, "we're going to be running day and night recons. We want to locate where they've set up camps and identify enemy personnel. We don't want contact. We want to bring out information that will allow us to run a hard-target op on their base camp at a later date, with great success."

At 1400 hours, the fourteen SEALs left the hootch to board the Mighty Mo.

"She looks like floating death," Cruz commented as they waited to board, "with all those gun barrels sticking out. Don't you think?"

"Yeah," Gene answered. "Like she's daring the enemy to try it."

On board, shaded by the helo platform above, Delta's squad filed down to sit on one of the two long steel benches running parallel to the sides of the Mo's interior. Lima, also in patrol formation, sat facing Delta on the opposite bench. Those of the Mo's crew not operating the boat manned its weapons. Gene leaned back against the olive-drab flak blankets covering the bulkheads and settled down for the ride.

They moved slowly through the waters of the Son Ku Lon, then turned south, down another large river. It was on this river that large numbers of NVA had been reported. Here they slowed even more to quiet the throb of the Mo's powerful diesel engines.

Just inside the river's mouth, Gene stood up to study the villagers from Old Nam Cam Annex. Living seven or eight miles from Seafloat, the villagers were busy doing their thing—fishing, moving supplies to smaller villages by sampan. They paid little attention to the lethal black boat in their midst. But Gene paid close attention to them. Many of the South Vietnamese in the village were potential VCs, and were known to be North Vietnamese sympathizers.

At eight hundred meters past the village all the men were standing, made uneasy by the sight of large poles protruding from the river's surface. Six wires stretched from pole to pole. Gene's grip tightened on the 60 when a small sampan, powered by an equally small outboard motor, cruised directly toward them. As it neared, he lifted the 60 and aimed at the ragged, hatless old man in the sampan with the long pole sticking out the back. The villagers used poles to propel their boats in water too shallow for motors. The elderly man sailed alone.

Dev called him over. *"Li dai!"*

The old man stared up at them.

"Li dai!" Dev repeated.

Gene, the 60 ready, felt the tension. They were all prepared to blow the sampan to shit if it became a threat to their operation or their safety. Every SEAL knew that the raggedy old man could be a sapper, a suicide, his sampan filled with explosives.

It came as a surprise when the old man warned them, in broken English, "Don' go no more. Boo-koo VC. They wait. Wires say, 'Stay out.' You stop, don' go no more."

Dev had him repeat his warning, making sure he'd understood, then motioned the old man on his way. The elderly man bobbed his head, then putted on toward Old Nam Cam Annex.

"Make sure you're locked and loaded, off safe," Dev ordered. "We're going through." He ordered the wires cut.

In silence, except for the soft, throaty sound of the diesels, the Mo moved between the poles and continued. All SEALs turned and stood on the metal benches where they'd sat, weapons ready, aimed at the banks on their respective sides.

Gene, poised to trigger the 60 at the slightest sound, watched the riverbanks for the least sign of the enemy. The jungle grew thick and dense right up to the water's edge. With the Mo's ten men and with fourteen SEALs, all with automatic weapons, anyone would be boo-koo *dinky dau*, crazy, to fire on her. They were about as safe as anybody could be on these rivers.

Eyeing the tree line along the bank, he heard the PL taking care of last-minute preparations. The final radio contact with TOC, Tactical Operations Command, prior to their insertion about a mile farther down the river, was made.

He couldn't see more than six inches into the jungle even now with the river narrowed to about thirty feet. There was silence around him on the Mo. Everyone's attention was trained on the bank's heavy foliage. Back-to-back, the two squads waited and watched.

The air shattered.

Gene slammed into the flak-blanketed steel bulkhead, then fell sideways on the metal bench. Its edge bit into his thigh like a sharp-edged baseball bat swung full force, as his shoulder hit the deck. A terrific explosion had hit the Mo on Delta's side. He rolled, stood, and jumping over a fallen crewman, came on line with Delta's squad, the 60 firing even before he was fully erect. The crewman behind him had been hit, and hit pretty bad. Doc quit firing and ran to him.

For a full minute, the SEALs, standing side by side, all guns opened up, poured out a steady, deafening stream of bullets. When no fire was returned, Gene realized they were outside the enemy's kill zone. Must have almost cleared it before the claymore hit.

The crew turned the Mo's bow into the right bank five hundred to seven hundred meters south of the ambush site. Gene focused on Dev. The PL had to make some decisions, and quickly, on whether to drop the bow and insert, flank the ambush, and go on with the op, continuing downriver, or abort the op for now and come back another day.

Dev motioned Doc over.

The MSSC man was, Gene thought, in critical condition. Doc verified his opinion.

"If we go on," he told Dev, "he will die. If we turn around, he still might not make it back."

No op is worth a SEAL's life. Tommy Blade's words repeated in Gene's mind. And this one, he thought, isn't worth the MSSC man's either. Turn around, he silently telegraphed to Dev. Turn around, and let's get him out of here and back to the Float.

"Now let's go back out," Dev ordered, "and get a chopper to meet us at the mouth of the river at the Son Ku Lon for medevac. We'll insert later tonight under cover of darkness. Now, get ready," he growled. "They might hit us again."

Gene took a deep breath. Might, hell. They'd be waiting next time.

He stayed, like the rest of the SEALs, on line, atop the steel bench facing the west bank. Off the bench, the Mo's sides were too tall to allow a clear field of fire, and they wanted a damned good view of the tree line hiding any enemy. Up front, he noticed, one of the boat personnel struggled to turn the 105 cannon toward the same bank.

"Sir," he yelled, "the 105's been taken out. Hit by that claymore that got us."

"Well, hell," Cruz said, standing next to Gene. "After that claymore hit and we opened up, the enemy will think twice about hitting us again."

"If any of them survived," Alex muttered. "Couldn't have been that many or they'd have hit us with a rocket, not just one claymore."

The Mighty Mo, having turned about, opened her engines up full bore and headed back on step.

Gene narrowed his eyes against the sun. The Sea Wolves had been scrambled, were heading their way, but the Mo'd be in the enemy's kill zone before the Wolves got overhead. The Mo was really moving for her size and weight.

"Get ready!" Dev snapped.

Boom!

Gene lurched, danced, trying to keep his feet, the 60 bucking in his hands. The whole world hit them. He flew across the boat, hit the other steel bench ribs first, rebounded, jumped back atop the first bench, the 60 gone rhythmic in his hands with its rapid, deadly song. The end of the kill zone was nowhere in sight.

Firing, he felt, saw, men being thrown across the inside of the boat, bodies falling. Seconds seemed forever, took an ungodly long time to pass. For an instant, he and the Eagle were the only ones standing, firing, then suddenly all of Lima and most of Delta were back on line. Roberts, Taylor, Mansen, all hit, but back up firing, others trying to get up. The only thing that would be in any of their minds was to gain fire superiority at all costs, or they were going to die. This was not a small group of enemy.

Foliage moved, clipped away by an enemy invisible but for the hundreds of gun flashes. The jungle was being chewed up by their tracers, every five rounds going into the trees . . . just pouring in, returning fire into the flashes.

Down. Get up. The drab-green flak blanket was slippery with blood but not his. It felt like his head was exploding with the deafening noise. The bastards! How many? Cliff Robb hit again . . . and again. Up, hit again. My God, the blood . . .

"Take care of Robb!" he yelled. "Hold him down, he's gonna bleed to death. West! Hold down Robb!"

The 60 thundered in his hands. Rockets blasting through their armor plating, through the flak blankets, shrapnel like a blizzard. The Mo's 60s, .50s, thundering, the SEALs pouring out everything they had, the sound like no other he'd ever heard. It was so loud, so immense, never stopping. The air shook with it, his skull exploding with it, blood running from everybody's ears. Blood running, smearing, everywhere. Taylor trying, trying, trying, to stand, sliding back down the blood-slicked flak blanket, trying and sliding, screaming with rage, bleeding. His weapon was blown out of his grasp but he was trying to climb up, pick up another, return fire. Robb, dead-white face under green paint, trying to stand.

"Hold him down, goddammit! Hold him! Doc! Get to Robb!"

Oh, God, oh God, oh God. The shrapnel flying, rockets, claymores . . . oh, God . . . the shrapnel. Flak blankets were being blown apart by rocket hits. Inside the Mo like standing in a frenzy of fireworks, a firefight grand finale with bullets ricocheting, a fiery killing display with no end. So many bodies. Wounded, bloody, bleeding SEALs crawling, staggering back up to fire—

Ka-boom!

The claymore concussion slammed him, ripped the 60 out of his hands. He grabbed it back, its barrel red-hot, and squeezed the trigger. She wouldn't fire! Housing group caved in. Throw it, grab the nearest of the Mo's unmanned 60s, fed by a five-thousand-round case of ammo. Return fire. Fire! Keep it opened up. Oh, God, Roland! What the hell? Firing his AR-15, so pumped up he was throwing its magazines at the enemy the second he emptied one. Fucking crazy with it . . . all of them in the purple haze.

The smoke, the smell of cordite, the new 60 slower, firing slower, the nickel gone with his own 60. Doc was treating wounded—there were wounded everywhere—with blowout patches, field bandages, trying to cover gaping bloody holes. Wounded helping wounded. God, the incredible, deafening noise! And the yelling, but only of orders, firing directions, from SEALs. No screams for help, no crying. Silence from the wounded. They knew everybody standing, the SEALs, the crew, had to gain fire superiority, had distractions enough.

Explosions were never-ending. Climb back up, stand, fire. Wounded were holding down wounded trying to get up to fight. Ears aching, bleeding, pounding with the incredible volume of continual firefight, the explosions. The 60 was solid, singing. He saw nothing, saw everything, tried to feel nothing.

Fire, fire, fire . . .

Then silence. Silence so loud it hurt his head. Eyes stinging with tears of relief, Gene stepped off the bench, breathing hard, heart thudding. Blinking sweat away, he set the 60 down. The Mo was a slaughter scene. He ripped off his shirt, tore strips, tried to staunch Mansen's bleeding arm, wrap it.

Sea Wolves roared over, above their heads.

God, West's eye was a bloody hole, flak jacket shredded like spaghetti, so shrapnel-tattered. Wipe the blood away, he told himself. Work fast. Don't see his pain. There are others.

Punched full of holes, the Mo smoldered. Small fires still burned here and there.

Gene stood up, his breath coming hard. Men lay everywhere. Never had he seen so much blood. The benches, deck, ragged and torn flak blankets covering the inner walls of the boat, all were smeared with blood, the steel deck sticky with it. It seeped, ran from the fallen, staining them and their clothes with dark wet patches. He worked, trying to help, trying to keep them alive long enough to get back.

There were explosions behind them. The Sea Wolves were dumping their rockets, opening up with miniguns—six 60s hooked together—and firing three thousand rounds per minute. He knew their sound.

And the Wolves radioed down, "Cannot suppress fire. Leaving to cover your extraction. Will escort you to Seafloat."

Gene slid his hand beneath Dev's neck, lifted his head, and put a folded, torn-off piece of another SEAL's cami shirt under Dev's skull, tying it in place with his own headband to make a pressure bandage. Then he left the unconscious PL and moved to the next man. He saw Jim moving, kneeling, directing Alex and Cruz. Their own PL was going from wounded to wounded, slipping sometimes, smearing the blood across the deck. Doc, fast and efficient, gave directions, assistance, as he went. Gene loved Doc. Doc kept them alive, forced them to live, never gave up, would never leave them.

The Mo neared Seafloat at last, barely making it. They'd had their asses kicked and handed to them this time. Gene knew it, knew all of them knew it. A first. Couldn't believe it, but knew it. He took a deep breath. The dark, acrid smell of cordite lingered in the air. Seafloat. God, he was so thankful to be back. No words for it. The triage, set up, waited for their wounded. Seafloat's people had listened to the battle over the radio. One surgeon and six corpsmen were standing there—all they had.

Robb, the worst hit, went first, then the rest were lifted gently into waiting hands; then the walking wounded left the Mo. Not until that moment did Gene realize Lima's squad had not so much as a scratch. Seventeen of the twenty-four men on board the Mo were hit. Hit many times. The remaining seven were all Lima, all his squad. They stared at each other in stunned silence.

Every part of him hurt, the result of being slammed against steel again and again by the endless concussions of exploding rockets, claymores, and grenades. His bruises went to the bone. He could see that the rest of the squad were in no better shape.

Weary, aching, exhausted, but all trained in first aid, they went to sick bay to help the overwhelmed medics. Once there, they were issued probes which they used to locate and extract shrapnel and rounds buried in tender flesh. Medevacs were on their way from Binh Thuy, about an hour's flight away.

When there was nothing more Gene could do for anybody, he left. Alone, in the late afternoon, he walked past the damaged Mo, between the hootches, and past the cleaning table. Nothing to clean now, with his 60 destroyed, but he'd be checking out a new one, doing modifications, putting another nickel in.

At Seafloat's edge, he pulled out the little Bible he'd shoved under his Levi's waistband before tearing up his cami shirt. Head bowed, eyes shut tight, holding the Bible against his bare chest in both hands, he thanked God they'd got back. God, he was sure with his whole being, had been looking over his shoulder and taking care of his squad. They should all be dead. It had to be God watching out for them.

In the waning sunlight, his thoughts were a kaleidoscope of images, sounds. Adrenaline still flooded his system and he swayed in place with it, his fingers clamped around the small Bible that meant so much. Nothing else to hold onto. Not out here.

They went to chow before cleaning either their weapons or themselves. On the way, Jim said the Mighty Mo had taken some thirty rocket hits, many claymore hits, and enemy rounds that numbered in the thousands.

"She's taking on water," he said, "due to the inability of the welded seams to withstand an assault like that. They're pulling her out of action. Word from the MSSC people is that she'll be taken to Binh Thuy for repairs."

"Repairs, by God," Brian said, pulling open the chow hall door. "Some hellacious job that'll be."

"Got that right," Cruz agreed.

Gene followed Doc inside, deep in thought. She'd earned her name, the Mighty Mo, and he would never, ever forget her.

"Another goddamned ball-banger," Doc bitched, as the squad passed the waiting line and went to head-of-line. "Why me? Why the hell? I'm not even a SEAL, dammit all." He slammed his still-empty tray against the counter. "I'm a dirty, sore, shakin' sonofabitch! One *dau-mau-mee* after another. Can't even go on the Mighty Mo without getting shot at."

Gene reached back for a slice of bread, and a jolt of adrenaline hit. Right behind him stood Freddy Fanther. The asshole had followed the squad to the front of the line just like he'd been on the op too. Before the realization finished forming in his mind, he hit Fanther. Just nailed him. Had to fight himself to keep from kicking the shit out of him.

"You bastard!" he yelled. But Fanther, bleeding and out, didn't hear him.

Doc grabbed his arm. "What the hell happened?"

"Punched his running lights out, is what the hell happened. He gets up, I'll outright put him down for keeps." He glared down at Fanther. "Jumped to the head of the line with us. Asshole was in line outside the door when we came in."

He could still feel anger halfway through eating the mound of spaghetti on his tray. He didn't even want to see Freddy Fanther again. If he came up behind him, the squad would let him know.

By the time he started on his third slice of cake, most of the squad had gone to clean their weapons. He looked up to see Willie taking Brian's vacated seat.

"Gene," Willie said, "Sean and I are going in to pull out the new Kit Carson Scout's family before Colonel Nguyen and his men return to the village. Tong's agreed to guide us. We're leaving at 0530. We're wondering if you'd like to go with us."

CHAPTER SIX

IT TOOK A SECOND to register what Willie was saying. Tong's village . . . 0530 hours . . . go with them and help. Gene looked at him, nodded. "I'll see if anything's happening with Jim, but sure. If he says okay, I'll go."

Willie sighed. "Good." He turned his attention to chow.

Gene smiled. His redheaded friend seemed content. "How much time you have left? Know you're short."

"Two weeks."

"You nervous?"

Willie raised an eyebrow. "Nervous? About what?"

Gene laughed. "Getting married."

"I swear I haven't really thought about it much." He set his forkful of spaghetti back down and was silent for a moment. "I'll just be glad to get home. Then I'll turn to Jell-O. I'll be discharged three days after return. Three days later, on Saturday, we'll tie the knot."

"You'll love it, my friend. Being married is the best thing in my life." Gene grinned. "You know, I'll be a daddy in about five months. Going to love being a daddy." He finished his milk. Tasted so darned good.

"Y'all hoping for a boy or a girl?" Willie asked.

"A boy'd be nice but, man, as long as the baby's healthy and has ten toes and fingers, I don't care." He stood. "Gotta run. Stop by the hootch later, and I'll let you know what Jim says about tomorrow morning. You want to, you can sit in on the card game. Gotta buy baby a new pair of shoes."

Willie grinned. "Not with my money. Y'all had better tap another poor boy. Have to save mine for married life," he said, and slapped Gene lightly on the shoulder.

Involuntarily he flinched. It was the shoulder he'd landed on when the first claymore hit and it hurt like hell.

"Damn, I'm sorry," Willie said. "Forgot how sore y'all must be."

"It's okay. Just a bit tender. Don't worry about it." He rested his hand on the back of Willie's neck for a moment, in reassurance, then went to the hootch to clean up. Good to have a friend. Blessed to have a really close friend like Willie. Lot of good men here, he thought later, looking around inside for Jim, but nobody that he cared for as much as Willie.

He found Jim reading a book. He was stretched out on his rack behind the plywood partition separating the officers, Jim and Dev, from their platoons. Lima and Delta shared the hootch. "So. All right to go?" he asked, after giving Jim the background.

Jim rolled over and sat up, thinking about it. "Yes. Try to get some more info on the colonel. Ask some of the villagers questions. Look around, see if we can hit him when he returns."

Gene nodded. "Yeah. I will." He grinned. Jim wasn't the greatest poker player. "By the way, we're playing cards tonight. You want to sit in?"

Jim opened his book again. "Maybe. I'll see."

Gene left him reading and made his way through the crowded, noisy room to the icebox. A few brews were what he needed, he decided, going down the aisle between Delta and Lima areas. He passed the sides of Roland's and Doc's racks. Doc had the bottom bunk, figuring there was less chance of breaking a leg getting out of it. Behind them, next to the wall, Cruz and Alex sat on their respective racks, Cruz on top where he could easily spot the SEALs who owed him. A couple of steps farther on he came to the end of his and Brian's bunks, situated next to the door. The new 60 hung from the frame of his rack on top.

For a change, nobody sat at the big table where the aisle running end-to-end in the hootch crossed the one from the door. The table in the intersection divided the territory between Delta and Lima. The icebox sat against the wall across from the door. Grabbing four cold PBRs, Gene opened and chugged one before yelling, "Let's get this card game going. Baby needs a new pair of shoes."

With Roland and Brian helping, he smoothed out the blanket on a bottom rack. The three sat on one side, with Willie, Doc, and Marc on the other.

"Infant's gonna have cold feet," Marc said.

"Not as cold as yours." Gene looked up into the ice-blue eyes that shocked him every time he saw them. Never would expect anybody with hair as black as Marc's to have eyes that color, and they were so clear they were like looking through blue-tinted glass. The Eagle's left shoulder was bandaged clear to his elbow. He'd caught some shrapnel on the Mo that afternoon. "How's your arm and shoulder?"

"Fine," Doc said. "I treated him."

"Dammit, Doc, I can answer for myself." Marc smoothed a wrinkle on his side of the blanket. "I'm fine," he told Gene.

"That's what Doc just said."

"Well, he doesn't know. I'm the only one who knows."

Gene leaned forward. "But he did know, and he said so, and then you said what he said, and he was right, wasn't he?"

Marc's eyes flashed. "He did not know. He's not me. I'm the only one who can know whether I'm fine or not."

"You're wrong, man. He knew when you weren't fine, didn't he?" Gene took a drink of beer. "Didn't he? And he'd know whether you were or weren't fine now."

"You're not listening to what I'm telling you," Marc shouted.

"The hell I'm not," Gene yelled back. "Heard everything you said, and none of it makes sense."

"Sense, by God," said Brian. "I'll put five bucks on Gene if they get into it."

"I'll take two of that."

"Roland, you don't know. Five on Gene. Put your money up." Willie grinned.

"Goddammit, I came here to play cards," Doc yelled. "We gonna play or not?" He scratched at his moustache, a sure sign of impatience.

Brian handed Doc the deck. "Deal. All bets are off."

Gene began to laugh. A second later, Marc joined in. Doc called for them to ante, and dealt.

Roland was funny, Gene thought, watching him. He'd always tip his hand, always go for the draw. If he didn't get his cards, he'd always say "Shit," in a muffled voice, then try and bluff. Everybody knew what that meant, so they'd bump the bet, and Roland would throw his money in. When he did get his cards, he'd smile and fidget in his chair. Before he could place a bet, everybody would fold and let him have the few dollars in the pot. He'd get so pissed off. Never did learn that he signaled his hands, and they'd just let him feed the pot.

Roland drew three cards.

Gene waited. The others leaned toward Roland, listening.

"Shit," Roland muttered.

"I'll cover and raise," Gene said, and grinned. Game was off to a good start.

After four hours, he was up about thirty dollars, and Roland was down about a hundred. Since they always played payday stakes, the amount of monies won or lost was kept in a record book. You-O kept it.

Gene glanced at his watch: 2400 hours. "That's it for me, buddies. Appreciate the contributions."

The group broke up, Roland griping as he stood, "Lousy cards. All fucked up."

Gene, hearing him, chuckled as he folded the blanket.

"Are y'all going tomorrow?" Willie asked quietly.

He nodded. "Sure."

"Good," Willie said, and left.

"Question," Marc said, stretching, then bending over to work some of the kinks out after sitting so long.

Gene put the blanket down, turned to look into ice-blue eyes. "What?"

"I was just wondering . . . sort of curious, all of a sudden, since I . . . well, I just wanted to know. Before you thought about joining up, being a SEAL or anything, what did you want to be?"

He really did want to know, Gene realized, and he wanted a straight answer. "I grew up in the church. All my friends were from the church, all my social life revolved around it. You know I got married when I got into SEAL Team? And that we're going to have a baby in a few months?"

Marc nodded.

"Well, my wife—Karen is her name—I met her through our church group. We wanted, for our church, to become missionaries and serve in Africa." He took a deep breath. "So that's what I was going to be. A missionary in Africa."

"And now?"

"And now I'm a SEAL and I'm here, and my family is back in The World."

Marc bit his lip and thought for a moment before asking, "And now you're not ever going to be a missionary?"

"No. I'm a SEAL." He looked at Marc, quiet now, head down. "But I've kept my faith. I'll never lose that. And you? What did you want to be?"

Marc didn't look up. "You won't laugh?"

"Hell no, I won't."

"A poet. I wanted to be a poet." He wrapped his arms around himself as though he were cold. "Thought I'd go up in the red-woods, have a little cabin, maybe close enough that I could see the ocean, and write poems."

After a long silence, Gene cleared his throat. The Eagle. A poet. Just shit-hot in battle. God knew they'd been in some hellish firefights. A poet and a missionary. Lord. "And now?" he finally asked.

Marc straightened, looked at him. "I'm a SEAL, same as you. But sometimes . . ."

"Sometimes?"

"Sometimes I think about it. Sometimes." He frowned, rubbed his hand lightly over his bandages. "Guess I'm sort of beat. Later. Okay?"

"Okay."

So who's the real Marc? Gene wondered, watching him walk away. Jesus. A poet with a 60. Just never knew.

He shook his head and went outside. He wanted some fresh air and a few minutes of peace and quiet before hitting the sheets. Starry night. Billions of stars, horizon to horizon. He stood there awhile, just looking, before pulling out his Bible. For a moment, he just held it, felt it there in his hand. He'd kept his faith. At least he had that. He bowed his head and asked God to look out for Karen and himself, to take good care of her and their unborn child.

As if in answer, far off on the dark horizon, against the starry night, the jungle lit up with tracer-sparklers amid huge white flashes. Darting within them, tiny silhouetted planes—jets on a bombing run—drew fire from the ground.

Beautiful to look at. A miniature light show on a distant stage, with the night sky for a backdrop. A poet could write it down, could tell it. But not a silent poet. He turned away, went inside.

0500 hours came early. He sat up, still very tired, surprised at how weary he was. Didn't feel very well. Black-and-blue bruises everywhere. Ached all over. Shake it off, he told himself. Grin and bear it. He rubbed his eyes, dropped to the deck, and got on with it.

In jeans, carrying his 60, with eight hundred rounds of bandoliered ammo wrapped over his cami shirt, he walked slowly to the helo pad.

Willie and Sean were waiting, with a group of Kit Carson Scouts.

"About time," Willie said.

"Sure began to wonder," Sean added.

Gene looked at his watch. He was five minutes early. "Fuck off." They laughed.

He waited while Sean got the Kit Carson Scouts to start boarding the chopper. The new KCS, Tong, boarded first, he noticed, even though his face showed he feared getting in the helo and flying. Watching them, Gene listened as Willie and Sean briefed him on the members of Tong's family—how many and who they were—that they'd be bringing in.

"With the new KC going," Willie said, "location and identification will be easy."

"We'll pick them up," Sean put in, "place them on the second helo, and return to camp. They'll be set up in a new home and taken care of like the rest."

Against the noise of the choppers warming up, Gene said, "Let's KISS. We need to get in, get out. No contact. This isn't even counted as an op."

They climbed aboard.

Taking off in a helo was one hell of a ride. He sat, legs hanging out of the open doorway, holding on. The engines revved and suddenly the ground fell away. About fifteen feet up, they hovered for an instant. The horizon tilted as the nose tipped. He caught his breath when they suddenly dropped, fast, almost straight down, to pick up speed. At the last instant before hitting water, the horizon tilted the opposite direction, and they were climbing.

At three to five thousand feet, he was in no hurry to land, sitting in the door with his feet dangling. This was the part he liked best. No doors to stop the air rushing past his face. Down below, the rice paddies were white, shining blankets, spread out and tacked down by dirt-brown hems, surrounded by jungle in all shades of green.

"Almost there," Willie called.

Gene turned to look forward. Rising smoke hung, a tattered curtain of dirty gray, against the dawn sky. "Something's up," he called back.

The pilots dropped the two helos to treetop level on the approach to the village so any enemy below wouldn't hear their engines until they landed. Gene leaned forward, not wanting to miss anything, loving the great feeling of flying along in the breeze like the birds.

The helo peeled off the treetops and down into the clearing like water over a fall, and landed like a falling leaf.

The entire village reminded Gene of the inside of a fire ring on the beach. Some of it still burned. Smaller structures, collapsed, were charred heaps on blackened ground. Thick, pungent smoke stung his nostrils and eyes. Everywhere he looked, he saw dead bodies.

They jumped off the choppers, followed by the Kit Carson Scouts, who ran through the village yelling. Except for one. Tong stopped over a body, then grabbed it up into his arms and started to cry.

The more Gene saw, the worse he felt. Obviously the colonel had returned early, found out somehow that the village chief's son, Tong, had become a KCS, and ordered the village destroyed.

Watching Tong, seeing the destruction, the many dead, Gene felt his chest constrict. He felt sick. These people hadn't wanted to fight. They were happy just being farmers. They wanted to be left alone. By both sides.

He joined Willie in searching for any wounded, any survivors. There were none. The colonel had killed every man, woman, and child. Including Tong's little girls. One had been only two and a half, the other four.

Behind him, Gene heard Doc talking.

"They raped Tong's wife too," he said, "before shooting her in the head. From where the rest of the bodies are, it looks like she was raped in front of the entire village before they were all gunned down."

Charred wood crunched under Gene's feet. The acrid stink seemed to cling to his face. Ashes puffed into small clouds with every step. The taste of charcoal lay on his lips. He looked through narrowed eyes at Tong, crying, his dead wife held tight in his arms. Naked from the waist down, her top still on but ripped open, her bare arms hung down, fists clenched in death.

"Let's pull out," Sean ordered. "The colonel's not that far away. Load up."

The biggest hootch wasn't completely burned yet, so the colonel and his men hadn't been gone long. Sean was right. They had to leave, and now. With Willie at his side, Gene walked toward the helos. Halfway there, he looked back. "Willie, Tong . . ."

Tong hadn't moved. Still held his wife, crying. Together, they returned for him.

Putting a hand on his shoulder, Gene talked, motioning, even though he knew Tong couldn't understand him, trying to get him to lay his wife down and leave. Willie, opposite, tried as well. In the end, Gene forcibly held Tong while Willie pulled his wife's body from his arms and lay it on the ground. Gene waved two KCSs over to take Tong away.

As they left, he bent to straighten the body and again noticed the clenched fists. Something was in her right hand. He pulled the colonel's shoulder epaulet out of her bloody fist. She must have fought like hell. Tore her fingernails off on that shoulder insignia. But she got it, and now he had it.

The world went purple. He leapt to his feet, triggering the 60, firing into the jungle until all the rounds in the belt were gone, but still pulling the trigger on the now silent gun and screaming at the top of his lungs. "I'm going to kill you, you fucking asshole. You're a dead man. I'll not rest until I find you, you son of a bitch!"

Willie yelling. "Gene! Come on! Let's get out of here! Gene! Gene!"

"*Aaaggghhhh!*" he howled, words no longer sufficient.

Willie screamed in his face. "Gene!"

And he heard. Blinked.

"Let's go. We have to get out of here."

Gene stared. "Sure."

The blades were turning, the engines revving. "Willie," Gene yelled, "give me two minutes. I'll be right there."

Without waiting for a reply, he headed back out to where the two little girls' bodies were. Half-blinded by tears, he lifted them—so small, so light—and lay their battered bodies together. He put the 60 aside, pulled the Bible from the pocket of his jeans, took off his shirt. Kneeling, he carefully covered their tiny bodies with his cami, then placed his Bible on top.

Picking up the 60, he ran to the waiting chopper, boarded, and, once again, sat in the open door. This time with eyes closed. God help him, he'd get that colonel, that fucking asshole, somehow, someway. God, bless those little girls. God. Why God?

Behind him, Tong cried and cried and cried.

CHAPTER SEVEN

GENE WAS FIRST OFF the chopper when the two Sea Wolves landed on Seafloat. While the Kit Carson Scouts, accompanied by Sean, boarded boats to cross the river between Seafloat and their camp on the Son Ku Lon's bank, he stood silently, staring down into the river's brown water.

"Friend," Willie said, resting his hand on Gene's shoulder, "don't let the pain go too deep. Plain and simple, the colonel lied about when he'd be back. There wasn't a way we could check the intel and get there to take Tong's family out before his return. He knew that."

Gene nodded, looked out over the jungle, trying to block out the image of the little girls lying there. He clenched his teeth, afraid he'd cry if he answered Willie. Wouldn't be able to stop it.

"It's so hard," Willie said. "I know it's hard. Nothing can change the evil that's been done. All we can do is try and stop that butcher from slaughtering. Mourn those poor souls, yes, but don't let it keep you from remembering what we're here for. The colonel is not alone out there."

"No," Gene said, thinking tactics already, forcing emotions back inside their cold, hard shell, "but we have to take him out. He's the worst."

"So far as we know now."

"I'd better report to Jim."

Willie nodded, red hair shining in the sunlight. "And we'd both best report to Johnny over at NILO. Gene, you all right?"

"Sure. And Willie, thanks."

But he'd never be all right again in a world where men could do such unthinkable things to tiny children. Could order them done and have other men willing to abandon every shred of their humanity to obey.

In the center of the hootch, Jim was sitting on an ammo crate pulled up to the table in the intersection, having a beer while he did paperwork. He looked up.

"Well, how'd it . . . What happened?"

He looked like a teenager doing homework. Gene stared down at him in the dimness. The breeze from the fans ruffled the edges of the papers under the PL's tanned hand.

Jim frowned, a look of concern on his face. "Gene?"

"Jim, we were too late." He tried to swallow. Couldn't. He took a deep breath and said it fast. "Prior to our arrival, the NVA advisor, Colonel Nguyen, returned to the village with the NVA forces under his command. The village was completely destroyed. Burned to the ground. The indigenous population were annihilated. No one . . ." His voice shook. He stopped, fought for control. "The indigenous are all dead."

Jim stood. "Tong's family?"

"Raped, mutilated, then shot." In his mind, the children, Tong holding his wife, the sound of his heartbroken weeping. He felt his chin tremble and focused intently on the table. Brown . . . hard . . . doesn't bend . . . two inches thick . . .

"Tong?"

"At the KCS camp."

"Anybody hurt?"

"No. No casualties."

"Can you estimate how many NVA?"

"About fifty. At least."

Jim nodded. "You look beat. Why don't you try and get some sleep? Couple of hours, maybe."

"Soon as I see Johnny, over at NILO, I will." He turned away. Jim might look like a kid, but there was a lot of man behind that boy's face. A hard man, but a good one. He took three Pabst Blue Ribbon beers out of the refrigerator and went to report to Johnny.

Later, he rejoined Jim, the feelings of deep weariness, of unwellness, put aside again. "We've got another op. You want to be my assistant PL?"

"Be glad to," Jim said. "What do you have?"

"Intel reports," Gene said, "indicate a weapons factory down one of the Twin Rivers about four miles from here. The factory is guarded by NVA and Viet Cong. They send out B-40 rocket teams to protect the rivers from Navy riverboats going up and reconning. We've inherited the problem."

Jim lit a cigarette. "What's happened so far?"

"Nothing good. The riverboat people have been taking a real beating. They've sent boats down numerous times, only to have them blown out of the water or, if they do get back to base, they come in crippled and smoking, with high casualty rates."

"Bad."

"Real bad. On one riverboat attack, trying to get farther down the rivers, they sent a zippo, a mike boat with a flamethrower, down with the Swift boats and PBRs. The plan was to have the Swifts and the PBRs draw fire, at which point the zippo would come in on step and barbecue the enemy doing the firing. This is how bad it is. Not only did the Swifts and PBRs draw fire, but the zippo was blown to hell. High-order."

"Obviously their tactics aren't working."

He watched as Jim drew long and carefully on his smoke. He had a contest going with himself over how much of a cigarette he could smoke without the ash dropping off. It was a little over an inch long now. Gene eyed it. "Not going to make two inches."

"A PBR it does."

"Patrol Boat, River, or can of?"

"Can of."

"Done. Anyway, Twin Rivers is ours to deal with now."

"What do you have in mind?" The ash fell off. "Damn."

"Told you so." Gene grinned. "Hand it over."

Jim took a can from the three he had left and gave it to Gene, who opened it and took a long drink.

"Good stuff," he pronounced. "Okay. We need, first, to cut off all food and medical supplies to the Twin Rivers area. I've got info that they're crossing from the smaller river on one side of the Son

Ku Lon, directly across it into Twin Rivers on the other side. Means we have to watch both banks of the little river where it forks, because we don't know which waterway they use."

"First thing is to monitor what the sensors show."

"UDT personnel placed sensors on the north side of the Son Ku Lon weeks ago, so we have that intel."

"Right." Jim dropped his cigarette butt in an empty can. "With the sensors, we'll know if anybody tries to enter Twin Rivers by land or water. Have to cut them off from the outside and any support. If we can stop communications, food, and medical supplies, they'll starve. They won't know what's happening. We'll play games with their minds. After a while, we'll be able to find and penetrate their safe haven."

Gene nodded. "Exactly. And once they're located, and info is gathered, we can go back in and search and destroy."

"Sounds like a good op to me."

"Thought you'd think so." Gene finished his beer and stretched. "Guess I'll get it under way."

Johnny'd said the sensors had been going off night and day. After studying the situation another twenty-four hours, Gene met with Jim again.

"Two things," he said. "This afternoon, the sensors showed movement on the north bank of the Son Ku Lon, but no crossing. It appears to be a scout element. And I've just received intel that a major crossing is going to take place somewhere between 0100 and 0400 hours, day after tomorrow."

He took a breath to relieve the familiar but still slight tension building within him. They'd be operating. Soon.

"Johnny says they're planning a diversion. They'll have a smaller crossing take place between Seafloat and the major crossing site. They figure the riverboats will take the smaller crossing under fire. They'll use those five or ten minutes to make the major crossing of the Son Ku Lon from the small river to Twin Rivers, where they'll have rocket team protection."

Jim nodded and rubbed an imaginary headband.

"Johnny also said his intel was that the major crossing will involve eight to ten large sampans, loaded with food and medical supplies."

"We go."

"Yes. With the sensors going on and off, and with the probable point element out there this afternoon, the intel seems accurate. I've cleared the op already."

He left Jim to clear their area of operation with the TOC, Tactical Operations Command. Johnny would help. He wouldn't need to make a visual recon of the area. The SEALs knew the territory almost as well as Charlie. The patrol would insert tomorrow, pre-dusk, then patrol to the small river directly across the Son Ku Lon from Twin Rivers, and set up an interdiction site while there was still light to see by. Due to the size of the target, they'd need to use claymores. Not only for use in the interdiction but for their own security. The sensors showed large troop movement.

At 0930 the next day he ran into Willie, who'd just returned from an op about one and a half or two miles from where they'd be going.

"I'm heading over to the KCS camp for an interrogation," Willie said. "Y'all interested in going over with me?"

Intel could come from anywhere. "Sure."

They left Seafloat on a Whaler and crossed to the KCS camp on the riverbank. By the time they arrived at the hootch, the military advisor, Sean, face shiny with sweat, was already there, observing. So was Truk, the KCS camp chief.

The KCSs conducted all interrogations of their own people. They used procedures Gene hated. He knew of many cases where the KCSs ended up killing a POW during questioning, especially if they believed the man was a VC. They'd arrange kangaroo courts and, afterward, blow the POW's head off. Once the KCSs had *chieu-hoi*'ed, and Charlie or the NVA got word of it, their families, as Tong's had, would be killed in ungodly ways to prevent anyone else becoming a *chieu-hoi*.

Gene took one look and braced himself, knowing Sean could only attempt to control the interrogation if the KCSs went overboard, but couldn't interfere.

The POW was tied to the horizontal flat surface they called a waterboard. Several pails of water sat nearby on the dirt floor, along with a pile of rags.

"Ask him again what village he's from," Sean said to the interpreter.

The POW refused to speak.

Tong wet a rag, placed it over the POW's mouth and nose, and slowly poured water on it. The POW tried to breathe, sucked in water, but no air. He struggled, gagged, in panic.

Gene gripped his 60. The POW would drown if he didn't talk, and if he did talk, he'd probably be shot anyway.

Tong lifted the rag. The interpreter repeated the question. Breathing hard and coughing, the POW remained silent. The rag descended. Water trickled upon it from the uplifted pail in Tong's hands.

Repetitions provided nothing. No solid intel would come from this POW, Gene knew. He'd die. And he himself had an op to run. "See you later," he said to Willie. They touched each other's shoulders, and he left to set up the Warning Order and Patrol Leader's Order with Jim, glad to be gone.

In the late afternoon, with Brian at point, Doc at rear security, Gene's squad inserted into the jungle. In silence, they patrolled north of the Son Ku Lon, up a small river. Their interdiction site was located at the base of the V-shape formed by a fork in the river. The sampans would come down one of the branches and attempt to cross the Son Ku Lon to enter Twin Rivers on the opposite shore.

In the dark green shadows under the triple canopy, Gene used hand signals to direct the placement of claymores along the banks of both of the small rivers' branches. Motionless and silent, the hidden SEALs sat almost back-to-back, but both locations had to be covered. No matter which river the enemy used, every member of the squad could bear down within a split second. He couldn't take the chance of choosing just one branch of the river for the interdiction and having the sampans pass undetected on the flip side, nor risk having them come in on their rear.

He looked up, around, and to his sides. Heavy jungle. Wet. Dark, thick, and shadowy, it engulfed them. On his right sat Roland with the radio. Cruz crouched next to Roland. On his left, Doc was still as a rock. Behind them, three steps away, Alex, Jim, and Brian guarded the smaller branch of the rivers. Near both groups were the claymores, positioned not only to face the river but also to cover their flanks.

They waited. Silent, unmoving. Listening. Watching. Forty-five minutes before sundown, dusk began to settle with ever-lengthening shadows. Insect hum blended with the water sound of the rivers. The air smelled of the river, rank with growing things, of wet mud. They listened to footsteps that weren't. Eerie footsteps, made by lungfish moving. The sound the lungfish made could be distinguished from human steps only by the absence of the sucking sound of feet pulling loose from that mud.

High in the trees, the breeze freshened. Gene frowned. Not just wind sound. Other sounds. Far off, but coming closer. He tensed, flashed quick looks at the others. They heard it too. Cruz hand-signaled that he saw VC.

Gene looked where he pointed. About fifteen feet into the jungle on the far bank, two shadowy forms moved down toward the Son Ku Lon. The low roar that wasn't wind got closer. At his signal, Jim, Alex, and Brian slowly moved to come on line with them.

Eyes wide, they listened to the sound of trees breaking in the distance, the increasing volume of the low thunder still heading their way.

Gene's chest and throat tightened. Adrenaline pumped. Never, ever, had he heard anything like whatever it was that was coming at them. He could feel the others turning granite, frozen in place like rabbits caught in headlights. Frozen, yet ready to explode in fight or flight, and still the terrible sound closed upon them.

Like tanks coming, he thought. Plowing down hundreds of trees. Moving closer every second. The two across the river had to have been advance scouts. But for what size force?

He tapped Roland, who got the TOC on the radio. "Tell them," he said, his whisper hoarse, "that we have a very large force coming into our area. Warm up the Sea Wolves, have riverboats stand by. Things are going to get hot."

The terrible sound rolled over them, got louder and louder. Unstoppable, unknowable. On the far bank, more VC were spotted. He signaled, *Let them pass*. They wanted the sampans, the supplies.

The roar increased, with the sound of breaking trees.

"If the boats come right now," Gene whispered to Jim, "we're still out gunned, even with the element of surprise." He turned to Roland, lips next to his ear, to whisper, "Scramble everything. Tell them to open up on targets given by voice command over the radio." He'd direct fire, then get them extracted. If they weren't going to get the sampans, then, by God, they'd get a large body count.

"Jesus," whispered Doc. "Listen to that!"

"You can bet your ass I am," Brian replied, just as softly.

The boats ought to be close, Gene thought, turning toward the oncoming roar. It was worse-sounding than a freight train. The trees were going down like firecrackers exploding. Whatever was causing it would hit them before the Wolves were overhead.

On line, beside him, Roland's words were soft and heartfelt. "Everything's all fucked up."

The entire squad looked upriver, to the north, where they could plainly see trees starting to bend, then cracking and breaking.

Couldn't be tanks, Gene thought. No motor sound. The roar was tremendous.

"Where's our support?" Jim's face was devoid of color.

"Will you fuckin' look at that!" Brian whispered hoarsely.

They stared in awe.

Across the river, directly in front of them, thousands of monkeys leapt from tree to tree. Branches swayed, bent, snapped, and broke under their weight and number.

"Roland! Call off support!" Gene ordered softly. "If they're close, tell them to keep going, but do not come into target area. Do *not* come into target area."

Fascinated, delighted, the men began to silently laugh. They watched the monkeys, grinned, shook their heads, and continued to laugh soundlessly, both at the sight and in relief, glimpsing the white of one another's smiles in the gathering darkness, then looking back at the wonderful spectacle above them.

Holy shit, Gene thought. Unbelievable. And he realized the first sighting of supposed VC had to have been large monkeys, walking in front.

"By God!" Cruz whispered. "Did you ever see anything like this?"

"Look there!" Doc pointed. "Look at that big one go!"

"You see that leap?" Alex lost all reserve. "Look at that! Just look at that!"

Gene was fascinated. "Never saw anything like this before," he said. "Never."

The main body passed, and the monkeys grew smaller. Young ones brought up the rear. Toward the end of the pack, several of the smaller animals were attempting leaps from high in the trees to trees on the opposite side of a little stream branching out from the river, but not making it. Either they lacked the strength, Gene thought, or they just weren't large enough, and they fell to the stream below. He shook with silent laughter at their screeching down to splash into the water and scramble out, dripping wet, still chattering.

"Hoo-boy," Jim whispered. "I don't even want to hear the shit Dev is going to hand me when we get back to Seafloat."

Gene grinned. "No way out. They'll want to know why the scramble. It's going to be embarrassing as hell to admit we scrambled all that firepower on monkeys."

"Never going to hear the end of this," Brian whispered. "Shit."

"They're going to run it down our necks like there's no tomorrow." Doc scratched at his mustache. "Damn."

"But they'll never get to see anything like it," Alex said very softly.

"Hoo-Ya," Brian whispered in agreement.

Gene signaled for complete silence. The last of the monkeys were passing. He directed the squad into their previous back-to-back positions in the gathering darkness.

They settled in to wait again. He hated interdictions. Everybody hated them. Sitting for hours, and not moving. Just looking, watching, listening for the sound of paddles in the water.

Thunder rolled. The breeze came up again. A storm moved in with a downpour. Even drenched, half-blinded by rain so heavy it was like sitting under a waterfall, the storm came as a relief to him and, he knew, to the others. With it, they could move their cramped limbs a little without problems.

He shifted a bit to ensure his legs didn't go to sleep. Stretched a bit, very slowly. Just enough to relieve stiff muscles. Nothing he could do about feeling so lousy. Half-sick. A long time later, he lifted the cover off his watch face enough to see the time, then secured it again. 0010 hours. Minutes past midnight. The storm passed on, leaving faint stars in its wake. He waited, watched, and listened to water sounds.

Beside him, Roland's radio emitted a very soft click. Message coming in.

Cheek next to his, Roland relayed it. "TOC says sensors lighting up here. You have troop movement."

Gene nodded, knowing already. Across the river, four real VC walked the bank. Large monkeys didn't carry weapons. They were headed toward the Son Ku Lon. He signaled to let them pass.

"TOC contact," Roland whispered five minutes later. "Sensors indicate large troop movement in target area on both banks and on the river."

Gene signaled the squad to maintain position, knowing their self-discipline was such that none would move, none would fire, no matter what, until he initiated action.

Several more, either VC or NVA, passed behind them about twenty feet away. The SEALs were silently, utterly still, even their breathing controlled. They wanted the sampans, not a no-purpose firefight.

Thank God, Gene thought, most of the movement was coming from the far bank. And then he heard what they'd been waiting for—the sound of paddles breaking the water's surface. The time had come. Element of surprise on their side.

The first sampan came into view, sliding through the water into their kill zone. The VC paddled expertly, guided it into the bank directly in front of them, no more than three feet away, and stopped. Gene watched unbelievingly as another, then another and another, drifted into the bank until nine of them, almost close enough to touch, were there. The smell of fish and oil and dirt strengthened, permeating the air he breathed.

The sampans rocked gently in the water. The VC sat quietly. Waiting, probably, for the diversion the intel said they'd planned, before they paddled the last three hundred meters to the Son Ku Lon and crossed it into the Twin Rivers.

Gene waited an additional fifteen minutes, making sure no more sampans were coming. Very slowly then, he lifted the 60 into firing position and felt the rest of the squad do the same. Between them, they carried two 60s, four Stoners, and Alex's XM-203 grenade launcher. His flank men had electrical firing devices to set off the claymores once they opened fire.

The last second of silence split wide open when he squeezed the trigger. At the first sound of the 60, the rest of the SEALs bore down on the sampans, all weapons blazing.

Hit from so near, by so much firepower, bodies flew off the sampans, which were torn apart by all the rounds. Claymores exploded and flares from the 40 Mike-Mike lit the area, all within the initial burst of firing.

After that, the squad selected individuals—hard targets. Concussion grenades thrown into the river killed those who tried to escape by swimming. More were thrown into the surviving sampans.

Gene realized they'd received no return fire. Surprise had been total. The enemy's three point elements were three hundred meters south. But they'd be coming back. He signaled a cease-fire.

Flares from the 40 Mike-Mike still lit the sky. Bodies floated in the water. The sampans were in pieces, some sections burning, set alight by the flares. The air was smoky, acrid with the smell of burning wood and gunfire.

Like ghosts, the SEALs left the scene, crossing the small stream behind them where earlier, Jim, Alex, and Brian had sat guard. They moved in file formation, southeast.

Gene halted at the Son Ku Lon. Roland whispered the latest intel from TOC.

"Large force movement all around you. Sensor boards all lit up. Both banks, and more sampans."

He knew the enemy was coming. They could hear talking, yelling, from all directions. Roland whispered again.

"TOC, on radio. 'You're surrounded.' "

The squad froze. Over twenty of the enemy passed, just inches from their location.

"Tell them," Gene whispered moments later, "to scramble. Emergency extraction. Pickup, five hundred meters east of target sight, on Son Ku Lon. Be ready to give support." Things were going to get hot.

Weapons reloaded, they were ready. Survival depended on support getting to them before their ammo ran out. They only had what they'd been able to carry. From the weight of it, he thought he had close to 450 rounds left for the 60. Wouldn't last long.

He pulled the squad in, pointed them into position, a back-to-back circle. On his command, they'd all open up, fully automatic,

360 degrees, get the enemy down, then move east to their extraction point.

Voices came from both sides at once, converging on their location. Gene felt a gut-tightening tension, felt the adrenaline surge, urging action. He allowed not an eyelash to move until the voices, the crunching steps of many boots, the brushing sounds of fabric against branches, made it definite the enemy was about to walk right into them.

At the last second, he triggered the 60. Hell broke loose. Their firepower cut jungle and enemy down in every direction, as the Sea Wolves came overhead.

"Blow the shit out of the jungle to our rear," Roland relayed to them. "Riverboats do the same, when they come on line."

Moving as fast and as quietly as possible, sweat pouring down their faces, shirts soaked with it, they snaked through the jungle, mud sucking at their feet, vine and branches snatching at their bodies, bullets smacking trees around them. Brian, ducking and weaving, found them a path through, their extraction point attracting him like a magnet. Where he went, they followed without question. He'd never led them wrong.

The MSSCs were waiting when they burst out of the jungle to pile aboard.

Gene counted heads even before the boat crew kicked the engine into high gear. "Is anybody wounded? Anybody hurt?"

"*Another* goddamned dick-dragger!" Doc, mad as hell, hyper, did a hands-on inspection, taking hold of each member of the squad, turning them around to satisfy himself they were indeed unhurt.

Nobody dared not turn when he turned them. They knew his concern was real. But they complained as much as they could without really setting him off.

They docked at Seafloat at 0145 hours. "Clean your weapons, then hit the rack," Gene ordered. "We'll debrief in the morning."

The last thing he heard before falling asleep was "Boy, were we lucky." The last thing he thought, smiling, was that they weren't lucky, but in good hands. Thank You, he thought, and slept.

CHAPTER EIGHT

"HOLD UP, GENE. I need to see you."

Gene, ready to leave after the debriefing ended, closed the door. He crossed the empty room to join Jim, who was standing near the situation map. "What's up?"

"I'd like you to go back to the target area and set up an observation post for any attempt at another crossing."

They never went back to a place they'd just hit. "Okay. Sure."

Jim, hands on hips, leaned forward, then back, stretching. "Riverboats, PBRs, will be banked about a thousand meters away. If you see any sampans, call in the boats to take them under fire."

Gene nodded. "Anything else?" They walked out together.

"Take Doc. You need a corpsman."

When Jim went off toward NILO, Gene set out toward their hootch. He had no problem with Jim's request. He'd been on several two-man ops. The less men, the less noise, the faster they could get in or out. Since the riverboats were running the op, he and Doc would only be needed as lookouts, and to call the boats in on the target. No, he had no problem with that, but Doc would be another story.

The briefing, from a PBR lieutenant junior grade, was really brief.

"We want you people to insert about 1300 hours, patrol down

about a thousand meters, then set up your observation post. If you see anything, call us in."

Sure nothing like the Warning Order or Patrol Leader's Order given by the Teams, Gene thought afterward. He guessed that in the PBR people's view not much needed to be said. They just went up and down the rivers, never patrolling, never hitting anything deep in an enemy base camp area. Just rode the boats.

Half an hour later, he ran into Doc and grinned inwardly. "Ah, Doc."

Doc stopped short. "What?"

"Boy, do I have a deal for you."

"What?"

"You and I are going out."

"When?"

"At 1300 hours."

Doc scratched at his mustache. "Who's going?"

Gene couldn't help the smile he felt spreading. "I already told you."

Doc's light brown eyes grew to the size of boiled onions. "You're shitting me."

Gene shook his head.

Doc's face went cherry red. Veins bulged in his neck. "No fuckin' way! I'm not a fuckin' SEAL. I'm not going. Blow it out your ass."

"Wait a minute, Doc. I haven't told you where we're going."

Doc's eyes narrowed. His jaw tightened. "Where?"

"Remember where we were last night?"

He remembered. "No fuckin' way!" he yelled.

"Now, Doc, if I can find another corpsman, you won't have to go. But if I can't, you will."

"No, sir! What fraggin' baboon-tailed, pus-contaminated, peacocking, bug-brained feather-ass says so?"

"Doc, it comes from Jim, dammit, but like I said, I'll try to find another corpsman."

"Right!"

Doc spun around and stomped away, yelling every four-letter word in the book, and some Gene couldn't identify. Amazing, he thought, the number of cusswords Doc either knew or could make up, once he blew his top. Realizing his mouth was hanging open in wonderment, he shut it. Amazing.

But two ops back-to-back in the same area was dangerous. The enemy would set up, if they were smart, hoping they'd come back in for information or to take a positive head count. So the SEALs never ever did that. He corrected himself. Almost never did that.

He looked down the jungle-edged Son Ku Lon. Jungle dark, green, and treacherous. Just stood, watching the muddy river flow past. They never retraced their footsteps. That was one rule they'd learned in blood, in the first year of SEAL training. He'd remembered and practiced it on all his ops. No way would he bring it up to Doc, in case he couldn't find another corpsman.

God, Doc was pissed. Grinning, Gene went into the hootch to start getting ready, then changed his mind and went back to the briefing room. There he studied the map again, even though they'd returned from the area less than eight hours before. The enemy's position had been hurt by their having taken out the sampans trying to cross. Now they had to make sure no further supplies got through to the Twin Rivers area.

He studied the map a few moments longer before returning to finish mounting his gear out. To the 60 was added eight hundred rounds, two flares, two frags, two LAAWS rockets, compass, map, and flashlight.

Alex walked up. "What are you doing?"

"Going back out."

"Am I going?"

"No, but find Doc. I need him now."

"Okay," Alex said, and went in search.

He felt a little guilty about not trying to find another corpsman, but why should he? Doc was the best. Going back in was dangerous. High-risk. If he was going to get shot, he'd need Doc to treat him as he continued to fight, until they were extracted or Jim sent in a team to pull them out. Dead or alive.

Doc arrived. "Did you find another corpsman?"

Gene braced himself. "No."

"You're fuckin' crazy," Doc said, despair in his voice. "Why do you pull this shit on me?"

There was nothing he could say, so he didn't try. "Doc, I need you to have an XM-203 and twenty rounds. All high-explosive. Six hundred rounds for the M-16, one PRC-77 radio, four frags, two flares, both red, medical and surgical kits."

Doc glared at him.

"Meet me at 1230 hours in the briefing room to go over our portion of the op." He fitted the last belt of ammo around his hips. "Eat a big meal. We'll be out up to twenty-four hours."

Doc wore the look of a trapped man. "You're ball-snappin' nuts." He stomped off.

1230 hours came fast. Doc was on time at the briefing room. Outside, Brian and Cruz stood guard. He walked slowly down the aisle between the metal folding chairs to join Gene at the maps.

For such a smart guy, Gene thought, Doc totally missed the obvious in asking why he was always their first choice of corpsman. All he had to do was be lousy, be undependable, untrustworthy, and he'd stay safe on Seafloat.

"This," Gene said, pointing to the map, "is where I'll have the boats insert us on the Son Ku Lon. We'll patrol to the OP, approximately one hundred fifty to two hundred meters in from the Son Ku Lon, and parallel to it."

Doc nodded, his green-and-black-painted face expressionless.

"I have a radio being monitored in our hootch to ensure that if we need help, we'll have SEALs coming in."

Doc studied the map. "Radio's good," he finally said.

"Yeah." One good thing about the Teams, Gene thought, was that they took care of their own. Even a Freddy Fanther. Anybody who tried to take a SEAL out, or hit one, had to take them all on. In spite of their personal differences, they were a close family, one of the reasons for the reputation they'd earned. People just didn't fuck with them. Didn't dare. Doc appreciated what the monitored radio meant.

Gene briefed him on the call signs and extraction. "We're not to make contact," he finished.

"Right!" Doc replied. The word dripped sarcasm.

In green face and full combat gear, they walked to the boat at 1300 hours. A lieutenant dressed in new clothes, whom neither had seen before, took Gene aside and immediately began telling him what he wanted done.

Gene, pre-op tension already building, was in no mood to hear from an amateur. Especially riverboat personnel.

"You're in charge of the PBRs," he snapped, "but I'm in charge of the patrol. I know the mission objective. You don't."

The lieutenant looked him up and down, obviously searching for signs of rank or rate.

Gene took a step toward him. "I'll follow your orders on the boat, but when we insert, I run the op. If you don't like it, you insert." Damned piss-ant, he thought.

"That's *sir!*" the lieutenant barked, face reddening.

That's shit, Gene thought, starting to walk away toward Doc.

"Get your ass back here," the lieutenant ordered, "I'm not finished."

Gene whirled, went nose-to-nose with him. "You're right," he said softly. "You call *me* 'sir,' lieutenant, or I'll take those lieutenant bars and shove them so far up your ass you'll need a medevac. Now, you leave and get this fucking boat moving before I make you lieutenant junior grade."

There was a short silence, during which the look in Gene's eyes convinced the officer. He turned and started giving his men orders to head out.

Gene motioned to Doc, who'd kept his distance.

"What was that all about?" Doc asked.

He was too angry to talk about it. "Don't worry. I took care of it."

"Seems so," Doc said.

As the boat pulled away from Seafloat, Gene walked to the bow. Had to get his mind back on the op and off that piss-ant lieutenant. No way would he call the boats in, if and when a sighting was made. He and Doc could take them out. They had the firepower with the 60, M-16, XM-203, LAAWS, frags, and SEALs back at base if they needed them. They'd open up, take out the target, and only then call the boats in. All he'd need to say was that the enemy saw them. The lieutenant would really be pissed off.

Hot breeze in his face, he stood, examining the tree lines and river. It occurred to him that there'd been no sign of Willie before they left. Odd. Where the hell was he?

Shortly the two PBRs pulled into the bank on the north side of the Son Ku Lon. They'd reached the insertion point.

Together, he and an unhappy Doc slipped off the side, into the water between the boats, to cover their insertion. If any enemy watched, they'd see only the two boats banked onshore, and not them.

They moved immediately into the bush and trees and disappeared into the dense greenery. Behind them, the boats would wait about ten minutes, then cruise back down the river. Normal routine for PBRs. Familiar to the enemy.

About a hundred meters into the jungle, Gene motioned Doc to stop. Back-to-back, about five feet apart, they waited and listened. Nothing.

Doc snapped his fingers. Gene motioned him over.

"Why," he whispered, before Gene could speak, "don't we just stay here, wait out the time, and then call for extraction? No one will ever know."

In the wet, green heat, the incessant hum of insects and bird cries came clear and distinct. Sweat ran down his sides under the ammo belts and shone on his painted arms.

He looked down at Doc. "Nice try."

Almost inaudibly came Doc's under-the-breath comment, ". . . sonofabitchin' SEAL really is crazy," and Gene couldn't help but grin.

Patrolling was comparatively easy, so, with Doc behind him, he moved west, parallel to the Son Ku Lon, another fifty meters. Watery mud went from ankle-deep in one area almost to their chests in others, but it wasn't too bad. They'd both been through a lot worse, he thought, stopping to look and listen every 100 to 150 meters.

He'd been counting their distance since insertion. They were getting close. The danger level increased. They'd have to be careful the last 200 to 300 meters. If the enemy waited ahead, he'd abort the mission or have Doc call in for an air strike.

Doc, he suddenly realized, was falling behind. He'd have to slow his pace. Turning, he placed his finger over his mouth to let Doc know they needed absolute silence from now on. There was no way to know what would be up there.

Expressionless, Doc nodded.

Through the trees then, Gene caught sight of the river they'd sat ambush on the previous night. Stopped, he waited, ever so carefully scanning their surroundings. Nothing unnatural moved. No sound of metal, no sound of voices. Only normal jungle sounds around them.

They moved up, pulling each foot loose from the sucking mud as silently as possible. Finally they were at the previous night's interdiction site.

The area was clear. Crouching next to a tree trunk behind a curtain of vines, he blinked sweat from his eyes. Sometime between then and now, the enemy had removed their dead and saved any supplies left after the devastation of the SEALs' interdiction. Fragments of the sampans lay washed up on the bank and scattered in the underbrush.

They turned south to set up their observation post on the northwest corner where the small river met the Son Ku Lon. There they settled into position, each quietly clearing a small, individual area in the bush. They'd be there for a while. Gene had hooked four hundred rounds into one long belt of ammo for the 60.

He hadn't told Doc his plans for taking the enemy under fire. Doc, sitting within arm's reach, would be there when and if the shit hit the fan, whether he was told or not.

Silently they waited. It was 1445 hours. Then 1545 . . . 1600 . . . 1630.

He reached out, touched Doc's shoulder. When Doc looked, he pointed to his eyes, then across the small river, and held up two fingers. On their right as they faced the Son Ku Lon, two VC were about thirty feet away, on the far bank of the small river.

Doc made a forward motion with his weapon, silently asking if they were going to take them out.

Doc wanted to make a hit, get out, and go home. Gene shook his head no and put up a fist: Hold.

The two VC moved up to the small river's mouth. They stopped, looking out over the Son Ku Lon. For ten minutes they watched and waited before turning to head north, back up the same river they'd tried to come down the night before.

Watching, Gene thought about how strange it was that both he and Doc and the enemy had all returned to the same area. When the VC were out of sight and hearing distance, he whispered,

"That's a point element. They might be going to attempt a day crossing. They badly need food and supplies down Twin Rivers."

Doc nodded.

The point elements weren't gone for long.

Gene breathed so softly, he couldn't hear himself, watching the two VC return to the place they'd just left. Directly across the Son Ku Lon from Twin Rivers, the men looked up and down the small river branch, waiting.

At 1800 hours, he picked up the sound of paddles entering water. Slowly he turned his head to observe two small sampans approaching the mouth of the small river.

Doc was ready. He motioned slightly with the radio. Should he call in the boats?

Gene shook his head. No.

"Oh, shit."

Gene barely heard Doc's whisper, but hearing it, he knew Doc understood, only too well, what he had in mind.

There were six VC. Two in each of the two sampans, and the point elements on the far riverbank. He waited until the sampans, only six or seven feet away, were even with his right side. That put them between his and Doc's positions and the two VC on the opposite bank. By allowing the sampans to come even with them, the two VC onshore would have to fire into the sampans to hit Doc and himself.

With the four-hundred-round belt for his 60, he'd have plenty of rounds before having to reload. He spun right and squeezed the trigger. Doc pivoted at the same time to come on line with him and bear down on the kill zone with his M-16. Never letting up on the triggers, they raked the two small sampans. Rounds that didn't hit them went into the far bank.

From the time of the first burst from his 60, about thirty seconds had passed, with no return fire.

"Cease fire!" he yelled to Doc. In the silence, he whispered, "Call in the boats."

They had four KIA in the sampans and one KIA on the far bank. He couldn't see the second VC, didn't know whether they'd got both point elements or just the one, but he wasn't about to cross the small river and track the missing one down. They'd stopped the attempted crossing and more than completed their mission objective.

Waiting for the PBRs, they watched the two sampans drift out into the Son Ku Lon. Shortly four PBRs came in. Two picked up supplies from the sampans, while two banked to take him and Doc aboard.

The boat they boarded was not the one they'd inserted from. He wouldn't have to say anything to the slipknot lieutenant. Not yet anyway.

When they docked at Seafloat, he and Doc jumped off. Not more than a minute later, the lieutenant came up behind him.

"What the fuck did you think you were doing? You were to call us in to make the kill."

Ignoring him, Gene kept walking toward Jim, who was approaching. Brian and Cruz were right behind him.

"Everything okay?" Jim asked.

Gene pointed behind him. The PBR officer screamed on.

Jim stopped the lieutenant short. "What the hell is going on?"

The raving officer shoved Jim aside in his determination to catch up to Gene, who'd come to a halt. The shove was a mistake.

Jim flipped the lieutenant to the deck. Before he could shut his mouth, Brian and Cruz had the barrels of their weapons in it.

"Don't fuck with my men," Jim said. "You have a problem, you see me, and I'll take care of it. But don't fuck with my men. Especially him."

He nodded to Brian and Cruz. They removed their weapons and helped the lieutenant to his feet.

"Your man," he told Jim, "made the kills. We were supposed to do it."

A disgusted expression crossed Jim's boyish face. "Was the sampan crossing stopped?"

"Affirmative."

"Then the op was successfully completed. Drop it. You're lucky," Jim added, "that he didn't kill you."

"I'm filing charges," the lieutenant snapped, and stormed off.

Satisfied that the loudmouthed officer had received what he'd been asking for from the start, Gene followed Doc toward the cleaning table at the hootch. "Hey, Doc!"

"What?"

Gene rested a hand on his shoulder. "Good job."

Mud-covered and stinking, Doc glared at him. "You're not a damned bit welcome."

He'd have to do something, thank Doc in some special way to make up for forcing him to go and to ease his own conscience for not even looking for a different corpsman. But what? He thought a moment, then headed out to get a Whaler and motor over to Solid Anchor where the Seabees were working. Behind Solid Anchor about two hundred Montagnards were camped.

One of the Seabees, recently arrived from the States, located an interpreter, a Kit Carson Scout, unaware of the bad blood between the KCSs and the Montagnards. The three started crossing the narrow area between Solid Anchor and the Montagnard camp. One of the Montagnards yelled and the KCS yelled back. Within seconds Gene, the Seabee, and the KCS faced armed and angry Montagnards.

"Oh, shit," Gene said, and aimed the 60, knowing the odds were really bad now. Suddenly he heard the sound of many running feet, barked commands, behind him. He turned to see a mass of heavily armed Seabees coming in behind the three of them. For some long, tense moments they were in the middle of a deadly silent stand off. Finally the Montagnards lowered their weapons, but they didn't move until the KCS was sent away.

It took a few minutes more to find a new interpreter, and a bit more time before Gene handed money to a narrow-eyed but now smiling Montagnard who pushed forward the gap-toothed whore waiting behind him.

Less than ten minutes later, after having fended off her advances twice, Gene walked her into the hootch and up behind Doc. He tapped him on the shoulder, and Doc wheeled around.

"Here's your reward, Doc. She's all yours. Bought and paid for."

Doc's mouth dropped open and his eyes went wide before his yell split the air. "Hoo-Ya!"

"Hoo-Ya!" the surrounding SEALs yelled back.

Chaos reigned for a bit until Roland yelled that since Jim wasn't around, Doc could go behind the plywood partition and use Jim's bunk for the privacy he was demanding.

Gene laughed, watching Doc drag the woman away from the deals she was already making with the others.

Behind the plywood partition they went. A line formed next to its doorway amid much arguing over who would be next.

"For a guy who has such a damned fit over falling in a shit ditch, he sure doesn't care much who he fucks."

Gene looked around into the Eagle's startling blue eyes. "He's a desperate man. Been a long time." He laughed.

CHAPTER NINE

GENE WAS SQUATTING IN the shade behind the hootch, smoking, sipping a PBR and staring off down the river, when Willie silently settled down next to him.

Gene knew it was Willie without looking. His presence felt different than anyone else's. "Where the hell have you been?"

"On patrol with Sean and some of the KCSs." He lifted both hands and ran fingers through his red hair. "I fear I'm the bearer of bad news."

Gene drew long and hard on his cigarette. "What happened?"

"We made contact with some NVA. Colonel Nguyen's people. A small force, thank God. A few VC with them."

Gene's stomach muscles tightened at the mention of the colonel, the instant remembrance of the desecrated bodies of Tong's little girls. He looked at Willie, blocking their small, pitiful faces out of his mind. Looked him over good. His forearm was bandaged. "What's that?"

"Truk spotted a VC targeting me from the rear. Shoved me, took an AK-47 round in the hip."

The PBR can in Gene's hand buckled slightly. "He buy it?"

Willie shook his head. "He's been medevacked to Binh Thuy. It looked to be a bad wound, but he's hanging on."

"Get the VC?"

"We got him. Yes. We surely did."

"Damn." Gene scanned the KCS camp on the bank in front of them. Truk, the village chief, had been the loyalest, been there the longest, and had earned Gene's respect. And he had a family. "Damn."

"I agree," said Willie.

"So what happened to your arm?"

"Shrapnel nick. Nothing important."

"Doc check it?"

"Not yet. I haven't seen him."

Gene grinned. "He will, you know."

Willie smiled. "Mercy. I do believe I'll put on a long-sleeved shirt. Doc can get sure enough testy."

"Tell me about it." He grinned again, remembering Doc's reaction to their two-man op, then sobered. "Dammit, Willie, you've got no business whatsoever going out on patrol. You're too short. You're about to go back to The World and get married, dammit."

Willie jumped up. "I'll have you know I'm a very decent height, sir. Five ten is not considered short. Now Brian, Brian is *short*."

Gene couldn't help but laugh. Damned banty rooster. He stood up and looked down at Willie. "You're short."

Willie snorted. "No need to show off over a two-inch difference. Have a little modesty."

"I'd be pleased if you'd just stay the hell off patrols and stay on Seafloat until your time is up, Willie."

"I'll be careful, my friend, but like you all, I have to do what's right and needed." He rested his hand on Gene's shoulder. "You understand."

Gene nodded. No sense in carrying on with Willie. No amount of argument or persuasion would change the southerner's mind, but if anything happened to him, he'd—he didn't want to think about it. "When did all this occur?"

"While you and Doc were out."

So that's why Willie hadn't been there to see him off or welcome him back. "You think Truk will be all right?"

"I wish I could say. He lost a lot of blood. We had to carry him out. He saved my life. I owe him."

So did he, Gene thought, so did he. Truk had proved his loyalty more often than any human should ever have to. Now he'd saved Willie's life. Time to let him know they cared.

Three hours later, having received Jim's okay, Gene stepped off an Army "Slick" before the blades stopped whirling at Binh Thuy's airfield. The creases in his cami shirt and pants were sharp, his jungle boots immaculately clean. Though his camis bore no insignia of any kind—SEALs never wore anything that would identify them as SEALs—he had all the authority needed. A Swedish-K slung from his shoulder and the 9mm pistol belt-holstered under his waistband and hidden by the cami shirt ensured that.

Binh Thuy spread wide over a good deal of terrain, with the airfield and Third Field Hospital on one side of the Main Public Road and the naval base reaching to the river on the opposite side. Multiple rows of drab-green Army Quonset huts housed people based there as well as the UDT Detachment, the MSSC Detachment, the Acey-Deucy Club, and other operations. About ten miles from the base lay Binh Sumoi, its two-story buildings well furnished with bars, restaurants, rooms, and prostitutes. The town was fat with military money.

He caught a jeep for the short ride from the airfield to the hospital. Nothing much changed. This road ran straight to the hospital. They turned right at the intersection on another that ran directly through the Navy's base to the river on the far side. Still, hot, humid, dusty air pressed down on it all.

At the second Quonset on the right, the MSSC Detachment, he jumped off the jeep. Inside, he went straight to the small bar in the corner for a quick cold beer, then left for the hospital and the ward where Truk would be.

It was cool and white inside the Quonset and smelled like every other hospital ward he'd ever been in. He hated that smell. It meant loss of control, elimination of choice. He stood silent, just inside the double doors, looking and listening. Men moaned, talked. One screamed endlessly, horribly.

There were two long rows of narrow beds, one against each wall, their ends forming the aisle. In every one lay a man tied to tubes tied to machines. Where was Truk? He took a deep breath and started down the aisle, then stiffened. He caught a whiff of something rare, faint but distinct. Something clean and fresh like a sun-drenched meadow. Shampoo? He whirled.

The nurse stood two arm lengths away. She had wide brown

eyes, hair framing an unsmiling but pretty face, and a firm body under crisply pressed surgical greens. Everything about her told him she was the professional's professional. Everything except the look in her eyes as they stared at each other. Vietnam, the hospital, the results of combat in her care . . . the naked ache of it stared back at him.

"May I help you?" she asked. "Are you here to see someone?"

He nodded. "Yes," and asked for Truk.

"Follow me," she said. "He's asleep now. He's under heavy sedation."

He followed her, followed the almost-not-there scent of meadows, to the second bed on the left. Truk lay deathly still, looking even older than he was. He looked smaller, cleaner, than Gene had ever seen him. The machine next to his bed made soft noises. He could hear it, even with the screaming from across the aisle. He bent to read Truk's chart, secured to the foot of the bed.

She talked it, accurately, while he read. Truk slept on, unaware that for the rest of his life, he would never walk unaided. If he walked at all. If he lived. Gene let the chart fall back into position and turned to look at the nurse. "What's your name?"

"Sara. You're . . . ?"

He held out his hand. "Gene."

Her hand was firm and small in his. He fought the urge to keep it there, to lift it to his lips. Instead, he released her. His fingers closed into a fist as if to capture the feel of her hand so the imprint could be kept and carried away and treasured.

"He should be waking soon," she said. "I'll be at the nurse's station if you need me."

He took a deep breath, watching her leave, but looked away, before she caught him doing so. The KCS chief slept, unmoving. He moved toward the screaming, unwilling, unable to stop himself from crossing the aisle.

He didn't have to see the chart to know what happened to the eighteen-year-old lying naked on the bed, but he read it anyway. For three days, the man had been like this. Caught in napalm. They couldn't save him, could try only to stop the pain with morphine. Morphine that wasn't working, couldn't work against such agony. Charred black, his skin, cracked in multiple places, exposed fissures of red flesh underneath. Unrecognizable features no mother could ever identify as her son's. Conscious, unconscious, he screamed, cried unceasingly, and would until he died.

Instinctively Gene reached for the 9mm on his hip. And stopped before his fingers touched it. God, it was the right, the humane thing, the only decent thing to do. But he had no right. Only God . . .

The new little Bible in his hand opened to the Twenty-third Psalm. He tried to whisper, "The Lord is my shepherd . . . ," and couldn't. Why did He allow . . . ?

Suddenly he couldn't stand the Bible in his hands. Couldn't stand the touch of it. He jammed it back in his pocket, out of sight, in the face of the inexcusable agony before him. His hand drifted upward on his thigh toward the gun on his hip . . .

"Gene? Gene?"

He stiffened, took two rapid breaths. His eyes filmed with tears, and he blotted them away with the heels of his fists before turning to her.

"Truk is awake."

He nodded, followed Sara back across the aisle, leaned over, and took Truk's hand in his.

"Geeee . . ."

"It's all right, Truk. Don't try to talk. You're going to be all right."

"Wil . . ."

"Willie's fine. You saved his life. He thanks you. I thank you." He leaned closer. "Don't worry about your family. I'll see to it that they're taken care of. They're fine. Willie went to make sure. I'll go too. Don't worry. Just—"

He went quiet. Truk slept again. He straightened the sheet that covered him, touched his shoulder very lightly, and left to talk to Sara.

"If he needs anything," he said, writing his name on the piece of paper she'd given him, "just contact me, and I'll see that it gets here."

"I'll be glad to," she said, taking the paper. "Not many bother to come see the KCSs."

"Truk's special." He studied her. "How long have you been in Nam?"

"Two and a half months."

He started to reply, but saw something in her face that said she wanted to say something else. "What?" he asked.

She shook her head.

"It's okay."

"Thanks," she said, "for not committing the mercy killing a few minutes ago."

"You saw."

"Yes. I've come close to doing the same. So I watched you."

He'd never heard such screaming agony as was coming from the bed behind him. He bit down on his lip, tried to think. "What do you think of Vietnam off the base?"

She shook her head. "I don't know. I haven't been off the base yet."

No wonder that look was in her eyes. Two and a half months of pain and nothing else. Would she . . . He could only ask. "Would you like to go to Binh Sumoi for dinner tonight? You should see some of Vietnam. It's a beautiful country. It truly is." He had to be crazy. There wasn't a prayer she'd go off with him, anywhere. Probably asked twenty times a day.

"Yes," she said. "I would like to go to dinner with you tonight."

He lit up inside. "What time? Where shall I meet you? I'll get a jeep."

She checked her watch. "I'm off at 1500 hours. I'll wait for you here at 1530." She held out her hand.

He took it in both of his. When she moved her fingers slightly, he instantly released her. "I'll be here at 1530."

When the double doors swung closed behind him, the sudden absence of the screaming came as a blessing, even as the relative silence outside emphasized it. He wanted a drink. Several drinks.

He had two hours and a half until Sara was free, until he returned, and ended the burn victim's pain forever. Death would come quick and clean. A blessing. Nothing could hurt the man like he hurt now. Shaking inside at the horror of it, he headed for the Acey-Deucy Club.

He was sitting at a corner table having a third Seven and 7 when a newly arrived sailor spoke to the bartender, then came his way. A messenger, Gene realized, and took a long swallow of his drink.

"Gene Michaels?"

He nodded.

"I've come from the hospital, sir. Found out you were here from the MSSC people. A chopper went down en route to Binh Thuy carrying some members of SEAL Team from Seafloat. Medical would like to know if you will come and try to identify the bodies."

"Some?"

"It's pretty bad. Three of the five are charred, but two are not."

Gene's stomach twisted. He closed his eyes briefly. When he opened them, the messenger was staring down at the floor, waiting. He pushed his chair back and stood.

"I have a jeep outside."

Gene nodded and followed him out.

At medical, the five bodies lay draped in green sheets atop white metal tables. The first two, unburned, he identified easily. They were not from the platoons on Seafloat, but they'd been stopped down there for a few days before heading to Binh Thuy, then home. The next two were charred beyond recognition. The third caused his eyes to burn with tears he couldn't shed. It was too damned much to have to take. Terry Taylor, from Delta Platoon, stared up into nothing. Gene closed his eyes with gentle fingers, memories a kaleidoscope in his mind. He'd gone through training, Jump School, SEAL Basic Indoctrination, with Terry Taylor.

He had been so funny, so good for morale: Jump School at Fort Benning, Georgia, he and Terry and three other SEALs, all in dress white Navy uniforms . . . An Army bar outside the base. They'd stood out like sore thumbs. Having had too much to drink, Terry up and yelling at the top of his lungs, "You bunch of Army pukes, eat donkey shit!" And he'd thrown his chair across the room. A hundred Army personnel and five SEALs. They'd been shit scared. No way could they fight off a hundred at once. But Terry had balls. He'd try. They'd taken him out—punched out his running lights—and apologized, telling the Army he was just drunk. They laid two hundred dollars on the bar and told the barkeep to buy the house a round, then got the hell out of there. But now Terry . . .

"Terry Taylor, Delta Platoon," he told them, wheeled, and left. Nobody spoke as he walked away and out.

The messenger stood waiting beside the jeep. Gene checked his watch. Almost 1530 hours. "Call for transportation or walk," he told the sailor. "I'm taking the jeep."

By the time he reached the hospital ward, he was late. Sara was waiting.

"Where have you—what's wrong?"

"I'm sorry I'm late. There was a chopper crash and they came and got me to identify. There was another SEAL from . . . from Seafloat." He looked away.

"Gene . . . the burn victim. He passed away minutes after you left."

He closed his eyes, controlled his breathing, and with it, his emotions.

"Are you all right? Do you want to cancel?"

"No." He shook his head. "Please. Let's go."

Three miles off base, on the road to Binh Sumoi, she said, "You were right. The country is beautiful."

They talked about Vietnam. He told her about Truk and his family, about riding in the chopper door above the jungle, about rice paddies and the Vietnamese children in the KCS camp, until they reached the two-story building housing the restaurant he had in mind. "Here we are."

They made their way across the crowded sidewalk and went inside. "It won't be what you're used to in The World," he warned, "but at least it's not chow hall food, and we're not on a military base."

She looked up at him. "So long as it's not raw." She laughed.

Prostitutes and military lined the bar. Every table seemed to have women sitting on men's laps. Music blared from speakers, people danced, laughed, and shouted at each other. Gene put a protective arm around Sara and they followed the waitress to a corner table. When they were settled, she ordered rum and Coke and he a Seven and 7. Eventually they ordered another, and another, before finally deciding to eat. They had plates of noodles with vegetables, along with duck egg and Spam sandwiches, and washed it all down with beer.

The table was cleared and fresh drinks were brought. But Gene, no matter how hard he tried, kept seeing the burned boy in the hospital ward, Tong's little girls, Truk, the five SEALs in the morgue, and for spaces of time he went silent. Coming out of it, he'd apologize and try harder to make the evening enjoyable for Sara.

"Do you dance?" she asked.

"Dance?" He blinked, brought into sense what she'd asked. "Would you like to dance?"

She smiled. "Yes. I would."

They didn't leave the floor for a long time. To dance was to hold someone and Gene hadn't been held for too long. Neither had Sara. By the time they checked the hour, curfew had gone down. Sara couldn't be on the streets.

Gene excused himself, went to the barkeep, and rented one of the rooms the military called back-berthing rooms. He intended to give her the bed and take a chair or the floor for himself. He'd told her he was married and that he and Karen were expecting their first child. She'd told him about the computer engineer awaiting her return and about their plans for marriage.

It wasn't until after midnight that they really began to share their Vietnam experiences. They saw tears in each other's eyes, heard the huskiness of grief and loneliness in the soft, hesitant sound of each other's voices. It was even later when, on the dance floor, their lips first briefly touched.

In less than an hour, they went upstairs.

They lay together in the small bed—at first, side by side. Gene almost held his breath, afraid to move, the feel of Sara going clear through him. He needed her beyond description. Music drifted up from below, but the room was very dark. A warm breeze blew softly through the screened window.

She held his hand. He waited, hoping, and felt her fingertips move against his open palm, over his fingers. His whole body tingled, heating with her touch. As one, they turned toward each other and the length of their bodies met. He almost cried out.

They held onto each other, limb-to-limb, cheek-to-cheek, eyes closed. They didn't move, just held on tight.

Gene, so much bigger, so much stronger, tempered his strength so as not to overwhelm the fragile body in his arms. Her breasts felt like satin pillows against his chest. Her stomach, hips, thighs, imprinted his body, held there by his arms. One hand with fingers stretched wide covered her buttock, the other her shoulder. Both of her arms were around his neck, and he could smell the clean scent of her hair.

For a moment, he saw Karen's face, felt her body, and loosened his hold on Sara. Shouldn't be here . . . shouldn't touch . . .

It was too late to stop. Too late to think. Her fingers were in his hair, tracing his face, touching him, and he began to kiss her, tasting her, caressing her, with a kind of hunger and need he'd never experienced before.

By dawn, it was over. Dressed, they paused at the door before opening it to leave. The knob was cool in his hand. Outside, a woman's voice calling, a child's answering.

"Thank you," he said, looking down at her, knowing it was probably for the last time, once he left.

Her eyes widened slightly. "And you." She glanced at her watch. "Time to go."

When he dropped her off, she shook his hand. "Fare thee well," she said, her voice soft, each word distinct. "Fare thee well."

He waited until the double doors closed behind her, then drove to the airfield on a road made wavy by tear-filled eyes. At the field he parked, got out, took a deep breath, and banished from his mind everything connected with Sara. He boarded the chopper headed for Seafloat. Before they were airborne, Willie's foolhardiness and Twin Rivers were in command of his mind, as was Colonel Nguyen.

CHAPTER TEN

GENE CHECKED IN AT NILO immediately after landing on Seafloat. "Johnny. Anything on Colonel Nguyen?"

Johnny stood to shake hands. "Not so you'd notice. Rumors. Not even soft intel. Gene, I'm sorry you had to be the one to ID the chopper victims, but you were the only Seafloat personnel there. A tragedy. We appreciate your help. It meant a lot."

Terry Taylor. Gene nodded. The corner of the map, behind and above Johnny's head, had torn away from the dull metal thumbtack and peeled downward into a roll.

"How is Truk?"

"If he's really lucky, he'll be able to get around with a cane someday."

Johnny moved the Annapolis class ring around his finger with his thumb. "Damned shame. But at least he's alive. If it hadn't been for Truk, Willie. . ."

"Yeah. Too close, that." Gene frowned. "Not out again, is he?"

"No. He's with Sean, over at the KCS camp."

"Anything new with Twin Rivers?"

"The riverboats are still operating twenty-four hours a day to prevent any crossings. No supplies are coming in or going out of the Twin Rivers area. No hard intelligence from any source on what's down there, other than a possible weapons factory."

Johnny leaned his chair back on two legs. "We've got to get into that area. It's frustrating. Every operation that's gone down, whether riverboats, zippos, or South Vietnamese troops, have all come out running for their lives, or they just never come out. You already know that. Something has to change."

"I'd better check in with Jim."

Johnny stood to shake hands. "Glad you're back. Good news that Truk's going to make it."

Jim thought so too. "Poor bastard. But at least he's alive. For a change, Willie will be able to deliver something better than funeral news to a KCS family." He pushed his chair back. "Let's go outside."

They eased down against the plywood wall of their hootch and squatted side by side in the shade. "So what's up?" Gene asked.

"It's time to go into Twin Rivers on a recon op. We need to find out exactly where they are, what they have, how many villagers are in there, and how many NVA and VC."

Gene looked off down the jungle-edged Son Ku Lon. "What's the plan?"

"An op to collect intelligence. Not to search and destroy." Jim lit a cigarette, took a long drag. "Not yet anyway. We have to know more of what we'd need to bring in, to search and destroy, and what the odds are against us. Don't want to lose anybody. Remember the Green Beret advisor?"

"The captain? Yeah." He remembered, all right. A bad op. Two Green Beret advisors, actually. They were going to take some South Vietnamese troops into Twin Rivers. He'd walked up to the new arrivals, told them he was a SEAL, and told them what had been going on in the area. He knew that they, like the SEALs, had no intel on what was in there. The captain had looked him over.

"What's your rate?"

Gene stiffened. They never wore anything that would give away their rank or connect them with the SEALs. There was a price on their heads and they all knew it. "Seaman. E-3."

"Where in the hell," said the captain, "does an E-3 get off telling me I shouldn't go down there?"

Too bad, Gene thought, staring into the captain's narrowed, pale blue eyes, that the man's brain wasn't as active as his ego. He'd tried to fill him in on the area. What to expect. Tried to advise him not to go down. The captain preferred to run shit down his neck. His background and experience meant nothing, apparently. Too bad. He was looking at a dead man. He told him so.

Veins bulged in the captain's neck. "Get the hell out of my way."

Gene stepped back, watched the two advisors and about twenty South Vietnamese board boats and move out. It was 1200 hours.

At 1500 hours, the boats returned, having penetrated less than five hundred meters into Twin Rivers. They'd been hit hard. One of the advisors had taken a claymore in the face; most of his head was blown off. Others of the South Vietnamese had numerous shrapnel wounds or had been hit with rounds. About half of them made it back to the boats, carrying the two Green Berets. The rest were dead.

During triage of the wounded, Gene walked by the captain, who lay bleeding. He wasn't going to be taken to the operating room. The doctors knew he was going to die, so they had patched him up, shot him full of morphine, and left him, in order to tend to others who had a chance of living. The captain knew it. All military advisors had advanced medical training. He stared up at Gene wet-eyed.

Gene looked down, his own shadow stretching over the bloody deck, making a dark slash across the man's body. Too late for anybody to help now. You dumb shit, he thought. I told you. Jesus. He shook his head and walked away.

Yeah. He remembered the captain. "Yes," he said to Jim. "Safety's paramount."

"We'll go down a small river," Jim said, "that's two rivers to the east of Twin Rivers, and be inserted by a single MSSC."

Insertion took place at 0200 hours. The night was dark and windy as they moved slowly down the narrow river to a point deep in the jungle. Clearance on both sides of the boat measured about three feet. The squad sat silent, half-crouched, bulky with full combat gear, their faces grim under green and black paint.

If they were hit, Gene thought, they'd have to open the MSSC up full bore, lay down fire as the boat went through a series of pivot turns to get around and head back through the ambush to get to the Son Ku Lon. There was only three feet of clearance on each side to do it in.

Twenty minutes after entering the narrow river, the rain came.

A downpour. He could hardly see the jungle just feet away. He shivered. The cold rain soaked his clothes, ran down his neck and into his eyes, but it made the mission safer. Its pounding snare drum sound masked noises; the densely falling drops screened them from sight. At the insertion point, the MSSC tried to turn its bow into the bank but only came around thirty degrees. Silently the SEALs inserted, setting security as the boat pivoted to idle quietly back down the narrow river where it would wait for their extraction call.

Under the dripping triple-canopied jungle, the squad waited until the MSSC's diesels could not be heard. Ten more minutes passed.

Gene heard nothing unnatural in the wet darkness and was grateful for the rain keeping the mosquitoes down. They could nail you through a cami shirt, through your blue and gold. God, those bloodsuckers were big.

Jim gave the hand signal to move out. Brian took point and disappeared into the dark. Jim rose from the mud and brush, followed by Roland, his radioman. Then Gene stepped off, the 60 cold and heavy in his hands. Behind him, Alex, Cruz, and Doc separated from mud and brush to follow.

Sheets of rain masked the slight sounds they made moving through the dense foliage. It covered the sucking noise of their boots. With the hard sound of the rain covering them, the squad moved faster. It could be seventy-two hours before they returned home.

Gene moved in and out of the brush and trees, listening for the slightest sound of man. He smelled the air for the scents of cigarette smoke, body odor, defecation, or urine, his adrenaline pumping.

All prior operations had failed, and people had died. Now it was their turn. But they were coming in the enemy's back door, or at least past all the claymore and rocket teams protecting the river. He hoped and prayed that was the case. If the squad didn't go deep enough into enemy area before connecting with Twin Rivers, they could find themselves in a bloodbath.

After three hours, he caught himself remembering the Green Beret captain lying outside of medical, waiting to die. He had to get the picture out of his mind. Stay alert, use senses to the max.

Concentrate on every step. Listen. Look for booby traps the three ahead of him might miss. Concentrate . . .

The rain finally stopped after dawn. Pale sunlight slanted thinly through the dripping treetops above. Automatically the squad adjusted to put more distance between each man as they snaked through the jungle. If a booby trap was tripped, only one would get it.

Depending, Gene reminded himself, on the type of explosive and how close to each other they were. During the night hours they'd been very, very close. He saw a hand signal.

Stop.

Jim was moving forward, but Gene couldn't see Brian. Then Jim was out of sight. The rest of the squad knelt or squatted where they were, maintaining their fields of fire.

Gene peered through thick leaves. So far into the enemy's backyard, time slowed to a crawl. But it was a relief to stop and rest. His muscles ached, he was tired. Watch over us and protect us, he prayed.

Jim appeared and sliced his hand across his throat. The signal passed down the line, back to Doc at rear security. Danger crossing.

They'd reached the first river.

Gene moved to their left flank with Alex. Cruz and Doc moved to the right. Brian slithered into the dirty brown water and moved slowly across, trying not to cause even so much as a ripple. As he approached the far side, his AR-15 followed his eyes. Slowly he pulled himself out of the water and disappeared into the brush.

The squad waited.

Brian reappeared and gave the thumbs-up signal. Jim started across. As he reached the halfway mark, about four or five feet from shore, Roland followed. Gene went next, then Alex, Cruz, and finally Doc. When they'd all crossed, Gene lifted the cover over the face of his watch. They'd made watch covers out of the leather tongues of old boots. They'd put snaps on them and fastened them to their black nylon watchbands, so the glow of numbers and hands on the watch faces was concealed. It was 0945 hours.

Neither he nor anyone else could tell exactly how far they'd patrolled during the night. They'd had to do a lot of weaving to get to where they were. But they knew the next river was the objective area. Twin Rivers.

Shit could hit the fan any minute, Gene thought. They could walk right into hell and never come out. Here, they were without support. No boats, no choppers, could come in if they needed help. They were on their own.

The squad moved out. After a hundred feet, Brian signaled a halt. Everyone froze.

At his signal, Gene moved up to Jim, who pointed to bunkers made of branches and logs packed in mud. Brian's AR-15 rounds couldn't penetrate them. Gene nodded and took point with the 60. Brian went back to take Gene's place between Roland and Alex. If someone opened up from the bunkers, the 60 could rip apart the structure and anyone inside.

It didn't bother him to take point, but it was hard. Big and carrying the most weight, he now had to be the eyes and ears for the patrol, as well as find a way through the heavy brush. His body ached, his thighs burned. Block it out, he told himself, and move forward.

There must have been thirty bunkers, Gene estimated, once past them, but thank God, no contact. He stopped the patrol and signaled to Jim: Danger area.

When Jim came up, he squatted next to Gene. They faced a small stream about three feet wide. Jim pulled out his map to get the exact location of their position but the stream wasn't marked. He handed the map to Gene.

He studied the terrain features, then shook his head. The stream was not on the map. He handed it back.

Just as Jim stood to go back and give the danger-crossing signal to the squad, Gene heard a slight fingersnap. The signal had been sent by Doc, at rear guard. Each man ahead of him pointed first to his ear, then to the rear, indicating someone was coming up behind the squad.

Gene listened intently. The sounds of disturbed leaves and bushes came not directly from their rear, but to the right rear of their position. Birds flew up, chirping alarm. Almost without sound, the squad, already in file formation, came on line and dropped down to conceal themselves within the foliage. The last thing they wanted was contact.

Through the bushes and trees Gene caught movement. It was one lone VC in black pajamas, talking to himself even as he strolled closer to their location. Not another person in sight. Just ten feet farther to the left, and the VC would have seen their tracks in the mud. Thank You, Gene thought.

The squad was dead quiet. Their personal discipline never faltered in combat.

Almost mesmerized, Gene watched the VC strolling closer. The man passed Doc without detection, then Cruz and Alex. He came within eighteen inches of Brian, who was still in Gene's position. The VC, carrying an AK-47 over his shoulder, holding it by its barrel, continued to talk to himself, just walking along within inches now of Jim.

Jim grabbed the VC, slapped a hand over his mouth, and took him down. There was virtually no sound.

Before Gene realized he'd moved, he had the VC's AK-47 in his hand and the rest of the squad had backed in around the three of them, ensuring 360-degree security.

In a low, soft voice, Jim said, "We'll take him out for interrogation."

Gene positioned his 60 inches from the VC's head. The man's eyes were stretched wide, almost popping from their sockets. He knew about the men in green faces, and it showed.

Jim pulled off his sweatband and stuffed it deep into the VC's mouth, then motioned for Gene's.

Keeping his finger on the trigger of the 60, Gene used his left hand to pull off his headband. Jim tied it around the VC's face to keep the first one in his mouth. When he rolled the man over to tie it, Gene pushed the barrel of the 60 into the back of the VC's head.

Finished, Jim snapped his fingers and waved for Cruz, who was responsible for prisoners. Taking out a pair of plastic handcuffs with a small wire going through the center, Cruz bent down and fastened the VC's hands behind his back. The cuffs would have to be removed with wire cutters.

After securing one end of a small line around the POW's neck, Cruz looped it around the center of the cuffs. Now he could control the POW's movements, by lifting and pulling on the line. He jerked on the line to pull the VC to his feet.

Absolute quiet returned. The sunlight faded and in the dimness rain began to fall again and the wind picked up. By 1200 hours, it was very dark and raining harder. Gene looked up. He couldn't see the sky through the treetops, but something up there had begun to roar.

What the hell? He glanced at the others, who were also looking. It sounded like jets coming in. Maybe a screwup by TOC. Maybe they had an air strike on. His shoulders tightened. Rain pounded down, but the sound overrode it. Wind, they realized with relief. It was howling, shrieking wind, tearing through the very top layer of the triple canopy.

Jim motioned *move out* and pointed to the left. They were pulling out. The storm would eliminate their tracks forever.

They headed due east, crossing the river. By 1400 hours, they passed the river they'd come in on, met the third river, and were headed north to the Son Ku Lon. Roland radioed their new extraction location to the boat. By the time the MSSC picked them up, it was 2300. The squad made it back to Seafloat at 2315 hours. They'd been out just over twenty-one hours.

Willie waited until Gene climbed aboard to say, "It's almost midnight. A bit longer and y'all might have turned into a pumpkin. Now that you're back, I'm going to bed."

Gene couldn't help but grin, watching him walk away, before taking control of the prisoner and getting him over to the KCS camp. Interrogation would be at 0600 hours.

Back at Seafloat, the cooks had fixed hot coffee, eggs, and toast, for which he was grateful. With the exception of Doc's canteenful of water for medical purposes, they never carried food or water on an op. They took salt tabs. For one thing, water was noisy. It sloshed. For another, if they were going to add weight, they'd rather carry ammunition. Too, ops were normally overnight— seldom lasting longer than thirty-six hours. He was really hungry as he sat down. They hadn't eaten for over a day.

Finished with chow, themselves and their weapons cleaned, the squad hit their racks. Gene lay down, thinking how good it felt to get into dry clothes, how good to stretch out and relieve the pressure from his legs. In the midst of a prayer of thanks, he fell asleep. Five hours later, he'd be getting up to attend the interrogation.

CHAPTER ELEVEN

THE ROAR OF THE wind through the treetops in the Twin Rivers area returned in Gene's dreams. Once again, the squad cowered below the shriek of jets that weren't, waiting for rockets to blow them apart. He moved restlessly in his sleep, waking frequently, dreading the coming interrogation.

He'd only be a viewer, only offer a list of questions. The rationalizations didn't work. The VC they'd brought in would be going through a hell Gene didn't want to see and didn't want to be a part of. He might die.

His pillow was sopping wet. He turned it over. All any of them wanted to do was live through it. But live through it with honor if humanly possible. To go through so much, and then die during an enemy interrogation . . . Jesus, at least they'd never face that. Not as long as they had bullets, knives, and the pill—for themselves and for each other.

The KCS conducted all interrogations. They had built up such a hatred for the NVA and VC that they never hesitated to put a fellow Vietnamese through excruciating pain. Their methods weren't always effective. When torture didn't break the victim, they simply killed him.

Mosquitoes droned outside the net around his rack.

Before dawn, he gave up trying to sleep, dressed, and walked out to the west end of Seafloat. Their two Sea Wolves were black silhouettes against a night sky filled with a trillion stars. He prayed for forgiveness, holding his Bible tight. What did God think of him, now that he'd left church behind to become a SEAL? As a member of the most effective, most highly trained military unit in the world, had he fallen from grace? With a tightness deep in his throat, he wondered if he'd ever be forgiven for what he'd done, and would yet do.

Standing alone in the pre-dawn night, he wondered how many other veterans of combat agonized over their religious beliefs. Especially the commandment Thou shalt not kill. He killed often. He was good at it. For his country, he thought. For those two little girls, Tong's daughters.

Bible in hand, Gene walked back to the east side of Seafloat, taken with a need to watch the sunrise. Before going to the KCS camp, he wanted to see the beauty of dawn breaking. Automatically he returned the small Bible to its shirt pocket and lit a cigarette.

The sun rose, blazing over the jungle. The sound of male voices mingled with the smell of food cooking in the chow hall. He turned away, drawn by the aroma of freshly brewed coffee. The day would be a scorcher.

Carrying his coffee, Gene took a Boston Whaler to the KCS camp. Willie waited on the dock. "Is everything ready?" Gene asked.

Willie nodded, his red hair shining in the early morning sun. "They're already inside with the prisoner. Come on. I'll fill your cup and we'll head over."

"How does it feel to have just a week left in country?"

"Great," Willie answered, "but I'll miss y'all, and I'll miss operating, even though I don't get to do it much."

They detoured around a group of children playing some kind of game involving stones and twigs.

Gene smiled at them, and wondered what his and Karen's child would be like, which reminded him that Willie was getting married. "Getting nervous yet about tying the knot?"

"Not yet." Willie smiled. "But I'll probably be a mess when the time comes. When I'm home."

Gene grinned. "Probably. What are you going to do when you get out?"

Willie bent to pet the dog pushing at his knee. "I'm going to work for my dad. Be selling cars during the day and finishing school at night."

"School? What are you studying?"

He gave the dog a final pat and stood. "History. I plan to be a teacher."

"I'll be," Gene said. "I didn't know you wanted to teach." He took his hand off the 60 long enough to wipe the sweat away from his eyes. The day was already like a steam bath.

"Neither did I," Willie said, pouring coffee into their cups, "until I came here."

The interrogation hootch was a few yards distant. It was an eight-by-eight plywood structure, with a few chairs and a table. This morning, Gene saw, they also had a map of the Twin Rivers area available.

The VC prisoner, tied to a chair, sat amid three KCSs and a SEAL advisor. The advisor acknowledged their presence with a nod. By the looks of the VC's bloody mouth, the process of questioning had already started. The KCSs had knocked some of his teeth out.

The translator repeated the question just asked. "Where were you heading when you were captured?"

When the POW looked at the floor and remained silent, a short, wiry KCS slammed him across the chest with a rubber hose.

Inwardly Gene winced. The hose hurt badly.

Again and again, questions asked brought no response and silence brought the hose. Frustrated, the KCS began to hit the POW in the face with his fist again. Blood ran from the VC's mouth.

Grim, Gene, as the platoon's intelligence officer, asked the next question. "Where were you coming from?"

When there was no answer, the KCS interpreter ordered the two other KCSs to wire the prisoner. After ripping off the VC's pants, they brought out a field radio. Two wires ran from the radio's crank generator, and they attached them to the VC's testicles. Spreading the map before him, they asked again where he'd been coming from.

When Gene heard no response, he clenched his teeth.

The cranked radio sent a high volt of current and the VC screamed and stiffened.

"Where were you coming from?"

Silence.

This time the KCSs made the radio "call long-distance," which meant the current ran twice as long as before.

Sweat ran down the VC's face and mingled with the blood. Still, he refused to reply.

The thin, wiry KCS yelled, and kicked the prisoner in the face, breaking his nose. The interpreter repeated the question and received no answer.

Gene was aware that silence, in spite of torture, was not unusual. Neither was the KCSs' next move. They cranked the radio again.

The VC's scream split the air. He could have been heard on Seafloat.

It was too much. Gene jerked the wire leads off the POW's testicles and started to untie the man.

Angry, the wiry KCS gave Gene a violent shove, and within an instant, faced his bowie knife.

"Back up!" the interpreter yelled at the KCS.

"Tell him," Willie ordered, gun in hand, "that if he touches Gene again, I'll blow his fucking head off. Tell him that if he doesn't like it, we'll take him and his family back to the village they came from."

The SEAL advisor looked at the interpreter. "Tell him."

Hearing, the wiry KCS stepped back. A return to his village meant sure death for himself and his family.

"Get them all out of here, Willie, except for us and the interpreter." Gene walked behind the VC. With a sweep of his blade, he cut the handcuffs off, then replaced the bowie in its sheath.

The man smiled slightly, for a second, before fear returned.

Gene turned to the interpreter. "Tell him to get dressed. He's not going to break," he added, to Willie and the advisor. "I've seen it before." He picked up a rag and handed it to the POW so he could wipe the blood from his mouth and nose.

When he'd dressed, Gene put the map of Twin Rivers in front of him again. "Where were you coming from?"

Silence.

"Where were you coming from?"

The VC said nothing.

Gene turned to the interpreter. "Tell him that if he doesn't start talking, I'll let the KCSs return and begin where they left off." He didn't want that to happen, but they had to have the information.

While the interpreter talked, Gene replaced the radio and wires on the table, setting them next to the map. When he looked at the VC, the terror in the man's still-bleeding face was obvious. "I'll ask you one more time. Where were you coming from?"

The VC pointed to the map.

Gene sighed with relief and leaned over. The VC was pointing to an area about five hundred meters from where they'd inserted the night before. "What were you doing there?"

Through the interpreter, the VC said that he was with a B-40 rocket team.

"Were you there last night?"

"Yes."

"Did you hear or see anything?"

"No. It started to rain hard, and we all went inside the bunker."

Thank God for the rain. "Were many with you?" Behind him, Gene could hear Willie's relief in the relaxed pace of his breathing.

"Two."

"Are they there every night?"

"Yes."

Gene poured a cup of water and gave it to him. "Why are you on that river?"

The VC sipped, then looked down. "To keep you out."

"Where is your village?"

Staring at the floor, the VC refused to speak.

"Show me on the map where your village is."

"Far."

Pointing to the area where they'd captured him, Gene asked, "Were you going to your village when we caught you?"

There was no reply.

"Are there NVA there?"

The POW's eyes widened.

"How many NVA?"

Silence answered.

"How many VC?"

"I know nothing. I talk no more."

Gene studied him for a moment, then turned to Willie and the advisor. "I'm done. Get him out of here. I'm going back to Seafloat." He'd developed a fierce headache during the interrogation.

He was halfway across the Son Ku Lon, between the shore and Seafloat, when he heard the shot from the KCS camp. He turned the Boston Whaler and headed back. The VC's body lay on the ground in the center of the camp. He'd been shot in the head. Executed. Willie was in a pissing contest with the KCS interpreter.

"What the hell went on here?" he asked when Willie approached. "What happened?"

Willie ran his fingers through his red hair. "They took the prisoner outside and gave him to Tong. The new KCS."

Gene knew who Tong was. He'd never forget the sound of his weeping, the sight of his two little girls. "And?"

"They told Tong to kill the POW. He did." Willie took a deep breath. "They wanted to know he was one of them. Well, they found out."

Chow had ended by the time Gene got back to Seafloat. Grabbing some fruit, he set out to find Jim. When he did, he told him about the interrogation. "I believe we were real close," he added. "Real close."

"Get the men," Jim said. "We're going back in."

Gene coughed. His head felt like it was going to split wide open. "What time is the Warning Order?"

Jim thought for a minute. "1700 hours."

His head pounded. "Okay." Since they were going out later that night, he'd have a chance to hit the sack for some Zs once he'd contacted the rest of the squad and given them the WO time. He coughed again as he reached the door of their hootch.

The next thing he knew, Brian was waking him. "Gene, come on. Everybody's waiting in the briefing room."

He lowered himself slowly to the floor from his top rack, pulled his blue and gold T-shirt over his jeans, and walked barefoot to the Warning Order.

The only change from the night before was their insertion point. They'd be going in three rivers to the east of Twin Rivers, the same way they'd extracted with the now dead POW.

Time seemed to compress and suddenly he was back in full

combat gear aboard the MSSC, heading out in darkness, light rain, and a slight wind. He felt like shit. His head still ached, his throat hurt, and he was hot. Taking a deep breath, he felt a cough coming. He ripped off his headband and shoved it deep in his mouth to cover the sound. It was dry and raspy. Sweat ran down his face.

He stood to catch the breeze as the boat moved slowly down the river. It cooled his face. Look after us, he prayed. Lay Your healing hands upon me and give me the strength to get through this op. Quiet my cough.

"Gene?"

Jim, a worried look on his boyish face, had come up to stand beside him.

"Gene, are you okay? Are you going to make it? We can abort and come back in a day or two."

He swallowed carefully. "I'm all right. I'll make it, but when we get back, I'm going to need a few days to recoup. I—" He jammed the headband into his mouth and coughed again as the boat turned into the bank.

Jim squeezed his shoulder before following Brian over the side and into the jungle.

Gene, inserting after Roland, knew from the Patrol Leader's Order that Brian would lead them past the first two rivers. Then he'd have to take over point because of the bunkers they'd passed the night before. This time, the enemy might be waiting. The VC they'd taken as prisoner hadn't returned to the village and they'd be wondering where the hell he was. Maybe, he hoped, the enemy would figure he'd been tired and hungry and just split.

Headband in his mouth, he coughed again. His head ached something fierce.

Crossing the first two rivers brought him some relief, cooled his temperature down. When Jim signaled for him to change places with Brian, he again took a second to pray for strength, remembering his burning muscles and the aches of being point with the 60, the night before.

He raised the 60 to his shoulder and kept it there. Going through the bunker area again was more scary than before. Each one seemed to have eyes.

The heavy foliage scraped his shoulders, and the mud was thick.

He moved slowly, watching, listening for any movement. As he passed one bunker, he trained the 60's barrel on the next. Behind him, Jim aimed at the one just passed, then Roland would, and so on down the line. Alex, with the grenade launcher, had the ability to fire into the smallest opening of any bunker that might open up on them.

As they moved, Gene could feel their tension. Every man wondered if one of the bunkers would come alive, or if all of them would. Were they holding their fire until the entire squad moved into their kill zone? He could catch no scent of the enemy within the thick, dank smell of the dark jungle, but until the bunkers were passed, they wouldn't know.

Finally he reached the narrow stream where they'd captured the VC the night before. No tracks, no sound. No contact. Thank God. He lowered the 60 from his shoulder and signaled *danger area* with a hand across his throat. Behind him, the squad set flank security while he waded the stream, entered the brush, and checked out the area beyond. Satisfied, he returned and motioned to the squad to cross.

When Jim came over, he signaled for a break. Whispering, Gene told him, "No bunkers. Not much brush under the triple canopy. Bring Brian back to point."

Jim nodded and brought Brian forward. Relieved, Gene left point and took his normal place between Roland and Alex.

Patrolling was easier as they paralleled the river. But it was only a matter of time until they found something or someone. With the patrol slowing down, he concentrated on making sure he didn't miss anything.

With dawn, light began to reach through the trees. Brian signaled.

Halt.

Gene knelt and watched Jim go to Brian. Jim circled his hand above his head: Rally point. The squad closed in on him to be silently pointed into positions that would give them 360-degree security.

When Gene's turn to approach came, Jim whispered, "There's some kind of structure ahead. No sign of the enemy. We're going in to recon."

Gene returned to position, and shoving his headband into his mouth, silenced yet another short series of coughs, as Alex went to Jim.

When the patrol moved out, they were able to see the strange area ahead. Closing on it, Gene found himself wondering what the hell it was.

They halted just outside its perimeter. Studying the area through a screen of heavy foliage, Gene saw no signs of life, but humans had to be somewhere near. In front of them sat five two-level platforms on stilts. Wood shavings were everywhere. Trunks of large trees lay scattered around. A three-foot-wide monkey bridge, with waist-high handrailings made of flat boards, was supported and tied with rope. It stretched across the river. Definitely a work area. But where were the people?

Jim motioned for security elements to cross the bridge and recon, parallel to him, on the other side of the river. Gene signaled to Cruz to take point.

Just as Cruz reached the far side, Gene, at midbridge, heard a fingersnap. Immediately he looked back. Jim pointed. Gene dropped flat. A sampan, carrying one person, was floating down the river. There was no way that it could pass without its occupant seeing him.

When the sampan came parallel to Jim's position, Jim stood up, his Stoner aimed. "*Li dai.*" Come here.

By the time Jim came fully erect, Gene and the rest of the SEALs were standing too, their weapons pointed at the old man in the sampan. The old man, obeying Jim's command, poled his boat to the bank.

He looked to be in his late sixties or early seventies. A true Joe-shit the ragman, he wore old, torn clothing. Dirty and stinking, his face wrinkled with age, his teeth were black and decayed by the beetlenut the Vietnamese used to numb their aching teeth and gums. He put up no resistance.

Brian directed him to move toward Jim. When he had, Brian pulled the sampan up on shore and secured the ragged man. That done, Alex and Doc crossed the monkey bridge to join Cruz and Gene. Hidden, with security set, they waited for any others coming into the work area.

The village lay close by. Gene could smell woodsmoke drifting through the trees. Nobody came.

Wanting to take a look at the village before heading out, Jim passed the old man to Brian to handle. Across the river from Gene and the rest of the security element, Alex and Cruz, he took point himself.

Gene snapped his fingers. He wanted to signal Jim to have the old man lead point. But thirty to forty yards separated them. Jim couldn't hear the snaps. Gene spoke very slowly but urgently, hoping to be heard. "Jim . . . Jim . . ."

Ka-boom!

Jim, thrown about four feet by the concussion, went down. He'd tripped a small claymore and now lay unconscious.

Gene gave the command verbally. "Get back across!" Jim needed Doc. Running across the bridge, he saw Roland go to Jim and roll him over. Brian stood guard over them, watching for enemy troops coming in. Automatically Alex, Cruz, and Gene joined him in setting a circle of protection around Jim. Doc took Roland's place at Jim's side. Roland joined the circle.

As they formed, Gene felt their shocked stares. They believed he was their lucky element. But now, for the first time, one of the squad was hurt. Had their luck run out at last?

Gene didn't know the answer. He only knew the anvils of hell pounded within his skull and fire raged under his skin.

Behind him, Jim regained consciousness. "There's a burning in my left calf," he told Doc.

Doc, without a moment's hesitation, took out his knife and cut open the left leg of Jim's jeans.

Jim was stricken. "Goddammit, Doc, couldn't you have just pushed it up?"

Doc smiled and continued cutting.

Gene was amazed, a moment later, to learn that Jim had caught just one small piece of the claymore's shrapnel. There was very little bleeding.

Doc put a field dressing over the wound. "That'll keep it clean, keep infection from setting in."

Infection could set in in less than an hour. That could be costly, Gene thought, waiting for signs of the enemy. Surely they'd heard the claymore explode.

Long minutes passed, and still the area was silent.

Gene rose, went to kneel next to Jim. "They're probably waiting. Securing the village. Other forces are probably coming in from their ambush positions securing the mouth of Twin Rivers."

"We've got to get the hell out of here," Jim whispered.

"Can you stand?" Doc asked.

"Think so."

Gene and Doc lifted Jim to his feet.

Doc looked at him. "Can you walk?"

"Yeah. Let's go," Jim replied. But before he took a step, he glared at Doc. "Did you have to cut my fuckin' jeans?"

Doc just smiled and took his rear security position.

Gene couldn't help but think of the monkey bridge Doc had straddled. Maybe Doc was getting back at Jim for laughing so hard or taking revenge for being sent out on the two-man op. Right now they had to haul buns to get out safely and before nightfall.

By the time they'd crossed two rivers to arrive back at the third, where they'd head due north, Jim had to slow the patrol down. His leg ached, and he was really limping. They took a short break.

Jim looked down. "My fuckin' jeans!"

Gene looked away, not wanting Jim to see him grin. He was more concerned over the loss of the jeans than his wound. They'd each been allowed to take three pairs to Vietnam. There was no way to get new ones.

A few minutes passed before Jim stood up. He gave the signal to move out.

He'd had a harder time standing, Gene noticed, and he was limping badly.

Doc stopped the patrol and walked up to Gene. "What about bringing the boat in to extract us?"

"I'll talk to Jim."

"We're three rivers away," Gene said, "and the enemy will be moving into the village area."

Jim nodded. "Call the boat in."

Gene relayed the order to Roland, who immediately got on the radio. He moved Jim to sit next to the river, then directed Roland to sit on Jim's left, while the rest of the squad set heavy security to the rear in case they were being followed. Doc took the opportunity to change Jim's bandage.

For the next thirty minutes, nobody moved. Deep in enemy territory, weapons ready, they waited, watched, and listened. Their hostage sat silently, next to Cruz, watching everything.

Finally Gene heard the MSSC's engines and had Roland bring the boat in on Jim's location. The moment they were all on board, he told its crew, "Get up on step and let's get the hell out of here!"

While Doc stayed with Jim, Gene positioned the rest of the squad, putting three on each side of the boat. Just in case they were hit, the old man sat on the deck, between them.

"We have a WIA," Roland radioed to TOC. "Have medical standing by."

When they arrived at Seafloat, a doctor and a stretcher were waiting. Jim was taken to sick bay, with Doc at his side. The rest of the squad headed to their hootch. They were outside, cleaning their weapons, when Doc rejoined them.

"He'll be okay. Found the shrapnel and closed, with only a few stitches. Gave him penicillin in case of infection, but he won't be going out until the stitches are removed."

Gene coughed and shook his head. Something must be wrong with Doc. He hadn't cussed once. Or maybe, something was right with him.

He was just pulling on clean clothes when Jim limped in. Seafloat's doctor had done even more damage. His jeans were ripped to midthigh.

Brian saw him first. "Those new air-conditioned jeans? Where can we get some?"

The squad burst into laughter.

"Fuck off," Jim said, and hobbled behind the partition to lie down.

CHAPTER TWELVE

BY THE TIME GENE joined the squad for chow, they'd dubbed the old man Raggedy. Sitting between Brian and Doc, Raggedy seldom raised his eyes from his food. Head lowered, the elder used both hands to shove food into his mouth, eating as fast as he could. When he did look up, he'd smile, baring his rotting teeth, his dark eyes shining. Stuffing his old, frail body with hot, solid food, he seemed very happy and content.

"You hear that Solid Anchor was hit last night?" Cruz asked.

Gene reached for the pepper. "Again? That's the third time this week."

"That's what comes of being on solid ground," Doc said. "If Seafloat wasn't a moving target, and going up and down with the tide changes, the damned rockets would have been aimed at us."

Before Gene had taken his first bite, Raggedy's tray was almost empty. He was using his fingers to get the last bits and pieces, the last vestige of juices, from his plate. That done, he grabbed his cup of coffee in both hands and downed it all at once.

Brian looked around Raggedy at Doc. "Don't think Jim's too pleased with your tailoring job on his jeans," he said.

"He's got no reason to bitch," Doc shot back. "I cut a damned straight line, considering the circumstances. You'd think he'd be grateful to have a little air-conditioning."

Gene grinned and lifted his fork only to notice a silent Raggedy looking enviously at everyone else's chow. But whenever one of the squad glanced at him, he smiled.

Alex reached for the ketchup. "Well, Gene," he said, "it looks like your luck ran out. One of our squad finally got hit."

Roland looked up.

"Think so?" Gene asked. "Jim got blown up by a claymore and walked away with a minor wound. Not that it didn't hurt. Doc did the major damage cutting up his jeans. Someone upstairs was surely looking out for us. And remember, no American has ever gotten down into the Twin Rivers area before."

"That's the damned truth." Brian glanced at the old man, who smiled and bobbed his head.

Raggedy was still smiling, but the old man's concentration was focused on their food. Obviously the old guy wanted more. Though he'd only taken a few bites, Gene pushed his tray across the table. Raggedy dove into it with both hands.

"Aren't you hungry?" Cruz asked.

"Yeah, but I'll get another tray and take one back to Jim. He must be starved." He shoved his chair away from the table. "Brian, keep the old-timer with you. We don't want him taken to the KCS camp. In fact, let's keep it down that we have him, especially from NILO. If Johnny finds out, we'll have to turn him over within seventy-two hours. I'll clear it with Jim."

Brian grinned. "Will do."

Back at their hootch, Gene found Jim on his bunk under mosquito netting. Naked, he lay on his back with a pillow supporting his leg. His jeans were on the floor where he'd dropped them.

"Brought you some chow. How're you feeling?"

Jim shrugged a shoulder. "Okay. How about you?" He pulled himself to a sitting position and reached for the tray.

"Feel better than I did yesterday."

"Looks like we'll both have a few days off." Jim took a drink of milk.

Gene leaned against the foot of his bed. "When I saw you take point, I tried to stop you. I guess you couldn't hear the snaps. I wanted to tell you to put the old man in front. He had to know where the booby traps were, and about any guards, if they had some posted."

"True," Jim said, picking the milk up again. "I wanted to get in, take a quick look, and get out. Stupid mistake to make. I'll never make it again."

"Neither will any of the rest of us who were there. You know," Gene added, "we can't go back in for some time."

Jim nodded. "Yeah. We've already run back-to-back ops. They might have missed the first POW, but not the old man and the claymore."

"They'll be waiting next time."

Jim smiled. "Good. Let them wait."

"About the old man . . ."

Fork poised in midair, Jim looked at him, one eyebrow raised.

"What about keeping him here? If we take him over to the KCS camp, they'll interrogate him. Probably kill him. We can question him here about the area. There's always somebody in the hootch to keep an eye on him."

Chewing, Jim thought about it. "Let me talk it over with Dev, since Delta shares the hootch with us."

"Sure. Hey, by the way, some of the guys were talking about putting your jeans up for auction."

"Get out of here!"

He laughed. "See you later."

Gene left Jim and Dev's quarters and walked across the hootch to his bunk. After stripping off his clothes, he jumped up in his rack, pulled the mosquito netting down, and opened his Bible. He had about three books of the Old Testament left to read, but he turned first to the Twenty-third Psalm.

He'd always loved that chapter. It had meant a lot to him before he joined the service, but now, over here in this shithole where they really walked through valleys of death, it meant even more. He finished it, turned back to where he'd left off, began to read, and fell asleep before the first sentence ended.

Noise woke him, four hours later. Packed with men, the hootch resounded with music, laughter, yells, and arguments over the poker games going on. He crawled out of bed and pulled on his blue-and-gold over his swim trunks. He felt lousy, as if he were burning up. He went looking for Doc.

Gene found him playing poker. "Can I bother you a minute?"

"Sure. I'm wiped out anyway." Doc threw his hand in and

scratched at his mustache. "You're not going out and want me to go again, are you?"

"No. I'm just not feeling well and my throat is sore. I think I've got a temp."

"Come on."

Gene followed him to his rack. Doc's hand was cool and reassuring on his forehead.

"Yeah, you're hot." He got out a tongue depressor and a small flashlight. "Okay, open up."

Head tipped back, Gene watched the corpsman's face, trying to see whether what he had was serious. Doc never changed expression.

"Yep." He stepped back. "You've got tonsillitis. Some pus pockets back there. Let's take your temp."

It turned out to be not quite 102 degrees, but Gene felt like it was 110. He coughed again. Probably from being wet and muddy all the damned time.

Doc handed him some pills. "Take these three times a day. Don't drink any milk or eat dairy products. Here are some aspirins for the temp and some throat lozenges." He closed his bag. "Take it easy for a while. I'll tell Jim you'll be down for a few days."

"Doc, I've already asked for a few days off. Jim said okay."

"You'll be able to keep him company. He's out for seven to ten days. That should give him time to try and sew his jeans up."

Gene laughed and stood up. "You're going to really rub it in, aren't you?"

"Yep." He picked up his scissors and snipped the air. "Got to get even some way."

Gene took Doc's empty seat in the poker game. There wasn't much to do, stuck out in the middle of the river between ops. Kill time, don't think too much. Drink or play cards.

Things were slowing down in the hootch when he stood and stretched. Time to hit the rack, say his evening prayers, and get some sleep. Minutes later, stretched out, eyes closed, he wondered what Karen was doing, how she felt, and whether their baby was all right. He ached to see her. He wanted, so much, to know how she would feel, pregnant, in his arms. Would he even be able to get his arms around . . .

* * *

Gene woke disoriented, feeling worse than the day before. It was almost 1000 hours when he took his meds. He regretted missing breakfast, but he'd go to the chow hall anyway. Usually they kept coffee on, and if they still had any fruit left, he'd ask the cook for some.

Sitting alone, he drank coffee and ate three oranges. The juice felt cool and crisp against the hot soreness of his throat.

The hootch was full of people when he got back. Neither Delta nor Lima Platoon would be going out within the next twenty-four hours. The cooks' info had been right. In training, Tommy Blade had said, "If you want to know if anybody's going out, just ask a cook. If someone's going, their PL or APL will set up special chow."

Just as well, thought Gene, stretching out on his bunk again. Lima needed a break, and Delta had three people in the hospital at Binh Thuy as well as another four still recovering from the wounds they'd received on the Mighty Mo op. Lima's second squad had been out the last two days, running a recon in the area where the Mo was hit. But they'd done as Gene's squad had—inserted three rivers away from their AO. He stared up at the plywood ceiling. Every little opportunity to lower the odds and come back, they'd taken.

Back, he thought, to a plywood packing crate—the hootch they called home. But back alive, all the same.

He woke, sweating, two hours later, to the sound of You-O's voice.

"Gene! You guys! I've got a Boston Whaler. Anybody want to go water-skiing?"

Did he ever. "Sure, you bet," Gene yelled back. He coughed, then jumped down from his bunk, determined to ignore his sore throat. He remembered the last time he'd had the chance to water-ski.

It had been his senior year in high school. He and Karen, very much in love, had gone with their church group and two married couples for a three-day weekend on the Colorado River. God, he could see them now, on their way to Parker Dam for breakfast. He'd been in the boat watching Karen ski. At five-thirty in the morning, the sun was just up. Karen was wearing her new two-piece suit when she hit the wake of another boat. She'd dropped the nose of the ski in the wake and went head over heels into the water. When she broke the surface, the top of the suit was around her waist, and he'd seen her breasts for the first time.

Standing in the hootch, pulling his blue-and-gold over his head, he closed his eyes for a moment, picturing her screaming for his T-shirt. Because she'd worn a blue float, she'd had one helluva time trying to stay low enough in the water to hide herself. He'd been laughing so hard, he hadn't been able to tell her that her red bathing suit top was right there, on the float around her waist.

"Leaving in about thirty minutes," Cruz yelled on his way out the door.

"Count me in," Gene yelled back, and winced with the pain in his throat.

Raggedy was still on his assigned bunk at the end of the hootch. Brian had told him he'd be staying for a while, and that if he touched anything, looked at a weapon, or tried to escape, he'd be killed. The ancient, Gene realized, had no problem with that. Old and tired, he was dry, clean, and well fed now. In addition, he'd been given a bottle of Jack Daniel's the night before. Obviously he liked it. About half an inch remained.

Gene, walking toward him, called one of the Vietnamese SEALs over. The old man smiled largely, nodding his head up and down.

"Ask him if he's had any breakfast," Gene said.

Raggedy answered, "Yes. The small man brought me some."

Gene grinned. He could only mean Brian, who was five foot three. "Do you want anything?"

The old man smiled, lifted the bottle of JD, and finished what was left. Handing Gene the empty, he asked for more.

"I'll see what I can do," Gene said, and left, bottle in hand. You-O would be out getting the boat ready. If any JD was around, he'd know where to get some.

"Bet your ass I can," Cruz said, "but it will cost you."

"How much?"

"We'll work something out later."

In less than two minutes, Gene accepted a new bottle. "Thanks, You-O. I'll be back in a few minutes."

"Gene, bring your 60 for the boat and tell Brian to bring his Stoner."

Gene waved, indicating that he would. Cruz would use his M-16 to secure the skier. It was SOP.

"You number one, you number one."

The old man had seen the bottle as soon as he'd cleared the door of the hootch. He sat grinning, every blackened tooth exposed. When Gene tossed the bottle to him, Raggedy immediately took off the top and chugged about a fifth of the liquor before hiding it under his pillow. Then he lay down and put his head on it. Gene laughed and left him there.

All the SEALs in the hootch knew who the old man was and none feared he'd take a grenade or weapon. His war had ended years before. Because of his age, they all treated him with respect, even though, as Brian put it, he was a kick to watch.

Gene pulled off his shorts and put on his bathing trunks before picking up the 60 and heading for the door.

"Where in hell do you think you're going?"

He stared at Doc, coming in. Caught in the act. Shit. "You-O's got a Whaler."

"And you've got tonsillitis."

Gene coughed, trying not to, without success.

"Just listen to yourself."

"But the meds really helped, and Doc, we're going water-skiing. There's just no way I'm going to miss the chance to do something fun."

"So go." Doc stepped aside. "Be damned if I'm going to waste my breath arguing with somebody dumb enough to get in that river when they're already sick. No, by God, I won't fuckin' do it." He stomped away.

Gene hurried to the boat, glad to see that You-O had thought to bring a PRC-77 radio. Brian and Alex, with a skim board, were already aboard. The Whaler had twin forty-horsepower motors on it. Plenty of power.

"Ready?" Cruz called.

"Hoo-Ya!" they yelled back.

About one hundred meters away from Seafloat, You-O powered the boat to a crawl. Alex went into the water and lay flat on the skim board. "Hit it!" he yelled, and Cruz did.

Alex got to his knees, then to his feet, on the board.

"He's really something to watch," Gene said.

"Ain't he, though." Brian whooped. "Look at that!"

Alex was making 180-degree turns, going backward and turning forward again, alternating with complete 360-degree turns.

For half an hour, You-O guided the boat up and down the Son Ku Lon, with Alex skiing behind. Most of the time, Seafloat was within sight. Occasionally they went farther, knowing they had the radio and some firepower.

They were heading back toward Seafloat when Alex called, "I'm done," and dropped the line. "You're next, Gene."

He grabbed the ski, secured his life jacket, and when they turned to pick Alex up, he traded places with him.

"Hit it!" he yelled, and away they went.

What a blast, he thought, giving Cruz a thumbs-up to increase speed. God, it felt good . . . the water's cool spray, the freedom . . . Cutting back and forth over the boat's wake, he jumped about two feet in the air, felt the ski smack water, then come back across. As the boat made sharp turns, he dug the ski deep into the water. The resulting rooster tails were beautiful.

You-O signaled they were turning down a branch of the river. Gene signaled okay, and they left the Son Ku Lon. Brian and Alex picked up their weapons. There were a few Vietnamese squatting, next to the hootches on stilts, right on the new river's edge.

You-O headed straight for them, then cut sharply away. Gene, forced to do the same, sent up a rooster tail that splashed the children and the old lady on the bank.

"You asshole," he yelled to Cruz. "Don't do that again."

You-O laughed. Gene didn't think it funny. There was no sense in harassing people, especially little kids and an old woman.

About half a mile down the river, the boat's engines died. Gene found himself sinking.

"We're out of gas," Brian called. "We'll change tanks."

Dammit, Gene thought, forced to swim. The boat had two gas lines to prevent that. You-O'd probably only hooked up one when he filled the tanks.

The boat moved faster with the current than Gene could. Underwater, he stroked toward the center of the river. If anybody onshore fired at him, it would be very hard for them to make a head shot, once he came up. He broke the surface, took a breath, and looked around. The boat was out of sight, having floated around a bend in the river.

Where the hell were they? Couldn't hear them, couldn't see them. Swimming with the current, he passed a few more hootches on the banks, glimpsed children playing, men and women watching. He'd drenched the kids and old woman with that fan of water. They'd been pissed. He hoped word hadn't got around.

The current carried him around the bend, just in time for him to see—five or six hundred feet ahead—the boat float around another curve and disappear again. Something was wrong. At least ten minutes had passed. What if it wasn't just hooking up a gas line? Getting a little scary. Up ahead, about fifteen men and women were walking along the path beside the river. The men were armed.

No sign or sound of the boat, and he was coming even with the walkers. Sure as hell, one would spot him and open up. He dropped the ski and went underwater. He'd go with the current, as far as he could, before coming up for air.

The cloudy brown water was running fast. He couldn't see, but he had to surface soon; he couldn't stay under much longer. Had he passed them? Were there more he hadn't seen, ahead? He came up, gulped air, and had started to dive again when suddenly the boat came back around the bend on step.

Thank God, he thought, pumping his arm up and down, giving the signal for pickup. His skiing trip was over. He'd never go out again. It just wasn't worth the risk.

Furious, breathless, he climbed aboard. "You-O, you . . . son of a bitch . . . depended on you . . . make sure the boat was ready. Dammit, you . . . could have got me killed . . . out there. I ought to—"

"Gene, I'm sorry. It was a stupid move. I'm really sorry, man. I apologize."

"Ten damned minutes or more . . ." He coughed. "Out there in enemy territory with no weapon. No protection, nothing." He coughed again. "Fucking carelessness."

Cruz looked him in the eye. "Gene, it scared the hell out of me too. Out of all of us. I'm just sorry as hell. My fault, absolutely."

"Damned straight, we were scared for you," Brian said. "Hell of a relief to see you wave for pickup."

Alex nodded, but said nothing.

Gene took a deep breath, half coughed, half cleared his throat, then swallowed carefully. Mistakes happened. Try as they would, things happened. To hell with it, he told himself. Let it go. He wasn't dead, the day was beautiful, and what skiing he'd done had been great. But damn, his throat hurt.

"I owe you," Cruz said. "The Jack Daniel's for the old man is on me. We're even. Okay?"

He nodded and settled back to enjoy the high-speed cruise back to Seafloat.

After they tied up, he grabbed his 60 and went back to the hootch. Some of the SEALs had hit the bottle a little hard. Happily drunk, they surrounded the old man, trying to carry on a conversation. Neither they nor Raggedy could understand each other, except for a few words. Finding one, they whooped and laughed with delight.

Gene was amused. The old guy was no dummy. He'd sat himself right on top of his pillow with the bottle of JD hidden beneath it, so the SEALs were sharing their booze with him.

"Hey, Gene. Come over here, will you?"

Apparently Jim had enough of bed rest. Gene joined him at the table in the center of the hootch.

"You've got to interrogate him," he said. "Find out about his area. We'll have to turn him over in two days, max."

Gene thought a minute. No way did he want the KCSs to get their hands on Raggedy. "Can I do it here and not at the KCS camp? I'll use one of the Vietnamese SEALs to translate."

Jim drew carefully on his cigarette. "You can try. If he doesn't cooperate, you'll have to take him over."

"Okay."

The half-inch-long ash dropped off. "Damn," Jim said, "you moved the air."

"Sorry about that."

"Go find your interpreter."

He sighed. Time to break up the fun and games.

CHAPTER THIRTEEN

WALKING OVER, GENE SAW Raggedy had his Jack Daniel's out again. When he reached the bed, he took the almost empty bottle away. "He's had enough," he told the other SEALs. "We have to ask him some questions."

They lost their smiles and moved away. When Gene turned back, Raggedy had flopped over on his bed and was out like a light. The old man had not only had enough, he'd had more than enough. No choice but to wait until he woke up.

Gene coughed. His throat hurt like hell. He might as well get some sleep himself.

He took his meds, got into his rack, and opened his Bible. By the time he fell asleep, he'd gotten into the New Testament.

When Gene woke, the first thing he saw was Raggedy smiling. He was sitting in bed, eating evening chow. Brian sat beside him, smiling and gesturing. Somehow, he'd persuaded the old man to use a spoon and not his hands. Obviously they were enjoying themselves.

Funny, Gene thought. In combat, their point man was one mean mother. If you were nearby, he'd kill you quicker than an eye blink. But the real Brian was a tender soul, with a lot of compassion. Caring for Raggedy, the true man showed.

Now he thought about it, Brian was the only one in the platoon who'd never joked about him being religious. Most of the teasing had come during their SEAL training, when the men were just getting to know each other. Now they were as used to him as they were to Roland always volunteering to make knife kills.

Maybe Brian was a believer too, but he couldn't tell one way or the other. If their point man prayed, he did it alone, which was okay by him. For himself, religion meant sanity. It was his link to home, and Karen. He returned You-O's wave as he went out the door.

Willie was in the chow hall, sitting next to Jim. Gene sat down beside Doc, across the table from them. "Willie, I'll be questioning the old man, with one of the Vietnamese SEALs, after the movie. Do you want to come?"

Willie stretched, then ran his hand through his red hair, leaving little tufts standing up. "Sure. Nothing to do tonight. We'll use the briefing room." He smoothed his unruly hair down and picked up his coffee cup.

"That's goo—" Gene started to say, and broke into a fit of coughing. It felt like his throat was tearing apart. When it stopped, he swallowed half a glass of water trying to soothe it.

"You sound shitty," Doc said. "How do you feel?"

"Okay."

"Taking the meds?"

"As ordered." He swallowed again, carefully. "What's playing tonight?"

Willie raised his eyebrows. "Didn't you hear? *Bullitt* is in."

"Sure, buddy," Gene said. He'd believe it when he saw it.

"It's true." Jim grinned. "It finally got here."

"All right!" Doc and Gene said in unison.

"One of my favorites of all time," Gene said. "Willie, how many days now before you leave this shithole?"

"Four." He grinned, ruffled his hair again.

"Getting our third platoon in tomorrow," Jim said. "Hotel. They'll fly in about 1000 hours."

"Who's in it?"

"Don't know. I do know we've got to unload a supply boat tomorrow at 1200. They want us all out there."

Gene sighed. "I'll pass the word, but why in the hell do we have to help unload a fuckin' boat?"

"Those are the orders from the CO of Seafloat."

"Dammit, we operate all the damned time. Everybody else puts in eight."

"Gene," said Jim, "there's no use in bitching. I tried. Let's just go do it and get on with the day." He stood, as did Doc and Willie.

"Aye, aye, sir."

"See y'all at the show," Willie said. "Save me a seat."

"Okay, buddy. Front row. I'm getting out there early for this one."

Back at the hootch, Gene wasted no time in setting two chairs up in the first row of seats. A rope-hung sheet doubled for a screen. He draped one of his shirts over each chair, to save them, before going inside for insect repellent.

"Hey, Gene."

He looked up to see Brian and the old man. Raggedy was dressed in greens.

"I'm taking him to the show," Brian said.

"The word was passed that it's *Bullitt*."

"Hah," Brian said. "Bullshit."

Gene followed Brian and Raggedy out and took his seat next to Willie. The first thing they saw was a spliced-in news clip.

"Get that shit off," somebody yelled. "Let's see Steve."

The film's title came up. It was *Twelve O'Clock High*. Half the audience left.

"What's this bullshit?" Cruz yelled. "The last thing we want to see is more combat."

Sitting two rows back were Brian and the old man. Gene paused on his way out. "Have him in the briefing room after the show, Brian. Okay?"

"Sure."

He and Willie went ahead and spent some of the time writing up questions. While they were setting up the Twin Rivers area map, Willie asked, "Y'all ever get laid over here?"

For a split second, he saw Sara. "Yes. Just once. An American nurse."

"Only once? Doesn't the urge get to y'all when you go into town and see all those young ladies?"

"Sure, but except for that one time, I've always thought of

Karen. It's tough, but I just change my thoughts to how nice it would be to be held and loved back in the States, or I think of a dick-dragger. Sometimes, I just get up and leave."

That was true. Except for Sara, that's how he'd always handled his feelings. Just blocked them out. "How about you?"

"Yeah, a few times, but not lately. I can't afford to get the clap or anything else. Don't forget, I'm not married. Yet. I just hope that when I am, it's as solid as yours."

Gene, both hands on the back of a chair, leaned forward. "Karen is the best thing that ever happened to me. She's—"

Brian and the old man came in. Behind them a Vietnamese SEAL closed the door.

"Okay," Gene said, "let's get this over with."

"I'll wait outside," Brian said, and left.

Gene looked at the smiling old man and started with "We're not your enemy. We've been sent to help you and your people. We've taken good care of you here, haven't we?"

The interpreter was good, relaying Gene's words as he spoke them. Raggedy listened without turning his head, watching Gene and nodding.

"Yes," the old man said. "You number one."

"You realize that we can get in now, at any time? We took another man out the night before."

"You have him? Where is he?"

"He's safe. Let me ask the questions. I want to know where you came from. Where is the main village?"

Gene listened to the interpreter's translation.

"The village is two hundred fifty meters around the river bend from where you captured me."

"Who's there, and what's going on?"

The old man bowed his head and said nothing.

Gene grabbed the interpreter's wrist on the downward swing of his open hand. "Don't even think about it. He's talking."

The Vietnamese SEAL's eyes blazed. "He's VC."

"Shut up. Just interpret the questions and responses. Nothing more." He locked gazes with the furious interpreter, seeing hate in his eyes. If the sonofabitch touched the old man, he'd find out what real trouble was. If he didn't take him out himself, Brian would.

He turned back to Raggedy. "What's going on? Who's down there? I've got to know. I won't let anyone hurt you." He paused. "Tell me."

The old man nodded and began to talk about a weapons factory, about the starving people, about their fear of the NVA. Once he started, they couldn't quiet him. For two hours, they listened. When he finally finished, they stood to take him back to the hootch.

The Vietnamese SEAL walked out first, muttering below his breath, unaware that Willie, during his tour, had quietly picked up quite a bit of the language and understood his "I'll get you, you motherfucker."

"Watch him," he warned Gene before they parted. "Never let him get behind you out in the bush."

Once he'd settled Raggedy back in their hootch, Gene gave him another bottle of Jack Daniel's. Then he went looking for Jim.

When he found him, they went to see Johnny at NILO, and he ran over the debrief with them. The village was 250 meters away. They were putting B-40 rockets together and had a large stockpile. There were about 30 NVA and 140 villagers. "The old man said they were starving and that they'd eaten all the dogs weeks ago. No supplies are getting in, and what little they had went to the NVA."

He coughed, then continued. "Some babies have died already due to hunger and sickness, and about sixty of the villagers were forced to fight and set up rocket ambushes on Twin Rivers. He said they knew about the men in green faces. The NVA told them we come from under the water and eat their babies."

"Good God," Jim said. Johnny shook his head.

Gene went on. "Raggedy said that they wanted, and needed, to get the rockets out but everything had stopped. They're afraid to make a crossing over the Son Ku Lon. Listen," he said, "I have an idea. I want to send him back in."

"Let's hear it," Jim said.

"I want to run a psy-op on the old man. Make him believe we can't be killed, and that the villagers don't have a chance against us, then send him back to convince the villagers to surrender."

They heard him out and agreed it was worth a try.

"We won't be able to get close for some time anyway," Jim said.

"No," Johnny agreed. "They'd be ready for you now."

"Have you received anything more on Colonel Nguyen?" Gene asked Johnny, standing up to leave.

Johnny shook his head. "Nothing."

They'd no sooner left NILO than the General Quarters siren went off. Loudspeakers blared, "Sappers in the water." They were under attack.

God, thought Gene, running for his 60, nowhere's safe. If Solid Anchor and the Seabees weren't under attack, Seafloat was.

People ran everywhere. Pilots, scrambling their Sea Wolves, avoided the MSSC and riverboat personnel trying to get their boats launched, while floodlights searched the waters. Exploding concussion grenades pocked the river with geysers. SEALs and Seafloat personnel scanned the river, trying to spot the swimmers and take them under fire.

When a searchlight caught one, Gene, with the others, opened up. The sappers were coming in from the east, using the swift river current to swim in. The night came alive with firing. Lights caught one sapper after another, and the boats dropped grenades. Three dead bodies floated nearby. Gene watched one of them sink before the boats could pick it up.

"Probably carrying the explosives," he said to Cruz about the one that sank. "Air bags probably hit, and the explosives went down with him."

"Way the tide's going out, he might not surface until he hits the ocean," Cruz said.

Gene studied the river's surface intently, but saw no more swimmers. After an hour without further contact, the CO came back to Seafloat and ordered GQ secured. Gene looked at the man with disgust. Seafloat's commanding officer, a full bird captain, was always the first to leave, on the closest riverboat, when they came under attack.

Like the rest, Gene was still tense and nervous. It was hard to relax after an attack, and it was 0500 hours before the last of them hit the rack.

When Gene woke, Hotel Platoon had arrived and was settling in. He was astounded to see his former instructor, Tommy Blade, among them. Couldn't miss him. He was six five and 250 pounds of the meanest-looking black man ever to be a SEAL. Gene had been scared to death of him in training, and so had the rest of the SEALs.

"What the hell are you doing here?" Gene asked after making his way to Tommy. "I thought you were still at Basic Underwater Demolition/SEAL training."

Tommy smiled slightly. "Left BUD/S and went back to SEAL Team One about two months ago. Asked for Hotel Platoon."

Gene frowned. "How many trips over here is this for you?"

"Seven." He tossed a bag on his rack. "Got to get set, Gene. See you later?"

"I'll look forward to it." He walked away, seven going through his mind. The seventh tour was considered the death tour. Teammates who'd made a seventh tour to this godforsaken hellhole—not many did—went home either shot up or in a body bag. Seven was just an unlucky number for SEALs in regards to tours.

He took a PBR out of the icebox as he passed. He couldn't imagine making seven tours. If he played things right, he'd make only one. If he even got home.

Alex came around the corner of Gene's rack. "We have to muster for the work crew, to unload the supply boat."

"Hell." The only consolation was that the supply boat would have the mail. With the rest of the squad, Gene mustered outside for the work crew.

It was steaming hot, and he was in a foul mood until he saw Jim. For somebody with such a boyish face, he sure had an evil grin.

"You-O," said Jim, "I want you to get a Whaler and two other men, and go to the other side of the supply ship and wait. The rest of you will go aboard. I've volunteered you to unload the crates of beer, Coke, 7Up, orange, and so on."

They formed a line. As each case came down, it passed from man to man, off the boat, to supply personnel. Until it came to the beer. For every case of beer that reached the dock, the SEALs dropped a case, twenty feet down, to Cruz, Alex, and Roland, waiting in the Whaler. When the boat was full, they took off.

"Take a break," Jim ordered.

Gene lit a cigarette, relaxed, and exchanged grins with the others. When Jim saw that Cruz had unloaded the Whaler, and was back in position, he ordered them to start working again.

Finally the supply boat was empty. Everybody went back to the hootch to wait for mail call.

Gene was on his bunk when Cruz walked in and gave Jim a thumbs-up. Everything was hidden. If anybody could stow that much beer, it was You-O.

Doc came in with mail and the packages from home. Back up on his rack, Gene counted eleven letters along with his two packages. The first thing he always did was order the letters by postal date. They could be up to six weeks old by the time they got to him, and he wanted them in order so he could make sense of what Karen wrote. In the days and weeks ahead, he would spend hours reading them over and over.

He started opening the packages, hoping she'd received his request for chocolate chip cookies and tuna. Sure enough, she had, and there was a note saying she'd sent what she could. He knew that. Knew that on his pay, which wasn't much, Karen had sent more than she could afford. If he hadn't been drawing combat pay, plus hazardous-duty pay for jump and demo, tax free, he didn't think they'd be able to survive. I love you, he thought.

His mouth was full of chocolate chip cookie when somebody started banging on the hootch door, next to the head of his rack. It turned out to be Seafloat's CO, and he'd brought two other officers with him. The CO didn't enter. Instead, he sent the officers in to ask for Jim.

"The skipper would like to speak with you," they told him. "Would you please step outside?"

It was easy to hear through the plywood walls. Gene and the rest of the squad listened as the CO accused them of stealing beer.

"I don't know what the hell you're talking about," Jim said. "Go ahead. Check it out."

As the two officers reentered the hootch to search, Gene listened and ate cookies, sitting cross-legged atop his bunk.

"Maybe they didn't give you the full order," Jim was saying. "Maybe somebody in supply took it. Have you checked them yet?"

"Your men unloaded." The CO's voice rose. "Your guys stole that beer."

Gene watched the two officers leave.

"It's clean, sir," he heard one of them report.

"Fifty-eight cases can't just disappear," the CO said. "If I find out you or your men were involved," he said to Jim, "there'll be hell to pay."

Back inside, Jim grinned, shook his head, and flashed a quick thumbs-up at Cruz.

"By the way," Cruz said to him, his grin even wider, "I believe you owe me some cookies if you got some in one of those packages."

Gene laughed, looked up, and saw Marc Kenau about to walk past. "Hey, Marc. Can I have a few minutes with you?"

"Have more than a few, if I can have a couple of those."

Gene held out the box of cookies. "Sure."

Marc took two and put a whole one in his mouth.

"Listen," Gene said, "I'd like to use you in a psy-op I want to run on the old man."

Marc, chewing, listened, his startling light blue eyes bright and intent. When Gene finished, he answered, "Sure, brother. You're the only one I'd trust to do it. What time?"

"Tonight." Gene checked his watch. "Between 2300 and 2400 hours."

"I'll be there," Marc said.

They'd run out of JD, but they now had plenty of beer. Gene proceeded to give Raggedy his fill, wanting him drunk enough to bite, and to take what he saw back to Twin Rivers.

"Evening chow's coming up," Brian said as Gene gave more beer to the old man. "Gonna have steaks, fresh vegetables, real potatoes—not instant—and even ice cream. Pass the word that it's one steak per man to start. Then, after everybody has one, we can have another if there are any left. I want to take Raggedy."

"Sure," Gene said. "This is his last meal with us. I'm glad it will be a good one."

"Just in the last two days, he's looked better, and I think he's even put on a few pounds." Brian patted the old man on the shoulder and told him, "You're in for a treat."

Raggedy smiled and nodded for all he was worth.

The treat for Gene was seeing Tommy Blade again.

"Gene, I'm proud of you," Tommy suddenly commented. "I hear you're one helluva operator."

"Thanks, Tommy. Coming from you, that's quite an honor, but I have you to thank for my training." Curious, he added, "Why did you keep me?"

Tommy looked around. The nearby tables were deserted. "I saw, in you, a whole lot of me. When you wanted to quit, it wasn't because you couldn't handle it. You just couldn't see the reason for the exercise."

The exercise had been a bitch. Even now Gene wouldn't want to repeat it. They'd staggered up on the beach next to the mud flats after a six-hour ocean swim, shaking with cold, and so weary they couldn't even talk. And that's when Tommy'd ordered them to do headstands in the mud. He'd sunk in to his neck. He'd scraped mud away from his eyes and out of his ears, gasping for breath. And Tommy'd ordered them to do a repeat, before sending them back into the ocean to wash off.

"Remember, you waited until it was over. You completed everything." Tommy rubbed the back of his neck. "I couldn't tell you why, at that time. You showed guts, then reason, and only wanted an explanation."

Gene was quiet, remembering how upset he'd been. He'd spent plenty of time in Vietnam's mud since. Nothing here could match the mudflats during training.

"You've made me proud to be your teacher," Tommy continued. "You've got one helluva reputation going on down here. I was right in keeping you."

"Tommy," Gene said, "let me buy you a beer."

"Absolutely," said Tommy.

Walking out, he added, "Gene, I've asked for you to take my place for a few days during Hotel's break-in op. You know the area, you're good, and, like me, you carry the 60. Jim said it was okay, if you agreed."

"Sure, Tommy. Anything you want."

"You love to operate."

"Yeah."

Over beer, Gene learned that Tommy was leaving for Saigon to take the chief's test—the reason he'd asked him to substitute. All new platoons were taken out by a platoon member who knew the area and sounds, the hot spots and so on. Most of the men were new, just out of training, but three or four had prior tours. Things changed so fast, though, and several years might have passed since the priors' tours.

"What's that smell?" somebody asked as they walked back to their hootches.

A rotten, foul smell was coming from the east side of Seafloat. Gene's nose crinkled. It really stank.

"That's a floater," Tommy said.

He'd know, Gene thought, after being here six times.

They went to see if a body from the sapper attack had floated in between the barges that made up Seafloat. A couple of hours of daylight were left, so they'd be able to spot it if there was one. It wouldn't take long in the water, with the heat, for a body to bloat.

Standing at the edge, near Jim and Delta's Chris, they looked. Nothing.

Jim and Chris ordered two men to put on scuba tanks and check under the barges. Alex and Roland got tanks, put on masks and fins, took flashlights, and went into the river. From Delta, Marc and Steve Mansen did the same, on the west side of Seafloat.

Gene coughed, and almost gagged at the same time, from the stench. Beside him, Tommy breathed through his mouth rather than his nose. Not five minutes had passed before Alex and Roland came up.

"We've found a body under our hootch," Roland yelled.

Before Jim replied, he gave three hard raps on the other deck, bringing up the divers under Hotel's hootch to tell them.

Gene waited for the four divers to bring the swollen corpse to the surface. It had to be pulled down first, then over to the side, and up. Visibility would be nonexistent under there, so they'd have to do it by touch. After another five minutes, up it popped.

"You-O," Jim ordered, "get a Whaler and a line, and take the body to the south shore."

"There's something else under there," Marc called, "and it's not a stiff."

"Find out what it is," Chris ordered, knowing the divers had a good twenty minutes of air left in their tanks.

They dove. Time passed.

Gene looked at his watch. Twenty minutes almost gone. Long time down in the dark. But not as dark as the ocean. Not as cold and dangerous either.

He and Tommy exchanged glances. Finally heads broke water and a large, block-shaped object was handed up to them. Carefully they laid it down on deck. Jim knelt and cut open a corner of the wrapping.

Gene stared, horrified. Behind him, he heard the gathered SEALs' "Oh, shit" at the sight of the huge block of C-4 plastic explosive. All of them backed away.

"Call in Explosives Ordinance Disposal," Jim ordered.

EOD had to come. SEALs knew explosives, but were trained in setting them, blowing things up, not disarming them. That was EOD's job. Anytime the SEALs did any disarming, they did it by blowing up the explosive in place.

EOD flew in about an hour and a half later, took the charge apart, and defused the device. "You were lucky," they said. "There were pencil fuses on it and they were fired. Only a faulty wire kept the whole two hundred and twelve pounds from detonating."

Holy shit, Gene thought. That was enough to blow up half of Seafloat, and any boats next to it, to hell and back. If the sappers had placed the charge at the other end, where the fuel and ammo were, Seafloat would have left the map.

"They must really want you guys bad," the wiry EOD man said. "They knew what they were doing. You SEALs were their target. Cover your asses."

Gene shivered, watching the EOD people board their chopper. "Thanks again," he called.

"Tell me," Tommy said, "when it was placed. And how."

Gene told him and added, "We thought they were coming in, not leaving. We don't stand watch. Seafloat personnel does."

"Who sets the watch?"

"I hear, the supply officer."

Tommy spit in the water. "I want to speak to that asshole," he said, and stormed off.

"Some of you better go with him," Chris said.

Followed by five others, Gene went after Tommy, catching up with him just in time to see him slam the door open.

"Where's Lieutenant Smith?"

"Here," said Smith. "What's the problem?"

Tommy loomed over him. "I want to speak to those men on watch last night, and the watch section tonight. Get them."

The lieutenant, about five foot six and 130 pounds, was obviously intimidated by Tommy's size and anger, and didn't hesitate. He sent for the men. When they walked in, Tommy laid into them.

"You people fucked up. You're not out there to drink, sleep, or play grab-ass. If you're on watch, you'd sure as hell better be watching for those guys." His fists clenched. "This is our home. We're supposed to be safe here. If I find or see or hear of one of you fucking up again, I'll slit your throats myself."

He turned to the lieutenant. "And I'll drop his body in your rack. You're responsible for seeing that they stay alert. If you can't, I'll be back for you."

Gene stepped back as he whirled and left. It didn't take long for the word to spread. The legend that was Tommy had definitely returned.

CHAPTER FOURTEEN

"COME ON OVER," TOMMY said when they reached Hotel's hootch. "I want you to meet our lieutenant. He wants to get out in the bush soon. I've already told him about you."

Heads turned when they walked in. They're so young, Gene thought, forgetting he was only months older himself.

"John," Tommy said, "this is Seaman Gene Michaels."

"Lieutenant Hagar," Gene said, taking the outstretched hand, "nice to meet you, sir." The man was a ringer for Steve McQueen. Same cool measuring look in the blue eyes, same curly, sandy hair. Even built like him.

"It's John, here," the lieutenant replied. "Tommy told me you're the only one that could fill his shoes while he's gone. Says you're one helluva operater."

Gene shook his head. "I can't fill his shoes. No one could. But I do know the area, and I can take you out. I've got a B-40 rocket team location."

Lieutenant Hagar, hands on hips, tilted his head just a bit in silent question.

"Let's go out tomorrow and set an ambush." Gene paused, giving the lieutenant time to say something. He didn't. So Gene outlined the plan he had in mind.

"We'll get in before the rocket team comes down to set their night ambush. The men can get used to the weather and the night sounds. It will be a light contact."

"Your information good?"

"Yes, sir. I was planning to run it with my squad."

"Okay," Lieutenant Hagar said, "we'll talk tomorrow morning."

Tommy walked him to the door. "Good job."

Gene waved as he left. He had to get an M-16 ready for midnight and the old man.

Within the next half hour, he'd gone to supply and found a gunner's mate to take four M-16 rounds apart and plug up the necks of the shell casings. Putting the four rounds of homemade blanks in his pocket, he went back to his hootch.

It took about two seconds to locate Marc Kenau. He had a fistful of Freddy Fanther's blue-and-gold. Fanther dangled about a foot and a half above the floor, both hands protecting his face. He was looking out between his fingers and yelling for Marc to set him down.

Gene sighed. He walked over and stood behind Fanther where Marc could see him. When he did, Gene motioned toward the door and raised his eyebrows in question. At Marc's quick nod, he went back outside. Moments later, the Eagle joined him, leaving Freddy Fanther inside and yelling, amid the roar of the SEALs' laughter.

"Piss you off?"

"Always," Marc answered. "Biggest mouth I've ever seen."

"Parakeet ass, though."

"Got that right. What's up?"

Gene pulled the blank rounds out of his pocket. "Got 'em. Wanted to check them and the M-16 out with you. I thought we should inspect them together and get ready."

At the cleaning table, they checked the empty chamber of the M-16 to be used, then counted the rounds which were placed in the magazine. Two live rounds first, then two blanks, two live, then the last two blanks. When they were both satisfied, Gene handed the M-16 and the magazine to Marc.

"All yours until 2300 hours."

"You can bet nobody's gonna fuck with it between now and then. Who else knows what's coming down?"

"Right now, only Jim, Willie, NILO, and us. Brian will have to."

Marc smiled. "Turned into a mother hen with the old man, Brian has. You're right. Little as he is, he's nobody to get mad if you can help it."

"Got that right, buddy. I'll come get you when Jim gives the word. By the way," he added, "I'm just wondering . . ."

"What?"

"Well, about you writing poetry. Have you—"

Marc shook his head. "Been thinking about it, but that's all."

"Hope it comes together for you."

"Yeah."

End of conversation, Gene thought, and was taken by a fit of coughing that left him sweating and holding his throat. Damned tonsils. Sooner or later, they had to go.

Back inside, he settled down to reread the packet of letters from Karen. *I love you,* she wrote, and he wished she could know just how much he loved her, longed for her, wanted to be with her. He read on slowly, relishing every word.

"Let's do it." Jim was standing beside his rack. "Sorry. Didn't mean to startle you, but it's time."

Gene sighed. "That's okay." He folded the letter and put it back in its envelope.

"I'll get NILO," Jim said. "You get Marc and the old man."

"Yeah."

Willie was playing poker. Gene tapped him on the shoulder, and he looked up. "You ready to go?"

"Sure," he said, and folded his hand.

Willie went to the KCS camp to get an interpreter and bring him back to Seafloat, while Gene talked to Brian.

"Get the old man's clothes too and bring him outside. When Willie gets back with the interpreter, we'll have a Whaler warmed up and standing by."

Brian brought Raggedy out just before midnight. The old man was almost too drunk to walk in spite of Brian's help. He was not only nodding and smiling, he was giggling and trying to sing.

Marc stood at the edge of Seafloat, next to an empty M-60 can weighed down by the sandbag inside. Gene faced him from some distance away, with Jim and Johnny from NILO standing behind him.

He motioned to his right. "Brian, take Raggedy and stand over there, by Willie and the interpreter."

While Brian walked the old man over, Gene checked the inside of the magazine again before putting it into the M-16. He cocked the weapon. When Brian and Raggedy were in place, he spoke to the interpreter. "Tell the old man SEALs cannot be killed. Tell him we are letting him go back home, to tell his people that they have three days to surrender or we will come back in and kill them all."

Gene waited until the interpreter had finished. Then he raised the M-16, aimed it at the middle of Marc's chest, and squeezed the first blank round off. When he looked at Raggedy, Gene saw his eyes were wide. He was shocked.

Marc hadn't flinched. He stood immobile, his startling light blue eyes slightly narrowed, with a look on his face that was absolutely cold—totally without feeling.

Gene cocked the M-16 and fired the second blank into him. He didn't even blink. The Eagle, Gene thought, is one scary-looking dude. Raggedy was clinging to Brian's arm, staring.

He cocked the M-16 again, knowing the old man would never notice. All his attention was on Marc. After firing, he had to recock the weapon. Having the bullet removed, and replaced with light wadding to keep the powder in, wasn't enough to blow the bolt back. He'd have needed a blank firing adaptor, but they were only used in training. None was available on Seafloat. Too late for training here.

He fired two live rounds into the M-60 can, blowing holes in it that Raggedy could clearly see. Gene thought the old man was going to have a heart attack. He was praying and muttering a thousand words a minute.

"You evil spirits, you evil spirits," was all Gene could make out.

After he'd fired two more blanks at Marc and two more live rounds into the M-60 can, Marc, still with that awful absence of feeling on his face, simply walked away and disappeared in the crowd of SEALs, who'd appeared at the sound of the first shot.

It took a little while for Brian to get the old man calm enough to listen.

Gene turned to the interpreter. "Tell him to tell his people what he saw, and that they have three days. No more." He glanced around. "You-O, show him the M-60 can, up close."

The old man looked, but wouldn't touch it. He was repeating, "You evil spirits," over and over.

"Brian," said Gene, "get him dressed in his own clothes, will you?"

"Right," he said. "God, I hope this works."

When Raggedy was dressed, Willie, Brian, the interpreter, and Gene loaded him into the Whaler and moved out to drop him off at the mouth of the river to the east of Twin Rivers. After the old man had scurried off into the darkness, they returned to Seafloat.

Johnny, from NILO, stopped Gene, who was on the way to get some rest. "It just might work. We can't go get them. Maybe they'll bite and come to us."

"Time will tell." Gene started coughing again. "Gotta get some sleep."

In bed, he said a prayer for the old man. He'd hated frightening him so, but maybe the villagers would come out, maybe Raggedy would have the chance to live out his life in peace. He reached for one of Karen's letters. Tomorrow would bring another day—and another op.

CHAPTER FIFTEEN

GENE WOKE BEFORE SUNRISE, drenched with sweat, his bunk soaked with it. He squinted at his watch and calculated he'd had a badly needed six hours of sleep. In one motion, he sat up, swung his legs over the side, and dropped to the floor. The impact sent a shock wave through his body that culminated in his skull. His chest and throat were so congested, he choked, setting off a chain reaction of coughing. It felt like twenty pounds of C-4 had gone off, high-order, in his head.

He dressed in the dark and tried to suppress the coughing so it wouldn't wake the others. They wouldn't be getting up for another two and a half hours. Don't want to be the one to do that, he thought as he took his meds. He sprayed his throat, wiped his face, and quietly left the hootch.

Outside, Seafloat lay silent in the night. Gene went to the east end of the barge to watch the sun rise. The dark sky, vast and majestic, glittered with what seemed a billion stars. Far off, on the horizon, the pale aura over the jungle told him a light rain fell there. The sight conjured memories of the rhythmic sounds of rain against a gray-black backdrop of sky, the cool night smell of it that always surfaced thoughts of home.

He stood watching, silently describing the feel of pre-dawn to himself—quiet, still, calm, peaceful. And suddenly he thought of Sara—her softness, how pretty she was, and how much she cared—not just about her patients but about all of them out here. She would never know how much she had eased his pain and loneliness.

Arms crossed, he stared out across the dark jungle, seeing only her face. Before they'd held each other, he'd seen the effects of stress, constant involvement with pain, and the weariness in her face. Afterward, for a while at least, there had been the absence of those things.

But he should never have . . . Even as he asked God to forgive him, Gene thanked Him for bringing him and Sara together. They would probably never see each other again. Fare thee well too, he wished her silently.

The horizon turned rose and lavender and peach. Forget, he ordered himself. Somehow, thoughts of Sara had to be buried. Dreaming of her, out here, was distracting—too dangerous to allow. Once back in The World, it could be dangerous to his marriage, and hurtful and unfair to Karen. He jammed his hands into his back pockets and focused attention on the fiery rim of the rising sun.

A gentle breeze came out of the west, caressed his face, and brought the aroma of coffee brewing. He headed in that direction. As he passed the hootches, he heard voices and the sounds of men getting ready for the day.

The hot coffee tasted great. Sitting with a cupful in his hands, Gene thought about the coming break-in op, for Hotel Platoon.

It would be a good op for them. And they'd be operating in an area close to support and extraction. Intel had it that three to five VC had set up a B-40 rocket sight, about a mile east of Old Nam Cam Annex. Their intent, as always, would be to launch rockets at the riverboats on night patrol. Fortunately previous teams had never been able to hit one of the boats, but sooner or later one would.

Overtaken by coughing, Gene almost spilled his coffee before he could set the cup down. Afterward, he felt limp. Each time he coughed it felt as if his head exploded, and a rough, tight chest pain followed. The more he coughed, expelling a thick green mucus, the more raspy his lungs felt. It hurt to take a deep breath.

He took several sips of coffee to soothe his throat before he picked up his fork again. A few minutes later, Hotel's lieutenant,

John Hagar, walked over, set his tray down, and joined him. As they ate, Gene went over the basics of the break-in op. They adjourned to the briefing room a short time later, where he gave Hagar the full intel report on the target.

"The insertion should be around 1600 hours," Gene advised. "We'll move slowly to enable the men to get used to the terrain they'll be working for the next six months." Unlike all other military units in Vietnam, the length of a SEAL tour was 180 days. With the number of operations they performed, under their Military Directive, in actual combat time their half year would probably equal a two-year tour with any other unit or service.

"The patrol," Gene continued, "will be able to familiarize themselves with the sights, sounds, and smells of the Delta. I'll be your APL, but you should bring in men from your squad to do all the legwork. I'll be there if needed."

"Sounds good," said John. "I'll get things moving."

Gene didn't doubt it. As he expected, the new squad was professional in preparing for the Warning Order and the Patrol Leader's Order. It seemed like no time before they were getting off the boat at their insertion point.

As substitute for Tommy, Gene took his position in the center of the squad's file formation. There was still plenty of light as they moved out. The men would be able to see everything.

The silent squad patrolled slowly, observing everything in their new environment. After a time, dusk began to fall. The shadows grew long, and what sunlight filtered down through the levels of treetops to the floor of the jungle would be gone, Gene knew, within thirty minutes.

Oh, shit! Frozen in place, his hand shot up to halt the patrol.

Behind him, the men stopped, but in front, they kept moving. He snapped his fingers to get their attention and got them to halt. The moment John looked back, Gene signaled for him to come to his location. When he did, Gene pointed out the booby trap.

An M-26 fragment grenade was wedged between three branches of a tree, about five or six feet from the ground. Silently he showed John the trip wire running down the back side of the trunk and across the small area. The wire, suspended about six inches off the ground, fortunately was running parallel to the patrol's movement. If they had crossed over at that point, toward the river, one of the squad would have snagged the wire and pulled the pin, exploding the grenade at head level.

John looked at Gene—with the kind of look that said, My God, but we're lucky—before beginning the process of calling each man up to see the booby trap, as the rest set security and waited their turn.

"Look carefully," Gene whispered to each of them. "Where there's one, we'll probably find more."

When Hotel's point man came up to look at the device, Gene handed him a three-foot pliable twig. "Hold it in front of you, while you lead us to the objective site, to detect trip wires. When the twig touches a wire, you'll feel the resistance. The twig will bend without setting off the booby trap."

The point man took the twig. Gene shook his head and stopped him. He took a minute more to show him how to hold the twig and his Stoner together, so that wherever his eyes and weapon tracked, the twig would still be leading. That done, they moved out and headed into their objective.

Once there, just as stated in the PLO, each man settled into position, to wait for the enemy to enter their kill zone.

They're good, Gene thought. Quiet and wide-eyed. The adrenaline would be pumping through their veins while they waited for the click that would let them open up, with the overwhelming firepower they possessed. He knew, too, that after a few ops, the adrenaline flow would decrease, and they'd learn to relax slightly until the time came when the shit hit the fan.

But tonight they were wired. All senses on full alert, they would be flinching at the smallest noise in the darkness and trying to distinguish the differing sounds of jungle versus man. Gene had no doubt that this, their first op, would stay with them forever. He eased back into his position, closed his eyes for a brief moment, and relaxed.

He felt lousy. Several times during the patrol, he'd shoved his sweatband into his mouth to silence his cough. Sometimes he'd shoved it so far down his throat that he had gagged, and ended up both retching and coughing. Between the heat, the humidity, and his fever, he dripped sweat. Worse, nightfall had brought ten thousand mosquitoes. The noise of the humming little bloodsuckers was a constant background in the jungle.

If intel was correct, the B-40 rocket team would be moving down, in about an hour, to set up on the Son Ku Lon bank.

Slap!

Gene froze and listened hard. Everything stayed silent. One of the FNGs—fucking new guys—must have been bit by a mosquito or a fire ant and slapped his head or face. Very slowly, very carefully, not disturbing the silence, Gene crept over to the XM-203 man and leaned over his shoulder.

Staring into wide brown eyes in a young face, he whispered, "If you slap another mosquito, you could get us all killed. If you survive, and I get out as well, I will rip your head off, defecate in it, then screw it on backward. Here." He handed the man his insect repellent and returned to his position.

Time crawled. Then Gene heard engines. From the sound of them, it had to be their own Swift boats patrolling, but they were in the wrong area. He and Hagar had cleared an AO of nine grid squares, one thousand square meters per grid, for their break-in op. All of it was off limits to all other operations while they were in there. Aircraft wouldn't even fly over unless he and Hagar called them in.

Gene's skin crawled. The boats were coming closer. The slightest sound from anyone in the squad, and the boat—or boats—would turn their bow-mounted, twin .50-caliber machine guns on their location and open up. Their rounds couldn't pierce the boats' armor plating, and with only brush for cover, there was no chance for survival.

He watched the two dark masses coming up the river, ever closer, and prayed that Hotel's squad would maintain silence discipline, that the FNG wouldn't kill another vampire mosquito. Let them pass . . . The squad couldn't make radio contact with TOC . . . boat crew might hear the radio's squelch.

Twenty meters from their location, the boats moved slowly. Only minutes until they'd pass—oh, shit! Horrified, Gene watched the boats turn ninety degrees and beach—right in their laps. At high tide, the boats were only feet away, their twin .50s looking down. Please don't let anyone move . . . not one muscle.

Without sound, and very slowly, the squad had raised their weapons to return fire if the Swifts opened up on them. Gene felt fear run deep—knew the others felt the same. Now it was a waiting game. God help them if anybody moved.

Hours passed. His legs went numb. Though the 60 grew unbearably heavy, he kept it trained on the boats. In the night, around him, the rest were doing the same. He couldn't believe their situation. One slight sound . . . one move . . . and they would be ripped apart by other U.S. Navy personnel.

The night continued, each second achingly long. The Swifts remained, bows at the bank. Gene's fears intensified. The boats might stay until sunrise. If that happened, the squad had a good chance of being seen. Once the boat people saw any humans in the jungle, they'd open up, thinking they were the bad guys. Lucky he hadn't had to cough during the past hours.

No sooner had it come to mind than the urge was there. Maybe fear had prevented it until that point, but once Gene thought about coughing, he had to. The back of his throat tickled, and built-up mucus choked him. With the boats' .50-calibers staring down, he struggled to negate the need.

He couldn't cough. The .50s would tear all of them apart. His stomach and chest muscles were rigid. Sweatband in the mouth . . . wouldn't work. Even the muffled sound would be enough that they'd open up.

Slowly he took his left hand off the forward grip of the 60 and placed the total weight of the weapon in his right hand. His arms ached and muscles burned, but he had to stay as motionless as possible. Using his left hand, he pulled his sweatband off, then pushed it deep in his mouth to try to suppress the tickle in his throat. He couldn't. It was too far down.

He had to stop the cough. He couldn't cost the other SEALs their lives.

Slowly he pulled the sweatband out of his mouth. Holding one corner in his teeth, he wrapped the middle and index fingers of his left hand with the band. His right arm ached with the weight of the 60. He eased the two wrapped fingers back into his mouth, reaching down as far as he could, as deep as possible into his throat, and concentrated on not gagging or inducing vomiting. He twisted his fingers to scratch the tickle, and hoping the cloth had caught some of the phlegm, backed them out slowly, never taking his eyes off the boats.

By God, he thought, it had worked. His throat was eased—at least for now.

Well after 2400 hours, the Swifts' engines kicked into life. Everlastingly grateful, Gene watched as they backed off and headed downriver to the Son Ku Lon.

Nobody moved until the boats were a distance down the river. Then they had to, to get the blood circulating in their legs and buttocks. For minutes, most couldn't stand. When he could, John signaled for them to rally, two hundred meters to the rear.

In position once more, Hagar said he was ready to go home for the night.

Gene nodded. He had no problem with that. His hands, face, and neck were welted from mosquito bites, as were those of the rest of the squad.

John called for extraction, and when the boat came, they headed home.

"We need to find out who the boats were," Gene told him on their way back, "and what the hell they were doing in our area of operations."

With John beside him, Gene headed to TOC as soon as they docked, leaving the rest of the squad to go to their hootch and to bed.

TOC was a somewhat restricted area, and Gene knew it. All operations in their area of the Delta were monitored there. It housed all communications, time frames, call signs, and situation maps. He went straight to the section leader.

"Which Swift boats were on patrol and what areas were they to patrol tonight?"

"We'll check the situation map," the section leader said.

Gene stared at it. The area they'd cleared had been reduced by three grids. "Take a look at this, John."

They had both checked the situation map to ensure there were no other operations scheduled in their AO. Where they'd cleared nine grids, only six were now on the board. Gene looked at the section leader.

"Who's been in the TOC in the last six hours?"

"Well," the man said, "Lieutenant Commander Wilson—"

"One of the Sea Wolf pilots," Gene told John.

"—Sean, Willie, and Tong," the section leader finished.

"That's all?"

"Oh, yeah. Loc—the Vietnamese SEAL?"

"I know him," Gene said. Loc had interpreted when he'd questioned Raggedy, and left angry. "What was he doing here?"

"He stopped in to say good-bye. He'd been reassigned." The section leader looked at his watch. "Flew out just about two hours ago."

"Was he near the map?"

"He could have been. They all could have been. It's possible that someone leaned against the board," he said. "Accidents happen. Mistakes happen. I just don't know. I'm sorry."

"There's no way to know," John said, once outside.

"Best thing," Gene said, "is to file a report with Johnny over at NILO. Loc will bear watching, wherever he is. I don't think the erasure was accidental. He was really pissed at me a few nights ago. Willie even warned me to watch my back."

"I'll talk with Johnny. Appreciate your going out with us."

Grim, Gene watched him walk away. Telling Johnny was the thing to do, so the intel network could keep an eye on Loc, just in case he was a double agent. Coughing, and angry, he went back to his own hootch and to bed, too weary to even wash up.

CHAPTER SIXTEEN

DARK GRAY MORNING CAME early with a hard, heavy rain. In khaki swim trunks, his body still covered with mud and dirt from the break-in op, Gene studied the south bank of the river. Dead trees, killed by defoliant, stood scattered in front of the thick, shadowy bush under the massed, lofty trees of the jungle. He coughed, bent over with the effort.

When the spell subsided, and he had his breath back, he went to the fifty-five-gallon barrel at the northwest corner of the hootch. Filled with rainwater, it overflowed now. Morning chow was coming, and he wanted to scrub up. He stripped off the swim trunks, grabbed a metal helmet, scooped it full of water, and poured it over his head.

He did it again before soaping, and then again when he rinsed off. Coughing hard, he struggled back into the swim trunks.

"Gene, how are you feeling?"

He looked around at Doc. "Shitty. Can't you get rid of this cough?"

Doc frowned. "Have you taken your meds?"

"Sure have. Every one." He put a hand on the hootch wall to steady himself.

"I want to see you, over by your rack."

There'd be no argument. Doc had that look that said he wasn't fooling. When he marched off, Gene was right behind him.

Moments later, Doc took a thermometer out of his medical bag. "Open," he said.

When he took it out of Gene's mouth, it read 102 degrees. "Let me see your throat."

Gene opened his mouth. Doc aimed his small flashlight and peered inside.

"Red," he said, "but no pus. Let me hear your lungs. Breathe deep."

Gene's attempt to take a breath started him coughing, hard. Tears ran down his cheeks from his watering eyes.

"You sound terrible. Get down to sick bay. You have to see the doctor."

"Okay. Right after breakfast."

Doc seemed to rise two inches. "No way! Get your ass down to sick bay. Now."

"But—"

"Now!"

Gene backed up. "Okay. All right."

Doc folded his arms across his chest and waited.

Keeping an eye on him, Gene pulled on his blue-and-gold. "How about just one cup of coffee?"

"*Now!*" Doc yelled.

"Okay. Okay." He headed out to sick bay. It was miserable weather, but the cool rain felt good.

Behind him, Doc reentered the hootch and went looking for Jim. He found him sitting on his rack, studying a map.

"Got a minute?"

Jim folded the map. "Sure, Doc. What's up?"

"I sent Gene to sick bay. I think he has pneumonia. If I'm right, the doctor will send him out of here."

Frowning, Jim chewed gently on the corner of his lower lip. His fingers smoothed the map, tightened the fold. "Is he at sick bay now?"

"Yes, sir."

"Thanks, Doc."

Doc nodded and walked away.

Jim went straight to sick bay. The doctor was finishing his exam when he walked through the door.

Gene smiled. "Mornin', Jim. How are you doing?"

He ignored Gene's greeting. "What's the word, Doc? How is he?"

"Well, he's got walking pneumonia. I'm sending him up to Binh Thuy."

"Wait a minute," Gene said, "I could be up there a week or two. Maybe longer. No way. Can't you treat me here?"

The doctor shrugged. "Sure. But you'd need to stay dry and get plenty of rest. You won't do that here."

"I'll do anything you say, but keep me here. I promise. Whatever you say." The endless screaming of the burn victim echoed in his mind. Anything would be better than a repeat of that. And Sara . . . who had to stay in the past forever . . .

The doctor looked at Jim, who nodded. Gene sighed with relief.

"Okay," the doctor said, "but if I see you wet or going out on any ops, I'll pull you out and have your ass on a medevac so fast . . ." He turned and crossed the room toward a metal cabinet on the far wall.

"Thanks, Jim. If you hadn't okayed me staying here, he would have sent me out."

"Don't thank me yet," Jim replied. "If you don't do exactly what the doc says, I'll ship your ass out myself."

Gene glanced at the returning doctor, then stared at the needle he carried. "What the hell is that for?"

"Penicillin. Bend over and drop them."

"You gotta be kidding. You treating an elephant?"

Jim chuckled.

"Just drop 'em. Jesus Christ. For being a big bad-ass SEAL, you're acting like a baby."

Teeth set, he dropped his trunks, turned, and felt the doctor swab his skin with something cold and wet.

"You ready?"

Before he could answer, the doctor drove the needle home. Gene yelled, "You hit oil?" and clenched his teeth. Damn, that hurt. Finally the needle was withdrawn.

"That so bad?" the doctor asked, handing Gene more meds. "I want to see you before evening chow. Got it?"

"Yes, sir."

"If you get any worse, I'll have to send you out. If you don't take care of yourself, it could cost you a lot more than just a few ops."

"Don't worry," Jim said. "I'll make sure he's a good boy." He rubbed the top of Gene's head.

On the way to the chow hall, Jim laid down the law.

"Don't screw around. I don't mind losing you for a few ops, knowing you'll be back in the bush soon, but if you screw around, I could lose you for a lot longer, and that would piss me off. You got that?"

"Yes."

"Don't yes me this time. You do exactly what he said. Understood?"

"Yes, sir!" Gene snapped back. No doubt that Jim meant it. Anything would be better than being sent to Binh Thuy.

The cook splattered watery powdered eggs on his tray. On second thought, maybe Binh Thuy wouldn't be so bad. "You eat these, or do you give us straws?"

"Move on," the cook said. "There's people behind you."

Gene took some burnt toast to go with the undercooked potatoes, and a cup of hot black coffee, then crossed the room to join Doc and Cruz. After setting the tray on the table, he pulled out a metal chair and dropped into it.

He shot up. *"Ai-yi!"*

Cruz stared. "What's wrong with you?"

Doc smiled. "He shot you up, didn't he?"

When he got back to their hootch, still hungry, Gene went to his footlocker, pulled out a can of tuna, an onion swiped from the chow hall the previous meal, and his bowie knife. After opening the can, he chopped the onion into big chunks and began to eat. It was one of his favorite meals. It didn't do much for his breath, but out here, who cared? Considering the smell of the jungle, the filthy brown river, and all the body odor, onions weren't really so bad.

Gene was playing poker and had just thrown in his hand when Willie came in.

"Gene, I need to talk to you right away."

"Okay, my friend." He stood up. "You-O, put my money on the books."

"I've got hot intel on an op," Willie said, standing next to Gene's rack.

Gene put up a hand, seeing Jim come through the door. "Jim, over here," he called.

Jim came over.

"Ninety NVA are leaving New Nam Cam before dark," Willie said. "I know where they'll be going. We can hit them. I'm taking twelve KCSs. I'd like five SEALs to go as well."

"Sure," Jim said. "I'll get four others."

Automatically Gene pulled the 60 off its rack.

"Where the hell do you think you're going?" Jim asked.

"Out with you and Willie."

"Are you nuts? You're not going anywhere. I'll find another 60," he said, and left.

"What's wrong with you?" Willie asked.

Gene slumped against the racks. "Doctor shut me down for a while. Says I have walking pneumonia."

"Then keep your ass planted. This war will still be here tomorrow and the next day. Y'all have done your share. Just get well."

"Dammit, Willie, you've done yours as well. What the hell are you thinking of, going out when it's just hours until you can get home?"

They looked at each other for a long moment.

"See you later, my friend. I've got to get ready."

"Okay, Willie." There was no use arguing. The redhead was stubborn as hell.

Two hours later, he saw Jim and Willie off. It came to him, looking at them, that there stood his two closest friends, both in full combat gear, both in green face, and they looked scary as hell.

Willie patted his shoulder. "See y'all after a bit."

He watched them walk out the door together, into the rain. It was almost twilight. They'd want to be in position before the NVA passed through. Dark gray and wet outside the rectangle of the door frame, it would be real dark in the jungle. Deep mud. Pouring rain. Shit. He walked slowly back to the card game.

"Marc, do you want to get some chow?"

He looked up, and Gene, once again, felt the impact of those incredibly transparent, light blue eyes.

"No thanks. I'm making a comeback."

Gene nodded and walked alone to the chow hall. He ate a hamburger and chips, then suddenly weary, returned to his rack and fell asleep. It seemed he'd barely closed his eyes when NILO's Johnny burst into the hootch yelling for Doc.

"The KCSs got hit . . . casualties coming in. We're going to need you in sick bay."

The SEALs left the hootch running. Gene pulled on his trunks and ran out after them, wondering which KCSs got it, and how bad. He reached the sick bay and met Johnny coming out.

"Let's go—helo pads. They're bringing in three KCSs."

They ran, slipping on Seafloat's drenched deck.

Marc stood beside him as the first chopper landed. The second they could, they pulled out the closest wounded, using a stretcher. Out cold, and covered in blood, it was Tong. They rushed him to medical, knowing the helos carried the most seriously injured. The other wounded would be brought back aboard the boats with the rest of the patrol.

Looking down at Tong's bloody face, Gene couldn't help thinking of how much the man had lost in the war. His wife, his two small girls, his parents, and now, maybe, his life.

In sick bay, they lay him on the only table, under the large surgical lamp. Two corpsmen and the doctor started working on him. Other SEALs carried in two more KCSs.

"Put them on the floor," the doctor ordered. "Everyone out but medical personnel."

Gene left to help get stretchers ready for the boats. They'd be arriving within ten minutes. From where they waited, he could see them, far down the river, coming home on step. As they closed, he made out Jim standing on the bow of the first one. Willie must be on the second, he thought, but he didn't have time to look once Jim's boat docked.

As Jim helped the wounded KCSs off, the SEALs each took one and walked them over to sick bay. Once there, Gene, like the others, checked his KCS's bandaged wounds, checked for missed wounds and for signs of shock. He looked up when Tong was brought out on his stretcher. The surgical sheet was partially pulled over his face.

The corpsman shook his head, replying to Gene's silent question. "We couldn't save him."

When the corpsmen moved away, he saw Jim approaching. With him were four SEALs, carrying two body bags on stretchers. Gene went to meet him.

"Jim, what happened?" There was nothing boyish left in the expression on his green-and-black-painted face. Just a sickness and a tiredness beyond words.

"They were waiting for us," he said, his voice hoarse. "They had to have known. It was an ambush. Before anyone could get off the boats, they hit us with rockets and heavy weapons fire."

If Loc hadn't been already gone . . . Gene looked down at the body bags. "Are any ours?"

Jim nodded.

"Who?" Kneeling, Gene started to open the first bag. Jim grabbed his arm.

"Willie," he said.

The outline of the body bag blurred as his eyes filled with tears. He felt his body crumple, couldn't stop it, and dropped to his knees. He tried to speak. Couldn't. He choked, felt hot tears streaming down his face. Willie . . . oh, God, Willie . . .

Jim pulled him up. "Come with me . . . come with me."

And he was walking . . . being walked . . . and they were at the edge of Seafloat. Jim put something in his hand. Gene looked down at the cross Willie always wore on a chain around his neck.

"A rocket hit next to the wheelhouse," Jim said. "Willie was standing right next to it." He paused, then continued. "It took almost one-third of his chest out."

Gene clenched the cross in his fist, crossed his arms tight against himself, and looked at the river, seeing nothing through tears that just kept coming.

"We had to break contact before we could help," Jim said. "Once clear, I went to Willie first." He touched Gene's shoulder. "He didn't seem to be in pain. He reached up and pulled on his cross. I started to render aid—" His voice broke. He took a deep breath and went on. "He said, 'I'm dead. Take care of my men.' "

Beside him, Gene drew in a long, sobbing breath.

Jim wiped at tears and continued. "I looked him in the eyes. He wanted you to have his cross, said he loved you. I was holding his hand . . ." Jim drew a shuddering breath, ". . . and his grip went limp, and he . . . died."

Jim's voice broke again, and he went silent. Gene touched him on the shoulder, clenched the cross tight, and walked away. At the far east end of Seafloat, he faced the jungle, blind with tears. Willie . . . Willie . . . He cried until he couldn't cry anymore.

A long time later, he entered the hootch and went to his rack. Lifting his pillow, he removed Karen's letters and the Bible, put them in his footlocker, and turned the key. Still holding Willie's cross, he lay on his bunk, staring at the ceiling with cold, dry eyes.

If he'd been there, Willie might still be alive. They could have used his 60 . . . But no. They'd been ambushed, Jim had said. The enemy had known. How? Loc? Rage churned within him. But he didn't know that Loc—they'd operated together, for God's sake. God?

It was after chow. The rain had stopped. The other SEALs, abnormally quiet, were getting ready for the movie. Seafloat was not quite back to normal.

Part of his life had been taken away. He lay cold and empty. Nothing had meaning. He felt nothing.

"Gene," Jim said beside him, "you okay?"

He nodded.

"The doctor wants to see you in sick bay. He wants to listen to your lungs."

Silently Gene dropped to the floor. Tong's blood still covered his hands and arms. He walked to sick bay.

"How do you feel?" the doctor asked.

He shrugged, stood silent, his fists clenched, while the doctor examined him.

"I want you to come back in the morning. Here. Take these."

Gene accepted two pills and a canteen.

"They'll help you sleep tonight. You need rest."

Without replying, he returned to the hootch and climbed back up on his rack. He opened his fist then and looked again at Willie's cross before putting it in the back pocket of his trunks. Eventually he slept.

* * *

For two days, he spoke to no one, not aware of keeping silent. When talked to, he just shrugged, shook his head, or nodded briefly. The other SEALs, sensing he wanted to be left alone, backed off. He ate by himself, walked by himself, and spent hours staring, rigid with anger, down the Son Ku Lon or out over the jungle. On the evening of the fourth day, he went to sick bay.

The doctor sat him down, listened to his chest, and took his temperature. "You sound good," he said. "No fever. Give it one more day and you can go back out."

Gene stood. The doctor looked up at his face and, startled, took a sudden step back.

Without a word, Gene left, going to stare again downriver into the dark night. Within him stirred a rage beyond anything he had ever known. Willie's cross cut into his palm. He'd get them for Willie. He'd get all of them. Hundreds for one. They wanted war, he'd bring them hell!

CHAPTER SEVENTEEN

NOT INTERESTED IN SLEEP once given the word he could go back out, Gene set to work getting his equipment ready. It had lain dormant for almost a week, and the time he had left in Vietnam was growing shorter, just as Willie's had. He ached to take revenge.

He started with a new case of M-60 ammo. Pulling out the first box of two hundred rounds, he took each belt apart and removed the tracers that were every fifth round. After four boxes totaling eight hundred rounds, he had fifty tracers. He set them aside. He then cut an X in the nose of each of the other belted rounds with his bowie knife. When the round hit its target, it would spread—mushroom. The 60 was devastating as it was, but X'd ammo meant certain death for the target. And death was exactly what he intended for every NVA or VC he could get in his sights.

Gene put down the bowie and reached for the tracers. He oiled each one before it was reconnected with the snap links that held the ammo together. The grouped tracers were put at the front of the first belt he would fire. Finished, he linked all four belts. They totaled eight hundred rounds.

Standard operating procedure for other outfits was six hundred, and a second person carried the ammo. It was not SOP for the SEALs. They had only what their M-60 man could carry by himself. Gene always carried a full eight hundred, and sometimes more.

He picked up the bowie knife and began working on it. Every stroke of the blade over the sharpening stone was a slice through an enemy throat. After an hour, he wet the hair on his forearm, placed the blade at a forty-five-degree angle, and stroked upward. It shaved without the slightest pull and left no stubble. Then he cleaned and checked the rest of his gear, replaced everything in its resting place, and went silently outside.

At 0320, the sky was clear and Seafloat quiet. The only ones awake other than himself were the men standing watch. He walked the entire perimeter of Seafloat. Each man he passed spoke, offering a word or two. He moved on in silence, as though they didn't exist, thinking of Willie, consumed with a soul-burning rage. Before, he had killed and hoped to survive. Now he wanted survival in order to kill.

Eventually the circle returned him to the hootch. He slipped inside, unslung the 60 from the side of his rack, and took it outside to the cleaning table. There he replaced almost every moving piece with a new one. Each part of the 60 was inspected and lubricated. When the weapon had been reassembled, he pulled on the cocking lever. All moving parts worked with ease, so smooth in their action they seemed to be made of silicone.

He looked up into sunrise. It had been his favorite time of day, the time he would normally have spent praying for the safety of all the SEALs, all the children, and for the end of war. Never again. Not after Willie. He turned his back to the rising sun, conscious only of the vow he had made the previous night: I'll bring you hell.

It was almost 0600, and people were starting to move around Seafloat. He hung the 60 back on his rack and went to the chow hall. There he got two cups of coffee and headed to NILO.

Johnny was still asleep.

Gene stood in the doorway. "Time to wake up."

Sound asleep, the officer didn't respond.

Gene raised his voice. "Johnny, get up. I want to talk to you."

Blinking, rubbing his eyes, he came awake. "What's wrong?" He squinted up. "Who is that? Gene! What's wrong?" He sat up. "What time is it?"

"Here. Drink some coffee."

Johnny took the cup and sipped. "Thanks. What's up?"

"Who hit Willie? What unit?"

"I don't know for sure. I still have some people out who haven't given a report."

"Who do you think it was?"

"Right now, we believe they were part of Nguyen's unit."

A surge of adrenaline hit Gene so hard, he was almost dizzy with it. His head rang, blood pounded.

"The colonel and his men went down to New Nam Cam for a little R&R," Johnny went on, looking down at his steaming coffee. "That hasn't been confirmed yet. It's still too early to know for sure." He looked up. "We do know that they headed northeast, where we believe Nguyen is located."

Gene clamped his hand around the bedpost. His knuckles went white. "Jim said the enemy knew." ·

"I'm checking that out as well. They could have been tipped off, but it's also possible they got there first, saw Willie's people coming, and set up."

"Do me a favor."

"What?"

"Get a fix on Nguyen."

Sitting up in his rack, Johnny seemed to cringe—to draw into himself. "We're trying!"

Gene leaned forward. "I want him."

"I know you do. I'm trying."

"Then send out all your people. Check with every intel source out there—PRUs, CIA, every military and civilian source."

"Gene, I'm trying. I really am. We all want him."

Through clenched teeth, the words came out. "Not as much as I do."

Johnny nodded. After a long silence, he asked, "How are you feeling?"

"I've been released by the doctor."

"Does Jim know?"

"Not yet. He will as soon as I see him."

"He's going out this afternoon," Johnny said. He took a swallow of coffee. "He'll be glad to know you can go with them."

Gene straightened. "Good. I need to get off this damned Float."

"Glad to see you healthy again."

"Thanks," Gene said, and turned to go. Halfway out the door, he stopped and looked back. "Find Nguyen for me."

Before Johnny could reply, Gene had headed out to find Jim.

He ran into Doc on the way.

"Hey, I hear you've been released. How do you feel?"

"Okay. Have you seen Jim?"

Doc's eyebrow raised. "Last time I saw him, he was still in the hootch. About thirty minutes ago."

"Good."

Just as Gene reached the door, Jim came out.

Startled, he stopped short. "Gene. How are you feeling?"

"The doctor said I can go back out." He studied Jim, watching for reaction. "Johnny said you're running an op. Put me down to go."

Jim's eyes narrowed. "Sorry. I've already got my list, and I've put the word out to those who will be going. Take another day's rest."

"Dammit, it's not too late. You haven't even had the Warning Order yet."

"Sure you're okay?"

"Yes."

Jim grinned. "Tell Marc Kenau he won't be going, but thanks. Warning Order is at 1400 hours."

"Anything I can do to help?"

Jim shook his head. "No, not this time. Everything is set until the WO. I'm going to chow. See you later."

Gene suddenly realized he wore a slight smile—a strange reflection of the cold anger, the glacier of hate he felt. Inside the hootch, he looked for Marc.

The Eagle lay on his rack, staring at the ceiling.

"Well," Gene said, "did you win or lose last night?"

Marc glanced around. The hootch was empty except for the two of them. "I made a killing. Do you need the money?"

"No. How much did you win?"

"I was down one fifty on the books. Now I'm up about six hundred."

"Must have been one hell of a game. Who was the big loser?"

Marc grinned. "Everybody, man. I couldn't lose."

"It's about time. Here's another win. Jim said you could stand down on the op, and thanks for agreeing to go."

Marc's ice-blue gaze fastened on Gene. "Who's the automatic weapons man?"

"I am."

"You mean, you're back?"

"Yes. Pass the word to anyone going out that I'm available between my squad's ops. I'll go out with anyone. Day or night."

Marc studied him. "Can I ask you a question and get an honest answer?"

"I've never lied to you before, my friend. I'm not about to start now. Shoot."

"How are you?"

"Fine. No temp, no cough."

"I don't mean that. How are you holding up? I know you took Willie's death hard. We all knew how close you two were."

"You really want to know?" He was cold, hard, without emotion. "I'm going out in the bush and kill anyone carrying a weapon, anyone who is known to be the enemy. NVA, VC . . . anyone supporting them. Doesn't matter. All I want to do is fight. I'm going to avenge Willie. That's all I care about."

He stared at Marc, who didn't move. "You keep your mouth shut about this."

The big SEAL looked into his face, his own showing concern and distress. "Don't go crazy on me, Gene. I lost a friend too. I don't want to lose you."

"Just pass the word that I'm available, Eagle. I'll be okay."

"You need someone to talk to, come see me. We've been through a lot together and I care. More than you know. More than I've ever told you. Especially since the Mighty Mo."

He stood, and before Gene could react, hugged him.

"I understand what you're saying," Marc said. "Do it. But be careful."

Gene headed for the briefing room. He wanted to check the situation map and all intel reports on Nguyen. He was out there somewhere, and he wanted to know where.

Jim had moved the Warning Order up one hour. Once everybody had the word, things moved fast, with each man preparing his basic equipment load. Their BELs included special equipment—LAAWS rockets, explosives, booby traps, and such. While the rest finished mounting out, he'd be preparing himself mentally, with a single intent. Kill.

At the designated time, he joined the others in the briefing room for the Warning Order and took his usual chair at the back of the room, next to the door.

Jim stood at the front. "Okay, guys. The objective is to search and destroy a small enemy camp of fifteen NVA and three tax collectors. We will be running a hammer-and-anvil ambush."

Gene listened while Jim told each squad member what he was to carry along with any special equipment. Details about the op would come during the Patrol Leader's Order in about—Gene checked the time—an hour and a half.

He felt the electricity begin to surge through his veins. Search and destroy. Just the kind of op he wanted. Perfect with hammer and anvil. They hadn't used that ambush in combat yet.

They had run one in Basic Underwater Demolition SEAL training. Tommy Blade ran it on them, and he, with the rest of the students, had fallen right into the trap. Afterward, they'd heard Tommy howling with laughter. Not only had he and his staff "killed" them, they'd scared the hell out of them. Now it was for real. The enemy wouldn't find it funny.

It was 1320 hours when they returned to the briefing room for the PLO. Most of the guys, Gene saw, were joking, playing grab-ass.

"Listen up," Jim ordered.

Smiles vanished as they absorbed the details. They all realized it would be one hell of an op. Gene studied faces. They'd be flown deep into enemy territory by helo and rappel into their AO. Jim had intel that the three tax collectors had collected almost $100,000 in South Vietnamese currency from local subcollectors. The three would be moving the funds north in the morning, under the protection of fifteen NVA. Though the SEALs would be in Colonel Nguyen's area, there was no intel on his location, so enemy forces were unknown.

Jim, giving details, let them know they wouldn't be able to extract by helo, but would have to make it through the jungle to a point where the boats could pick them up. They were going so deep that they'd have no communications for most of the op, and no fire support from the Sea Wolves or riverboats. They'd be on their own.

The squad went directly to the helo deck after the PLO. The choppers were waiting.

Gene put on his Swiss Seat and snap link, wrapping the half-inch nylon rope around his waist, between his legs, and tying it at his waist on the left side. He hooked the snap link on the rope at the belt-buckle location. Once at the objective, two hundred-foot ropes would be thrown from each side of the chopper, and the men—one at a time on each line—would tie their snap link into the rope and exit the bird.

He opened and closed both hands several times, flexing them, checking his grip. When he went out of the chopper, he'd have the 60 in his left and be holding the hundred-foot line in his right, whipping it out to the side as he came down. About five feet above the ground, he'd move the line behind his back, which would stop his descent instantly, then ease himself down quickly and get un-hooked.

During the trip to their insertion point, Gene took no notice of the country's beauty and, unlike past times, took no joy in the flight. Instead, his mind churned with thoughts of search and destroy. The edges of Willie's cross bit into his palm. He didn't recall taking it from his shirt pocket where Nguyen's shoulder patch and the cross had replaced the small Bible.

Behind him, Jim passed the word. "Get ready."

Gene tucked Willie's cross back in his pocket and stood up, just inches behind Jim. Across from him, Roland stood waiting behind Brian. Seconds later, Jim and Brian jumped. When the ropes showed some slack, he and Roland went out, followed by Alex and You-O, and finally Doc. All of them, as they hit the ground, set security immediately.

The 60 ready, Gene crouched silently with the rest, watching and listening, wondering if they'd been seen. Above, the choppers would continue to fly north for some twenty minutes before heading west, then south, for Seafloat. For a while, he could hear them pulling away. Then they were gone. It was a cold feeling. Once on the ground, there was no turning back, even if they wanted to. The only way out would be to head south through the thick, enemy-infested jungle.

Deep in the brush below the trees, he stood immobile, breathing softly. Now their self-discipline was crucial. They must make no contact until they reached the objective—couldn't risk being seen or heard. And once the objective was hit, they had to move fast and silent if they were going to make it back alive. Once they hit, they had to become invisible, make no mistakes.

He could feel the tension in the air. The surreptitious glances the others had been throwing his way had ceased. The squad was totally outer-directed now, tasting, smelling, feeling the air for danger, like wild animals. It was as if they all shared the same feeling. This op was it. Not all of them would be coming out alive.

Jim gave the signal to move out.

CHAPTER EIGHTEEN

IN FILE FORMATION, THE SEALs filtered into the surrounding jungle. A short time later, sunlight faded as night set in. Brian's fist went up. Danger area.

Gene set flank security at the small river—about, he guessed, eight feet across. Cruz did the same. Brian slowly crossed, and entered the dark jungle on the far side of the water.

As he waited, Gene scanned the area, listening to the hum of insects, the trees sighing above, aware of the dark green, earthy smell of the river.

Jim and Roland were ready to cross. Screened by foliage, they crouched, poised for Brian's return.

Suddenly the brush across the river stirred. Brian stepped out to give the thumbs-up, all-clear, sign. Jim entered the river. Just as he started getting out, Roland slid in with barely a ripple, his weapon at the ready.

Cruz snapped his fingers. Roland, up to his ankles, froze in place and looked back. Cruz pointed left, down his flank, and whispered, "Sampan."

Roland backed into the overhanging brush at the river's edge and became one with it.

From his hidden position, Gene watched the sampan come into view. Two armed VC. Around him, none of the squad moved or made any sound. They wanted no contact, wanted only for the sampan to pass. Brian and Jim on the far bank made the situation especially dangerous. If the squad were seen, and had to open up, they'd be firing into their own men across the river.

The VC remained unaware of the SEALs' presence. They paddled on, talking to each other.

For five minutes after their passing, the squad listened and waited, holding their positions. Finally Roland crossed the river, with the rest following as indicated in the PLO.

Gene, soaked to his waist, noticed the lengthening shadows. Darkness came fast under triple canopy. They'd have to slow down. When night came down it was hard to maintain visual contact with the man in front and the man behind.

Before they moved out, Jim tapped the top of his head, initiating a head count. When the signal reached Doc, he moved up to Cruz, in front of him, and whispered, "One." Cruz moved close to Alex, whispered, "Two." Moments later, after Alex's "Three" and Gene's "Four," Roland whispered, "Five," to Jim. Jim, able to see Brian at point, knew he had seven men, no one missing, no extras, and moved them out again.

Two hours later, Brian raised his fist, halting them at the edge of a small clearing. The squad set security while Jim and Brian conferred, waiting to see whether their decision would be to cross the clearing or skirt it, just inside the tree line.

When the word came back to move out, Gene wasn't surprised they'd decided to patrol around the edge of the clearing and not take the chance of being seen.

He began to count his steps to maintain the correct compass bearing, after changing direction. Turning left, he went ninety-seven paces north. After the squad had moved east across the width of the clearing, he counted ninety-seven more going south. At that point, they turned east and were back on course, just as though they'd cut straight across the open area. Though walking in direct lines took longer, it was much safer. The last thing they needed, he thought, squinting as vines brushed across his face and over one shoulder, was to get lost.

The squad slogged on, Jim calling breaks every five hundred to eight hundred meters. Down on one knee, resting, Gene estimated their hard targets—the tax collectors and guards—to be within a thousand meters. Not much farther, but still several hours would pass before they'd be in position to hit the objective. The patrol, to this point, had been a rough one. Hours long, and over difficult terrain. His lower back and legs ached, his shirt was wet with sweat, and his jeans were caked with mud. It occurred to him that being sick had taken its toll. Normally he wouldn't be this weary, this soon, even with the load he carried.

He rose again, with the rest of the men, at Jim's signal. Three hundred meters later, he heard voices to the squad's right flank. So had the rest. As one, and on line, they took up hiding positions in the thick brush.

Absolutely still, controlling his breathing, the 60 ready, Gene narrowed his eyes to slits—eyes reflected light and so were easily seen—and peered in the direction from which the voices were coming. The talking got louder as the enemy closed on their location. A patrol of six NVA regulars stopped within a few feet of him. Talking and laughing, two squatted down next to each other. One lit a cigarette. They were so close, he and Cruz could have reached out and grabbed them.

Gene's heart pounded so hard, he feared they might hear it. Go away, he thought. Go . . . get up . . . go. The squad had to hit their target before sunrise or they'd miss the objective, and all they'd been through would be for nothing. Suddenly one of the NVA stood, turned toward the brush he and Cruz were hiding in, unzipped his fly, and urinated.

Gene, listening to—and seeing—the stream just to the right of his shoulder, and just to the left of Cruz's, never moved. And he knew Cruz wouldn't either. Better to get pissed on than give their positions away. Dumb ass . . . could reach up and zip his fly for him . . . yell, Boo! He'd jump ten feet, probably shit his pants. Funny . . . He clamped down on the thought before the urge to laugh, or the more powerful urge to kill, took deadly hold.

There was silence, then the metallic noise of the zipper came again, loud and unnatural. Another reason why SEALs wore Levi's 501s. They buttoned. He didn't dare look at Cruz.

Minutes passed. The sound of rain came. The sound always came first, as drops hit the treetops high above. Then the rain would start coming downward, from one level to the next. Before it hit ground level, the six-man NVA patrol moved out. From their gestures, talk, and the way they looked upward, it was obvious they didn't like the rain much.

Gene smiled with grim satisfaction. Rain was welcome. It would cover their tracks and any sound they might make en route to the target. Too bad it had already been too dark to make out any markings on the NVA uniforms. Any insignia seen would have been used to determine exactly which enemy force the six men were with, later, back at NILO.

After ten minutes, Jim again tapped the top of his head with his left hand, asking for a head count. Moments later he had it. By then the rain was a downpour. They headed for the target with great speed, but with all senses on full alert, responding to every sound. Each and every noise had to be analyzed, distinguished from natural sound. They'd run into one patrol already. The fear of running into another worked on everybody's nerves.

Jim's fist went up to stop the patrol about an hour before dawn. He moved it in the circular motion that indicated the location would be a rally point. If any enemy contact were made from then on, or if they had to split up for any reason, they would rally back to this location to reunite.

Gene waited as Jim motioned each man to him, and silently pointed them into a location, to form a security perimeter. That done, Jim and Brian moved out alone. They returned a good ten minutes later. One by one, Jim went to each man. When he reached Gene, he told him the squad had reached their objective, the enemy camp.

"When I give the move-out sign," Jim whispered, "the patrol will break into two separate groups."

Gene nodded, listening intently. The first group was composed of Brian, Jim, and Roland. They were the hammer. He, Cruz, Alex, and Doc were the anvil. Nice, thought Gene. Very nice.

Jim waved his arm, and the men headed out to take their positions. Rain covering their movements, Jim, Brian, and Roland crept closer to the front of the camp's five hootches.

The small structures had a framework constructed of poles. Their walls and peaked roofs were a thatch of reeds, palm fronds, grasses, and mud. Dirt-floored, each hootch measured about eight by ten feet.

Gene, Cruz, Alex, and Doc began moving to the east, skirting around the small clearing surrounding the hootches, to come up behind them. They had five minutes to get to the rear without being detected, and to locate a safe position from the frontal attack Jim's group would initiate.

Jim, Brian, and Roland would be firing straight into Gene's group's position. Their rounds would sizzle through the hootch walls like they weren't even there. The NVA, splitting out the back and heading toward the brush as soon as the first few shots were fired, would never know they were running directly into Gene's group, and the sure death he ached to give them.

It seemed like it took a long time to reach the east side. Once there, Gene used the last few minutes—before Jim, Brian, and Roland brought the hammer down in a frontal attack—to place Alex, Cruz, and Doc into position. He then signaled them to get down low. Their lives depended on Jim's group keeping their fire above the three-foot level.

Blood rushing, heart pounding, Gene waited, his finger on the 60's trigger. The quiet and the dark, within the steady rain, seemed to grow even quieter and darker. He faced the dead space—the open area about twenty meters from the back side of the hootches to where they hid inside the jungle's edge. Cruz, Alex, and Doc were hunched, black shapes within the shadowy foliage near him. They looked like long-forgotten statues from an ancient, rotting temple.

Suddenly the night blew apart. Weapons on fully automatic poured hundreds of rounds into and through the hootches, and into their position just above their heads. The rounds cracked going overhead. Small branches, twigs, leaves, showered down. Gene sucked in his breath. Not only had Jim and his group opened up, they were screaming at the top of their lungs, "Kill them! Alpha squad! Flank right! Bravo! Left!"

Involuntarily he shivered, but held the 60 steady. Screaming and firing, Jim's group sounded like thirty to forty men. Not three. And sure enough, here came their targets. Running as fast as they could to reach the safety of the jungle, men boiled out from inside the hootches, splashing through the mud and puddles in the clearing, coming right at them.

Silently Gene counted. Eighteen meters . . . fifteen meters . . . ten meters . . . Two pop flares lit the night sky up like high noon. The rain fell in glittering lines. Five meters, and coming fast. Jim's group ceased firing, and Gene knew they'd hit the deck. With only seconds to spare before the fleeing NVA overran their position, Gene, Cruz, Alex, and Doc rose as if from the depths of hell, and cut loose with a devastating barrage of fire.

With the 60 quaking in his hands, Gene saw the horror on their targets' faces, even through the sheets of rain, but felt nothing. Coming at a dead run toward their position, the enemy tried to change direction, but couldn't get away from the deadly fire of the SEALs' weapons. The 60 became red-hot. Bodies dropped, jumped, shook like puppets.

The pop flares started to die out, the darkness to return. It didn't matter. None stood, now, in the clearing. Gene yelled.

"Stop firing!"

In the sudden stillness, smoke rose from glowing red barrels. Gene listened, watched. Jim, Brian, and Roland would be running a very quick search through the hootches. As the Mark 13 flares died, the hootches burst into flame, set afire after the search. Through it all, Gene kept an eye on the fifteen to twenty bodies in the rain-soaked clearing.

And one moved. A dark figure against the ground, an NVA was slowly crawling to the north, trying to get away. Gene spotted his movement just before the NVA soldier, probably thinking he was home free, stood and started to run across the open fifty-yard stretch to the jungle's edge.

"Cruz!" he yelled.

Bolting from his position, Cruz took off. The NVA had a good head start, with only a few feet more to reach the trees and freedom. Cruz went down on one knee, took aim with his XM-203, and fired one round of explosives.

At jungle's edge, the 40 Mike-Mike hit the runner, center mass, in the back. Exploding on impact, half the body blew away from the waist up. Gene heard the remains hit the ground with dull thumps. Cruz headed back. Jim, Brian, and Roland, silhouettes against the flaming, smoking hootches to their rear, walked toward them. Gene, Doc, and Alex reloaded, mostly by touch, watching to make sure nobody else came or went.

Jim circled the squad, then said, "Gene, make sure they're dead."

Gene waved, and Cruz, Doc, and Alex joined him. Together, they moved a few steps closer to the bodies and opened up. While the other three made selected shots, Gene, with cold, clinical detachment, raked the entire area. Bodies jerked with the impact as the stream of rounds swept across and back.

Gene never let up on the trigger, seeing not the bodies on the ground, but Willie, the little girls, Tong's wife.

After the fourth sweep, there was only the pattering sound of the rain.

The 60 weighed solid in his hands. "Reload."

In the sudden silence, they obeyed.

"You think he's gone off the deep end?" Cruz whispered.

Doc shook his head. "He's responding. No errors."

Jim gave the order. "Move out."

Under the steady murmur of rain, the SEALs shifted into file formation and stepped back into the jungle. Behind them five hootches burned. Twenty-three NVA lay dead.

Gene lifted the cover off his watch and glanced at the time. They'd spent eleven minutes at the objective. Successful mission . . . enemy eliminated. And Jim had the tax collectors' money.

They moved quickly, knowing they had to put some distance between themselves and the hootches and bodies. Having had the small patrol pass earlier, they all knew that after hearing the gunfire, enemy forces would be coming in. And, Gene thought, if one patrol was in the area, so were others.

Jim stopped them after they'd gone about one hundred meters into the jungle. "Guys," he said, just loud enough to be heard, "remember the R&R Center? Well, stay ready. Keep all noise down. No more voice commands. Brian, get us out of here."

Brian moved out fast, ducking and weaving, the squad right behind him. They'd covered nearly five hundred meters before they heard weapons firing.

It was just like it had been at the R&R Center. Gene listened. The NVA were reconning by firing, hoping that if they came close, the squad would return fire, and they'd get a fix on the SEALs' location. He jumped a root, almost tripped, slipped through the narrow space between heavy brush and a tree trunk. His eyes stung with rain-mixed sweat. The enemy would come fast, hard, and in large numbers.

Even under the triple canopy, rain poured down hard. The jungle, dark and wet, stank to high heaven. With each step, he felt like he was being sucked down into centuries of decaying rot.

Mouth open, drawing in gulps of air, he kept up the pace Brian set. The damned mud. Couldn't capture them, but sure slowed them down. Picking up each foot, with pounds of it caked on, made his leg muscles ache. It felt as though he had fifteen-pound weights strapped to each ankle.

"Ambush, front!" Brian yelled as he opened up, fully automatic. Jim, beside Brian before the words were out of his mouth, opened up as well.

"We'll flank right," Gene yelled. "Try to hold them down until we can come on line." He heard five or six weapons, saw an occasional muzzle flash through the dense brush. "Peel off on three!" he called, and heard them relay his command. Once enemy contact was made, no need for silence. Better, in fact, for everyone to give direction, distance, relay commands. It confused the enemy, left them unsure of what size force they faced.

Even as he moved, Gene evaluated the situation. Brian and Jim had to hold the enemy down. Within a few seconds, the two would be heading back past the squad. With the squad unable, because of the dense brush, to move on line to gain fire superiority, Brian fired fully automatic. Jim was set on semiauto, single fire, allowing rounds to be continuous even as Brian changed belts in his Stoner. By the time Brian opened back up, fully auto, Jim would reload so that there would never be a lull in return fire.

"One, two, three!" Jim yelled.

On three, Brian poured every round from his Stoner into the enemy position. No one returned fire. "Go!" he shouted, wheeling left to give Jim, himself opened up then to fully auto, a clear shot.

As Jim fired, Brian ran straight back until he was behind Doc, the last man in the squad. The first thing he'd do back there, Gene knew, was reload, then wait until it was his turn again to open up. The Australian peel-off. They'd fire, then peel off until contact was broken, or they got to an area where they could flank the enemy and sting them to death.

Gene grabbed Jim as he passed. "I've got three hundred rounds hooked up. When I open up, put some distance between us. Take everyone. I'll level the area, and meet you four hundred meters at eight o'clock."

Jim nodded, kept going. Roland yelled, "Go!" and peeled off to the rear.

Gene opened up with the 60 in rapid three-to-five-round bursts. The clock system was effective in telling everyone where the enemy was or where to head in breaking contact. The patrol's heading was always twelve o'clock. Jim would take the squad four hundred meters in the direction of the 8 on a clockface to reload, set up, and wait for him.

The jungle started to fall. Gene saw two white flashes firing back. Standing, he screamed, "Willie!" and bore down on the flashes. Not in bursts. He held the trigger down. Seconds before the belt ran out, the flashes stopped, and there was nothing. No sound. No gunfire.

He dropped on one knee, broke off another belt from around his chest, and reloaded. He stood, waiting. For the first time, in all the ops, he felt no fear. He wasn't worried about whether he'd make it. He wanted contact. And then he heard movement.

Staring into the darkness, he listened for a clue of what was, or what was not, out there. It could be Jim or one of the others come back. God, he hoped not. There! Noise over to the right . . . about two o'clock. There it was again. He spun and headed out in the direction of eight o'clock.

Moving through the thick brush, the trees, he watched for signs of the squad. He weaved in and out through the heavy green foliage. The shadows were dark on dark. He felt relaxed, moving easy. Any other time, he would have been scared. Not now.

After one hundred and fifty meters, he stopped, squatting to listen. Was the noise still there? Was anyone following, thinking he'd lead them to the others? Hearing nothing, he rose and continued, to link up with Jim. He should be getting close now. He had to be careful, had to hear the password. Count it off, he told himself, count the steps . . .

He traveled approximately four hundred meters. No one was there. Had they left? Which direction? Where were they? He kept moving.

"Purple."

He froze.

"Purple."

"Haze," he answered, and men in green faces stood up from their concealed positions, spread left and right before him.

"Had to say purple twice, Gene," Jim said. "Anyone following?"

"No." Throat dry, he felt the charge of adrenaline receding. He'd heard about the two SEALs before his tour. They hadn't heard the challenge, hadn't answered with the password. The rest of the squad had blown them away. Just riddled them. But they'd lived. Only humans he'd heard of who'd survived a SEAL ambush.

One by one, Jim called over a man at a time to tell them they were changing direction. "Everyone out here knows we have to go south to get out," he whispered to Gene, as he had to the rest. "We don't have much ammo left and we still have a long way to go."

Gene nodded and stepped back. The sun was starting to rise, but it was still raining.

When Jim had spoken to everyone, he waved for Brian to move out, and pointed north. They were going farther into enemy territory.

Gene stepped over rocks. They were headed back, around the objective. Maybe they could get into an open area and call in for an airlift. He walked on, Roland in front of him, Alex behind.

Suddenly the rain stopped. He glanced up to see beams of sunlight coming through the trees. They seemed to reach out, to stretch, to touch the ground.

A thousand meters from the point where they'd been hit, things were quiet. Jim signaled to Brian to head east. An hour later, he called for a break. The squad circled, took security positions, and sat, keeping eyes and ears focused outward from the center.

Gene counted his remaining rounds. He had about a third left, with a long way to go. It was full daylight now, but still dark under the triple canopy, with rain pouring down again and covering their tracks. It was a blessing.

After the break, still weary, they continued north, farther and farther into enemy territory. They were agreed they'd traveled approximately five miles north of the target.

Brian's hand went up. They froze, and stood fast while Jim went forward. Brian had stopped just prior to a clearing.

Gene moved up in response to Jim's wave. A large village area lay before them, with a lot of enemy. There were fifty to a hundred of them. About sixteen hootches. Training exercises seemed to be going on. In one area, strings of barbed wire were lying on the ground, with men weaving through them. In another, a group of men attacked an unmarked target. Others were flanking another group.

"An NVA training camp," Gene whispered.

Jim and Brian agreed.

Gene followed them back to the rest of the squad. They moved out to the west. Staying inside the jungle's edge to remain out of sight, they moved with great speed and caution, sweat pouring down their faces, for the following two and a half hours.

Finally Roland attempted radio contact. Nothing. Distance and jungle prevented them calling in their Wolves to extract them. They patrolled on.

Jim snapped his fingers. Brian turned. Jim pointed southwest. The patrol changed direction and followed Brian, who never led them wrong.

They'd missed their pickup at the extraction point. The boat crew that had been waiting there would have moved back down toward Seafloat by now, Gene thought, as was planned and ordered in the PLO. If the squad hadn't made it to the extraction point by 0900, the crews would know they'd be coming out at a different location. Soon, though, Seafloat would be sending out air patrols to see if contact could be made, or to see if the squad could be located by air.

No good, Gene thought. The air patrols wouldn't even be in the right area, since the squad had changed direction several times. He ducked under draped vines. Twenty-four hours after the planned 0900 pickup time, the boats would return upriver and wait for radio contact, knowing that if the squad was still alive, they'd patrol back to the Son Ku Lon and then head west toward Seafloat.

But if no contact were made within a seventy-two-hour period, they'd assume the squad members were all dead.

He stared through the greenery looking for anything unnatural. All the shades of green, all the shades of brown. So damned many bushes, vines, tendrils, trees . . . He felt smothered, buried, within all of it, with the steaming heat pushing down, the clinging heavy mud . . . Boy, were they coming out in a different location—somewhere. The enemy must all have gone south looking for them. Smart move to head north, farther into enemy territory.

Gene stopped dead in his tracks at the sight of Brian's fist held high in the air. Brian had spotted a small enemy force through the thick brush and trees and was pointing to their location. Sure enough. An NVA patrol of fifteen to twenty men was thirty to thirty-five meters away. The NVA were patrolling parallel to them, but heading in the opposite direction—moving into the area they had just left.

The squad hadn't moved except to aim all weapons in the enemy's direction. The trigger of the 60 felt warm and smooth under Gene's finger, as the enemy patrol moved through their kill zone. They didn't want contact now. They had very little ammo left, no radio contact, no friendly forces . . . they were isolated.

We could take the patrol out, Gene thought, and take their weapons and ammo, but that would give away their own position. That would bring a lot more than the fifteen or twenty walking by. Silence, he told himself, was golden.

The enemy patrol walked past and out of sight. Five minutes passed. The squad remained still. Gene breathed softly, smelling for any scent of more enemy, alert for trouble.

They'd crossed several small rivers. The dirty brown water had felt cool, and relieved some of the heat, and washed some of the stinking mud off their hands, weapons, bodies. But the coolness hadn't lasted long. He stood immobile, awash in sweat, thinking that patrolling out so far during daylight hours was dangerous, and they'd been out almost all day. There were about four hours left until dark. They'd be able to pick up the pace then.

Jim signaled Brian to go southwest. Glad to be moving again, the squad headed out. Later, about twenty meters into an area so thick with foliage they could hardly get through it, Jim stopped the patrol and signaled a break. Staying in file formation, maintaining their fields of fire, they came to a halt.

One by one, Jim told each of them to rest. "We'll be here until sunset," he said, before sending Doc and Cruz out to cover up their tracks and their point of entry into the thick brush.

As they settled in, Gene listened to Jim and Roland, in soft, low voices, trying to make radio contact.

"Manger . . . Manger. This is Silent Night . . . Silent Night. Do you copy?"

Roland tried several times before putting the handset back on his H-harness, the two straps over the shoulder with a cross-strap in the back forming the letter *H* that they all wore.

On the harness, they could carry ammo pouches, first-aid gear, knife, flares, grenades, and anything they'd need on a patrol. You-O wore a vest Velcroed in front. It had small elastic straps. He carried his 40 Mike-Mike for his grenade launcher with it. Probably he'd rather be carrying his little black book of who owed him what, and be back on Seafloat putting everybody in debt about now, Gene mused.

He reached to take the narrow line being passed along from man to man. He connected it to himself and passed it on to Alex. If someone fell asleep, the person next to him would pull the line to wake him up, or if they took turns getting a little shut-eye, they could use the line.

Sitting there, he picked up a small twig and removed mud from his ammo belts and the 60 while he listened to the jungle. From time to time, he zeroed in on sounds that turned out to be natural. He kept a sharp eye on the ground around him for snakes or creepy-crawlies and glanced at the others, from time to time, to make sure they were all right.

It seemed as though only a short time had passed when word came down to move out. He stood up, stiff and sore. Jim waved *forward,* and the patrol picked up and headed west.

The mosquitoes were out in force by the time they came to a fairly large river about twenty meters across. Its banks were covered with thick jungle. Brian signaled *danger crossing,* and the patrol stopped. Jim called each of them up, instructing them to inflate their life jackets halfway.

Gene nodded as he listened to Jim's whisper. Holding to each other, they'd use the outgoing current to take them out of the area.

"Don't let go of the man in front of you," he said. "Brian will keep us close to the bank."

Gene studied the river. It was a dark night. No moon, no stars. Jim had his act together, no question. With a little effort, they could make it to the Son Ku Lon before daybreak.

Holding onto each other, they slid into the water. The current was swift-moving. Carried along by it, they were getting closer to being able to make radio contact. Friendly forces and food would be damned welcome.

Moving next to the bank with the current was a scary business. What-ifs set in. What if they floated into a village or an enemy crossing? What if this? What if that? Holding on to Roland's H-harness with his left hand, Gene kept the 60 abovewater with his right. At his back, he felt the pull of Alex's grip on his own harness.

Overhanging branches and trailing vines, tree roots and twigs, seemed to reach out and grab as he floated past. It began to rain again. Though it made it hard for them to see and to hear, the rain made it just as hard for the enemy.

Suddenly the squad stacked up. Gene pushed into Roland, and Alex pushed into him.

Brian had moved into the bank and held on. They'd all floated into him. One behind the other, they pulled themselves tight into the brush and froze.

Gene held his breath as he watched three sampans pass. Brian had heard the splashing of oars in the water, grabbed a tree root, and stopped the squad, giving them enough time to hide under the brush while the sampans went by. Their point man was good. Damned good. He doubted that anyone other than Brian would have picked up that sound among the other water and jungle noises surrounding them. Damned good, Gene thought again as they moved back into the current, about two feet from the bank.

After they'd floated for almost three straight hours, they were cold. Even though the water and the air were warm, they weren't 98.6 degrees. The squad's body temperatures had dropped. Hypothermia was setting in. To create body heat, they had to leave the water and walk. Jim took them out of the river and back into the jungle.

Patrolling felt good. As they moved south, Gene felt the sweat begin to roll down his body again.

After about seven hundred meters, and no enemy sightings, Jim signaled another break. Resting, Gene listened to the insect hum, the jungle sounds. It was almost 0400. Enough time had passed that the enemy probably believed the SEALs had just disappeared, as usual. Daybreak coming soon. Too soon. He heard Roland get on the radio.

"Manger . . . Manger. This is Silent Night. Over."

"Silent Night, this is Manger. What is your location?"

Around him, Gene caught glimpses of smiles in the darkness and heard the sighs of relief.

"Manger, this is Silent Night. Stand by."

From a few feet away, Gene watched Jim and Roland study the map, then radio in a code telling the squad's exact location, before asking, "Manger, what is your ETA? This is Silent Night. Over and out."

"Silent Night, this is Manger. Estimated time of arrival is about twenty minutes. Over and out."

Like shadows, the squad left the area to return to the river. There they set security and waited for extraction. It wasn't until the boats came into view that Gene realized how tired, cold, and hungry he was. Friendly boats . . . their boats. The sight was so welcome. He tried to swallow over the lump in his throat.

Roland signaled with radio squelches, and the boats pulled into shore. As they climbed aboard, the crew slapped them lightly on their backs and shoulders. Gene caught words and phrases. "God, it's good to see you. We thought you all might have hit the big one. We heard the shit hit the fan at the objective. When you didn't make the extraction, we figured—"

"Wrong," Brian protested. "We kicked their asses. Man, what a hit! They walked right into it. Out of the frying pan and into the fire. Bodies were everywhere. No one got out."

Brian, Gene knew, was pumped again, the adrenaline flowing now, with safety. As was his own, but with it returned the soul-deep rage that eliminated tiredness, cold, and hunger. The rage that demanded more of the blood of those who'd killed Willie, and the blood of Colonel Nguyen. He stopped listening and turned away.

Behind him, the boat captain called out, "There's Seafloat!"

Gene, staring into the dark water, looked up to see a group of people standing on the east end. As the boat turned into the barge, some yelled, "Hoo-Ya!" and some applauded as the squad got off. Barely acknowledging them, he headed for the hootch.

Marc was waiting at the door. They looked at each other, smiled, but said nothing. Gene went inside. Behind him, Marc's voice was loud as the others approached. "We've got hot chow waiting for you guys. Get down to the chow hall."

"Drop your weapons off," Jim ordered, "and go eat."

At the top of his lungs, Doc yelled, "Hoo-Ya! Chow!"

Seconds later, Gene stood alone beside his bunk. He opened a can of tuna and then carried the 60 out to the cleaning table to make her ready. He spent half an hour cleaning before breaking out eight hundred rounds of new ammunition. Back inside, he put the ammo and the 60 on his rack. When he turned around, Marc was standing there with a cup of coffee.

"Here, buddy," he said, handing Gene the cup. "Why aren't you at chow? We've got steak and eggs waiting for you."

"Thanks anyway, Marc. I ate some tuna. But thanks for the coffee."

"You really had us scared. We were ready to go in to see if we could find you."

Gene looked into the light blue eyes. "Eagle, who's going out?"

Marc straightened. "KCSs. Got an op after lunch."

"Thanks." He turned back to the 60.

"Are you okay?"

"Sure. Seen Johnny?"

"Yeah. He's at the chow hall talking to Jim. What happened out there?"

"Nothing, really. We had an objective. We hit it." He looked in the Eagle's eyes. He saw the concern, the caring. "Thanks, man. Thanks."

His reply was swallowed up in the shriek of Seafloat's siren.

CHAPTER NINETEEN

"ALL PERSONNEL! MAN YOUR battle stations! General Quarters! General Quarters! All personnel! Man your battle stations!"

They were running before the order was repeated. Gene grabbed his 60 and tore out the door.

"All boats and choppers depart Seafloat!"

People rushed in all directions. Gene ran past a sandbag barrier wondering what the hell was going on. Every other attack had come in the dark of night.

"We have a large number of sampans coming in from the west!" the voice over the loudspeaker finished.

Gene dodged SEALs returning on the run from morning chow to get their weapons, and headed for the helo pads. The choppers were warming up. He could see sampans in the distance, coming in on their location. Looked like fifty or sixty of them. Boats were pulling away from Seafloat to intercept. Maybe today would be the day Charlie and the NVA overran them.

He squinted in the wind. One chopper gone . . . two choppers gone . . . He spun, looking in every direction. From what other direction would the enemy hit? Seafloat personnel were set. SEALs roamed the decks looking for sappers trying to float explosives in. The sampans were closing . . . about three or four people in each one. It was hard to see, to be sure. He tuned in to the open communications, between the boats and choppers, coming over the loudspeaker.

"Float, this is Airborne. We have about forty or fifty boats. They are flying the white flag. Weapons are stacked on bows. I repeat, they are *Flying white flag*."

"Float to all crafts: Escort them into north bank."

By that time, Gene was flanked by Brian, Jim, and Cruz.

Brian, looking through binoculars, suddenly yelled, "It's the old man! It's Raggedy!" Grinning, practically dancing up and down, he turned to Jim. "Can I take a Whaler out?"

Jim shook his head. "Wait."

Good move, thought Gene. The boat people could be a decoy or a diversion. As the sampans neared within five hundred meters, riverboat crews directed them into the north shore. There, KCSs, Seabees, Montagnards, and two squads of SEALs from other platoons waited. Their platoon, Lima, was ordered to remain on Seafloat and hold their position at all costs if they were actually being attacked.

About half the sampans had banked. Armed SEALs were meeting the beaching sampans and directing their occupants to Solid Anchor's landing strip. Brian, Gene saw, couldn't stand it.

"Jim, can I get the old man now? I know he's scared. Let me bring him back!"

Jim looked over at him and shook his head. "Go ahead, get the old fart. Bring him back. But be careful. Cruz, go with him."

Brian spun around and took off in a full run yelling, "Hoo-Ya!" with Cruz right behind him.

Gene continued to scan the area. With General Quarters still in effect, all sides of Seafloat were carefully watched. If there was any other movement out there, they'd see it. If the surrender was a ploy, the prisoners would be cut down. They couldn't allow enemy on Solid Anchor. The Seabees had completed too much construction on their north shore.

He shifted the weight of the 60 slightly. Seeing the old man, they knew the sampans had come from Twin Rivers.

"Your little psych job worked," Jim said.

Gene nodded, watching the activity. All boats had pulled in, and the last prisoners were being checked and counted. Command would have to call for helo transports to move them to Binh Thuy, to a U.S. POW camp. Brian, Cruz, and the old man motored past in the Whaler. Brian wore a huge grin, and the old man was patting him on the shoulder, smiling from ear to ear, and saying, "You number one . . . you number one."

Brian was heading toward the east end of Seafloat, to their hootch. Looking at them, Gene was reminded of little kids on Christmas morning. And with the thought came the sobering memory of Tong's two little girls and Willie. The small feeling of joy disappeared, and on the bank now, instead of the old man's people, he saw the enemy.

They were prisoners. He couldn't touch them. His hands tightened on the 60. In a few hours, he'd be going out with the KCSs, and he'd get a head count. A head count of any enemy bearing arms. Much as he wanted to, he knew he'd never be able to kill just anyone. But the enemy, and the colonel . . . They were his.

"Stand down from General Quarters!" ordered the voice from the speakers.

Gene walked slowly back to the hootch, Jim at his side. "Can I go out this afternoon?"

Jim looked at him, a strange expression on his boyish face. "Okay." He frowned. "You feeling all right?"

"Yeah. I am."

They walked on. Marc, silent too, joined them a short distance from the hootch.

The first people Gene saw, as they entered, were Brian, Cruz, and Raggedy. They were sitting on the floor next to the refrigerator. The old man was chugging a bottle of JD. After a long swig, he lowered the bottle and looked up, focusing on Gene and Marc. The smile disappeared from his face. His eyes widened. Gene could almost feel the old man's extreme fear as he cowered next to, and almost behind, Brian. He began babbling.

"It's okay," Brian said, patting him as though he were a child. "It's okay." But the old man wanted nothing to do with them.

"He's calling you evil spirits," one of the Vietnamese SEALs said. "Devil gods. He's boo-koo afraid of you two."

Gene touched Marc's arm, and they went outside. "Brian knows we'll have to question the old man soon. I'm sure nobody'd object to our doing it in the briefing room. We just need to know who and what is still down there."

"Anything we can use or destroy," Marc said.

Johnny walked up. "Drinks on me, guys." He set a six-pack on the cleaning table. "You two pulled it off. There are one hundred twenty-eight men, women, and children over there. Some ninety weapons." He turned the gold class ring on his finger with his thumb. "Shit-hot idea, man. Really was a shit-hot idea."

"Glad it worked."

"I hear," Johnny continued, "you're going out with the KCSs."

"Yup." Gene turned to Marc. "And I hear we've got a guide for this op. Something about saving somebody's daughter."

Marc nodded. "Yeah. One of the boats coming in off an op with Tommy Blade's squad—its wake swamped the guy's sampan and the daughter fell overboard. She couldn't swim. A couple of Tommy's men jumped in and saved her."

"Uh." Johnny took a drink of his beer.

"Don't know much more," Marc said, "but the op's on some tax collectors at the regional level, and it's in a Secret Zone."

Gene relished the icy coldness of the beer sliding down his throat. It would be his only one. Drinking stopped when an op was coming up. It ran through his mind that, on the hammer-and-anvil op he'd just come off of, they'd eliminated tax collectors and their escorts. But regional collectors were higher up the ladder. Secret Zone. Free kill zone. Good.

"I'm ready." He reached in his pocket, closed his fingers around Willie's cross, and felt the stiff fabric of Nguyen's shoulder patch.

Finished with his beer, Gene left the two men and walked barefoot to the edge of the helo pad on Seafloat's west end. Feet dangling in the water, he looked downriver, thinking of the hammer-and-anvil op and how easy it had been to blow the enemy away. Real easy. Some one of the bastards out there had killed Willie at Nguyen's command.

Memories surfaced again of the village burning, Tong holding his wife, the faces of the two little girls as he had covered them with his shirt, Willie, inside the drab-green body bag . . . His rage mounted. They had reason enough for being there, with all the horror, the killing. Those poor people. The raping, the murdering, had to be stopped. If the assholes wanted death, he'd bring them death.

He looked up at the sound of helo transports. Two Chinook

helos were coming in to take the POWs away. They couldn't be kept at Solid Anchor. Let V Corps interrogate the rest, he thought. The SEALs had the old man. He'd stay here. For now anyway.

Gene stood up and walked over to Johnny's hootch. He knocked on the door. "Johnny? You in?"

"Door's open."

When he entered, Johnny put down the western novel he was reading. "What's up?"

"Any word?"

He frowned. "About what?"

"Give me a break, Johnny. Who hit Willie?"

"You're not going to like it."

"Who? The colonel?"

He sighed. "Yeah."

"Have you located him?" His voice sounded in his ears like gravel crunched under boots in winter.

"I think so," Johnny said, "but I'm checking it out." The ring glinted as he ran his fingers through his hair. "The last word that came in was that he's northeast of here. Maybe twenty or thirty miles. He's picked up more men. Possible training camp up by Five Sisters."

The edge of the desk cut into Gene's thigh as he leaned forward. "Yeah." Five Sisters. Five large rivers feeding down into the Mekong Delta. Not far from the Secret Zone where they'd hit the R&R Center. Son of a bitch! They'd just been there. "Yeah," he said again. "Keep me posted," he added, and left.

He didn't tell Johnny they'd seen what must have been the training camp. Didn't want anybody else going after the colonel. Wanted him for himself. The colonel belonged to Lima.

Just before 1100 hours, Jim called the squad together for a debrief. Everything, from the time they'd left Seafloat until their return, was covered. The details of what they'd seen, heard, and smelled were given by each of them. After the debriefing, the reports would be sent to SpecWar Headquarters in Saigon, with copies to Johnny. They'd get them all. Except one. The intel on the training camp.

In charge of intel for Lima, Gene secured that bit of information in his footlocker before deciding he'd better go to chow. He didn't know how long he'd be out with the KCSs. The op might be short and sweet—go in, kill them, get the money, go home—or it could be another long one. A possible dick-dragger.

It didn't matter, he thought, walking around a work crew on his way to chow. His 60 was cleaned, oiled, loaded, and ready to sing.

By the time he arrived, the line was short and almost every seat was taken. When he reached the serving line, he realized that, standing in front of him, was Freddy Fanther.

Gene opened his mouth, then shut it. Nobody liked the poor bastard, for all kinds of reasons. Still, he was one of them. And maybe, this op, he'd come back in a body bag like Willie had. It was time to let bygones be bygones, clear the situation, and leave as few bad memories as possible.

Good old Freddy. Didn't look around to see who was next to him. Too busy piling on the food.

"Are you going to eat all that or sell it to the Montagnards?"

Freddy jumped at the sound of his voice. "Just leave me alone."

"Hey, mellow out, man."

"Dammit, just stay away from me." He took a step backward, then hurried off to a table.

Gene felt a flood of guilt. The freckled SEAL was scared to death of him. What if Fanther got killed on his next op? He had to settle this thing. Or at least try.

Gene took the makings of a sandwich, some veggie sticks, a glass of milk, and a cup of coffee. Wending his way past tables and chairs, he spotted Freddy. A vacant chair sat next to him.

Freddy glanced up, then lowered his head, looking as though he were silently saying, Don't sit here . . . please don't sit next to me.

Gene pulled the chair out. "You mind?"

"Would you go if I said I did?"

"No. Just thought I'd be polite and ask before I sat down." He put the tray on the table and took the chair. "Mind if I say something?"

"It's a free world."

"Let's bury the hatchet. You're not the enemy. Listen. You're a Teammate. You made it through Hell Week and training. You did your time." Gene sighed. "I might not like everything you say or do. Your timing is shitty. But you're still a Teammate. Life's too short. There's plenty of enemy out there. Just friends. Okay?"

"Sure," Freddy said, beginning to smile. "Why not?"

Gene was relieved. "So how have things been going?"

Freddy began telling about being on the Mighty Mo.

Gene took a long drink of milk. Freddy hadn't been on the Mighty Mo. Don't hit him, he told himself. It's not worth it. But he couldn't listen to him anymore. "I've got to run." He picked up the rest of his sandwich. "See you later." He fled.

Gene had just cleared the door when Marc came up.

"Let's go. Briefing room."

"Okay."

When they entered, Sean was up front at the maps. Seated before him were four KCSs and a man in his forties, who was dressed in black pajamas. Ralph, one of the SEALs from Delta Platoon, sat against the wall. Gene took his usual chair at the back, and Marc sat down next to him. Sean was giving the mission directive.

"This is Yen." He nodded at the man in black pajamas. "Yen will lead us to the tax collectors, for saving his daughter's life. Normally, once on board, he and his daughter would be sent to Binh Thuy and relocated, but for now, his daughter is being taken care of, and he will lead us in. We'll use one large sampan. Everyone will be covered. In the bow will be two KCSs and myself. Marc, Gene—Ralph will carry a Stoner—you three and two KCSs will be concealed beneath one of those hinged, thatched roofs. It will have tarps over both ends."

Gene looked over at Ralph. He seemed relaxed.

Sean cleared his throat. "Gene, Ralph, keep your guns on him." He motioned toward the guide. "Anything happens, kill him."

Ralph glanced back at Gene, then away.

Sean looked at one of the KCSs. "Let Yen know that if he leads us into an ambush or trap, he'll be the first to die."

The KCS translated.

"No! No!" Yen protested. "I take you in. You saved my daughter. Viet Cong would let her drown. I take you in."

Sitting with his chair tilted back against the wall, Gene listened to the rest of the PLO covering the details of the op. They'd be going into a remote Secret Zone east of Seafloat and south of the Son Ku Lon. No Americans had ever been there.

"Any questions?" Sean scanned the room. Silence answered. "Be at the boats in thirty minutes, locked and loaded."

Back at the hootch, Gene gathered his weapons and gear, then double-checked to make sure he had Willie's cross in his pocket. It felt hard and sharp-edged in his hand.

"Marc, you ready?"

"Yeah, but give me a minute. Okay?"

"Okay, but let's hurry."

A few seconds later, he was ready. "Let's go."

The Swift boats were warming up. One had a large sampan tied to its port side. With everyone on board, Sean gave the signal to cast off. Slowly they began moving east down the Son Ku Lon. The ride would take a good forty-five minutes before they headed south.

Gene smoked a cigarette, drank some water, and took two salt tablets. The day was steaming hot and clear. His skin was wet-slick, oiled with sweat. Great patches of it darkened his cami shirt.

They turned down a river. He estimated it was twenty feet wide.

"Now, load the sampan," Sean ordered.

With two of the KCSs, Sean climbed in the boat's front end. They covered themselves with plastic tarps. Gene followed Ralph and Marc beneath the thatched roof. There he made it clear to Yen that both his 60 and Ralph's Stoner were trained on him. Marc sat at his back.

Their sampan cast off from the Swifts. Hidden aboard, they would wait at the river's mouth, where it emptied into the Son Ku Lon, until insertion time.

Dripping wet, Gene sat immobile. With the sides draped, the crowded area under the thatched roof was a steam bath. It stank with the smells of gun oil, sweat, the dankness of the jungle and river, and the body odor of the KCSs sitting shoulder-to-shoulder with him.

It was important to eliminate tax collectors and to seize any money they'd taken from the villagers. Without money, Nguyen couldn't buy food and medical supplies. Without food supplies, people would starve. Without either food or medical supplies, they'd have to move. Forced into action, mistakes could be made. And if Nguyen screwed up, they'd get him.

When insertion time finally came, Yen restarted the sampan's small 3.5-horsepower motor, and they proceeded farther down the river. Gene and Ralph watched his every move. After several miles, the river narrowed to a mere five feet. Yen guided the sampan into a small stream to starboard.

Gene tensed, knowing their objective was to the left—the port side—not starboard. He pushed the 60's barrel through a small opening in the drape over the hinged roof above, and aimed it at Yen.

About five feet downstream, the guide stopped and backed their sampan out. He then continued south on the river for five hundred meters before turning into another small stream. This time on the port side.

At least they were headed in the right direction, Gene thought, and pulled the nose of the 60's barrel back inside. Peering through an opening in the drape, he saw the small stream was still about four or five feet across, running through heavy brush under triple canopy.

The sampan's motor stopped. Yen lifted it out of the water, took a long pole, and started poling them along. The tide was running out, and the stream wasn't deep enough for the motor. With all their weight aboard, the waterline was about a quarter of an inch from the sideboard.

The last thing in the world they needed was to be grounded. Gene lifted the 60, just a bit. The stream got narrower as the tide kept running out. Again Yen pulled right, into another stream, only to back out. Then he did the same, a third time.

It was too much. Gene prodded Yen with the tip of the 60. Eyes wide, shoulders hunched, Yen turned to stare at him.

"What the hell are you doing, going in and out of these streams?" Gene whispered harshly.

"They watch," Yen whispered back. "We no go in and out, they know we not friend."

Gene nodded and pulled the 60 back.

"You get ready," the guide whispered. "We close around next bend."

The sampan crept through the water. If they got hit now, the boat couldn't be turned around. They'd have to take it out backward, which would take a lot longer, since its rear was flat. Nor could their Swift boats come after them with the stream so shallow. The jungle was too thick for air support, and they knew, from the PLO and the guide, that hundreds of VC and NVA occupied the Secret Zone surrounding them. But where they were, nobody knew.

Gene froze. Voices were coming from the port side. Three men in black pajamas, he saw through a small opening, were calling and motioning for Yen to pole the sampan to them. Gene blinked sweat from his eyes. Yen moved the boat closer and closer. The three were saying something about the sampan, but he couldn't understand all of it. Two of the three had AK-47s slung from their shoulders.

The unarmed one frowned. "What kind of sampan is that?"

"This is a business-type sampan!" one of the KCSs up front yelled as he threw off his plastic cover and opened his M-16 up on full automatic. Instantly Sean and the other KCSs opened fire as well. Even as they did, Gene, Marc, and the rest bolted from their seats and threw up the heavy thatched roof to begin firing. The roof slammed straight back down on their heads. Violently they threw it back up. It rebounded hard, a split second later, almost knocking them to their knees. They threw it up a third time with such force it tore loose and landed in the heavy, overhanging brush on the bank.

By then, it was too late. Sean and the KCSs at the sampan's front end were howling with laughter.

Gene saw stars. The firing was over. Two of the VC lay dead on the bank. The third had escaped, leaving a wide blood trail.

Ralph stepped out of the sampan, only to see the Stoner box holding his ammunition fall out of his weapon and into the mud.

Setting security, Gene gasped. "Jesus!" Ralph could put it back in and fire if he had to. And he'd better. They had at least seven miles of tiny streams to go before the Swifts could come down and pick them up. They damned sure couldn't afford to throw ammo away.

As Ralph picked up the fallen Stoner box, Sean and two of the KCSs left the sampan for the bank. They began to search the bodies and the area.

Sean found a small money bag on one body. "Not even enough cash to buy a week's supply of food for the KCS camp," he announced after looking inside. "Everyone out of the boat," he ordered. "Turn it around."

Disappointed over the risk taken for so little return, Gene slung the 60. Using brute force, they lifted the sampan. Slipping in the mud, trying to keep their footing in the stream, they managed to face the boat in the other direction.

The second they had, Gene pulled the 60 around into firing position and scanned the green wall of jungle intently. With all the gunfire, enemy would sure as hell be coming.

"Now, one with an AK-47 got away, but with that kind of blood loss, he's a dead man." Sean climbed into the sampan. "Load up, and let's get the fuck out of here."

Aboard, Gene glanced around. Satisfied everybody was there, he concentrated on the jungle in his immediate area. They staggered fields of fire, so both sides of the sampan were covered, but with the drapes and the thatched roof gone, they were completely exposed. Hunched down, he tried to make himself as small as he could. Ralph and Sean were doing the same.

Be ready for an ambush, going out," Sean warned. "You all know they'll be coming."

Only too well, Gene thought. He could reach out and touch the impenetrable brush, it was so close. If they got hit, it would be at point-blank range. The only thing they'd be able to do would be to return fire and hope the sampan cleared the enemy's kill zone before they were all dead.

Listening, watching intently, he suddenly remembered his very first kill. He could still see the young boy in a sampan. He'd put a bullet right between the boy's eyes. Afterward, he had spent a long time vomiting, knowing he'd never forget that young kid. He hadn't. Now it was their turn to be the ones in the sampan. If the enemy managed to reach them before they could escape, they had as much chance as that boy.

The stream widened about three feet on each side as twilight approached. Suddenly one of the KCSs fired.

"Ambush left!" Sean yelled.

Every one of them opened up, firing left. The gathering darkness sparked with muzzle flashes bright as the sun. The volume of fire was such that it moved the sampan to the right bank.

There was no return fire. No ambush. The KCS had fired a round accidentally. It wasn't the first time, and wouldn't be the last, Gene knew. No sense in getting mad. The tension and the fear were such that he'd done it himself when he'd first come to Nam. They all had. Then, from the rear, he heard firing, knew the enemy was reconning and looking for them.

Sean got on the radio. "Scramble Sea Wolves!"

Smart, Gene thought. They still had some distance to the larger river where the Swifts would pick them up. But right now they were amidst a lot of enemy, and everybody was on the edge of opening up again. The KCSs weren't SEALs. They didn't have the discipline. Pulling the trigger would come as a relief to them.

He listened to Sean radio the Swifts to come down and realized Sean hoped to time it so that their boats would arrive at the extraction point the same moment they did.

Sean's plan didn't work. When they reached the pickup point, the Swifts weren't there. Gene looked up and saw the Sea Wolves overhead. He watched them fly just a little south of their location and draw fire. Heavy automatic weapons fire. The Wolves opened up with .50-calibers, 60s, and rockets.

"Emergency extraction!" Sean radioed to the Swifts.

"Cannot suppress fire. Get out of there," the Wolves radioed down. "We can't stay any longer. Return fire is too heavy."

Gene heard the Swifts before he saw them. They came into sight at full speed, then banked at their feet. They loaded fast, and once they were aboard, Sean dropped a grenade into the sampan. The Swifts turned and headed out on step. Barely out of sight around a curve in the river, Gene heard the explosion as the sampan went up.

When no further enemy contact was made, Sean suddenly announced loudly, "This is a business-type sampan!" They laughed hysterically.

"Bang, bang—you're dead!" Ralph yelled, and Gene listened to them laugh again.

They reached Seafloat a little after dark. The money they'd recovered would be given to the KCSs for clothing and food. They had three enemy KIA. The bleeder wouldn't have lasted ten minutes. More important, Gene thought, climbing out of the boat, the enemy had more proof that they weren't safe anywhere. It didn't matter how far into the jungle they went, or how many of them there were. The SEALs could and would penetrate their private domain. The psychological impact of that would cause the NVA problems. From an intelligence point of view, the op had been a total success. Most important, they'd all got back alive.

Later, after reporting to NILO, Gene stood alone at Seafloat's edge. In his pocket, his fingers traced the angular shape of Willie's cross. Sorry, my friend, he thought, I didn't make a kill for you this op, but three of the bastards joined their Maker anyway.

Gene stared out into the night, still tense. Some ops were like that . . . get all pumped up, go out, and next to nothing actually happened. Get back and feel . . . half-grateful, half-angry, he guessed. But there was always the next time. At least for him. He'd be going out again, bright and early. He took a breath and headed to the cleaning tables to get his gear ready.

By the time he hung the 60 in the sling on his rack, it was 2130 hours. Card games were going on in the hootch, all around him. Gene leaned against the metal bedpost. He was going on ninety-six hours with no sleep. Probably should try and get some. Stretched out on his rack, he closed his eyes but couldn't stop the hell he'd seen in Vietnam from running through his mind.

Willie, he asked silently, can you hear me? I miss you, my friend. Why didn't you stay home on the Float? You didn't have to go out. You gave the ultimate. For what? I'm lost, my friend. So full of hate, so angry. Wish I'd been with you that day. If I'd been there, you might have lived. I'm so sorry, my dear brother . . .

Sleep never came.

CHAPTER TWENTY

THE LACK OF REST began to take its toll. Though he was mentally alert, his body felt heavy after four days without sleep. Gene leaned against the cleaning table outside the hootch and decided the main reason his strength wasn't up to par was that he'd just come off the sick list. He'd gone without sleep before, during Hell Week in training. Six days.

Gene had just finished cleaning his gear. He'd only fired about a hundred rounds on the KCS op. Not even a warm-up for a power weapon, especially one so clean and smooth in operation. He'd dismantled the 60, to clean and inspect every part like he always did, and was glad he had. The operating rod had fractured. If he'd just sprayed her down with WD-40 oil, she could have quit when he needed her most.

He shuddered at the thought. He could have fired eight hundred rounds, or eight, before that rod broke in two and left him with what amounted to a twenty-six-pound club.

He turned the 60 in his big hands and looked at it. Many a person in this godforsaken place had gone into battle only to have their weapons malfunction due to worn-out parts. Most malfunctions were due to poor or no maintenance. It was stupid to risk their own lives and their buddies' because they were too lazy to take care of their gear.

One of the reasons he'd volunteered for SEAL Team was that

they had the fewest casualties of any branch of the military. For one thing, SEALs took care of their weapons.

He'd just started toward the hootch when Marc came out, ran past him to Seafloat's edge. Gene cringed in sympathy. The Eagle was puking his guts out. He waited a moment, then went over to walk back inside with him.

"Marc, you okay? You look lousy."

The Eagle stopped, pulled his T-shirt off, and used it to wipe his pale and sweaty face. "I think it was something I ate," he said. "Hope this is it. I've got an op tonight."

"Hey, bro . . . I'm ready. Why not check if I can take your place?"

Marc glanced at him, his light blue eyes red-rimmed. "No. I'll be okay." He stopped, spun away.

Right, Gene thought, watching Marc run to the side again where he began to dry-heave.

After a good two minutes of retching, he came slowly back. Now his reddened eyes were tearing. Tough on the stomach muscles, Gene knew. The Eagle went right past him on his way to the head. Hoo-Ya, he thought, both ends going. He leaned against the cleaning table and waited for Marc's next appearance.

"Sure you're okay, buddy?" he asked when the Eagle came back.

"It's got me going both ways."

"All right," Gene said. "What's the op?" He waited while Marc looked around to make sure nobody was within hearing.

"Easy op," he answered in a low voice. "We're making a hit. Should only be out for about three to six hours."

"I can fill in for you. You'll be a security element anyway, and it sounds like it's going to be short and sweet."

Marc wiped his face with the T-shirt again. "Sure you don't mind?"

Gene shook his head. "Anything for you, Eagle. You know that."

"Let me go tell the PL and see what he says. We've already had the Warning Order, but I could fill you in on the basic equipment list." He took a long, careful breath. "The PLO is at 2200 hours."

"Go," Gene said. "I'll wait here."

Poor guy, he thought, watching Marc walk away. He turned his back to the cleaning table and lifted himself up to sit on it. A cold beer'd taste good, but he couldn't drink if he was going out on an op. If, hell, he thought. He'd be going.

Roland and Cruz walked past the table, crossing his line of sight. They paused. Gene stared down the Son Ku Lon. Roland and Cruz moved on without speaking.

Yeah. He'd be going. One more chance for revenge. The adrenaline began to flow.

"It's all right," Marc said when he returned, "but clear it with your OIC. You sure you don't mind?"

"Not at all." Gene eased himself off the table. "Just take it easy," he added. He went to check in with Jim.

The lieutenant wasn't at his rack. He looked around the hootch to see if Jim was playing cards. He wasn't. On the way back out, Gene saw that the mail had come in. There were letters from Karen on his bunk. He scooped them up, opened his footlocker, and dumped them in with the unread stack that had buried the abandoned Bible. Since Willie's death, the letters and the Bible had meant no more to him than a beer can tossed in the Son Ku Lon.

He left the hootch to check at the chow hall, thinking Jim might be getting some coffee. No luck. There were only forty minutes left before the PLO. He checked in the other hootch, where the third and fourth platoons were. Still no luck.

Frustrated, Gene walked back to Lima's hootch. Just outside the door were shelves made of wooden ammo crates. They were used to store plastic explosives, grenades, flares, claymores, and such. Four large plastic bottles sat there as well, one each for aspirin, malaria tablets, salt tabs, and Dexamyl. From experimenting with them just after arriving in Vietnam, he'd learned he could take only one and a half tabs of the Dexies. If he took two, he'd flip out, be seeing things that weren't there.

Gene opened one of the bottles, took two Dexamyls out, and laid them atop the shelf. He drew the bowie, laid the blade across one tab, and gently tapped the top of the knife. It sliced the tab cleanly in half. A few swigs of beer washed one and a half tabs down. For the next eighteen hours or so he'd be ready to go do anything. He tossed the rest of the beer over the side, into the Son Ku Lon.

Back in the hootch, he put on a pair of jeans and a cami top before picking up the 60's ammo belts and crisscrossing them around his chest and waist. There were no lower pockets on the shirt he'd tucked into his waistband. From the time some of the 60's rounds had gotten snagged, when he'd broken them off to reload, the first thing he'd done with a new shirt was tear off its bottom pockets.

Gene had just fastened the last belt of ammo around his waist when Brian and the old man walked in. The point man's face looked like thunder.

"Brian, what's wrong?"

"We tried to get the old man into the KCS camp but they turned us down." He jammed his hands into his pockets. "We've got to send him out in the morning."

Gene glanced at the old man. Obviously he didn't know what Brian was talking about. He was just smiling away. Of course he was pretty shit-faced. Didn't seem to recognize him. Or, he suddenly thought, was it that they all looked alike to the old man? "Sorry to hear that. Why not have Jim or Johnny try?"

Brian grimaced. "They did. They were with me over at the camp."

"Are they back yet?"

"Yeah. They're either over at Johnny's or at the chow hall for coffee." He whacked the door frame, then headed for his rack, the old man carrying part of a bottle of JD and following along.

The sight reminded Gene of a frustrated kid walking down the street with a tail-wagging puppy underfoot.

When Brian got to his rack, he opened his footlocker, pulled out a bottle of Scotch, took a big swallow, then reached in again to take out a *Playboy* magazine. From across the hootch, Gene watched him open it to the centerfold. He showed the old man. Raggedy's face lit up. He laughed and reached out to touch the picture.

Gene doubted the old man had ever seen a naked "round-eyes" before. The Vietnamese women had very small breasts, and both men and women had very little pubic hair. No doubt Raggedy was amazed at the centerfold. They do well together, he thought, Brian and the old man. Brian would be hurting inside, having to send him away. Raggedy would be going to a POW camp. Still, it would be better there than the way he must have had to live these past years.

He'd get three square meals a day, dry and clean clothing, and a roof over his head.

It was time. In full combat gear and green face, Gene walked over behind Doc, who was dealing in a card game. "If anyone looks for me, tell them I went out with Marc's platoon."

Gene got his 60 and left before Doc could get a good look at him. The pills were taking effect. He felt full of energy and mentally sharp as he headed for the briefing room. The night was warm and muggy, the sky clear. Got to be very careful tonight, he warned himself. Plenty of starlight out there. No rain to hide sound.

"Gene!"

He turned to see Jim and Johnny coming toward him.

"Where are you going?" Jim asked.

"Marc's got the flu or something. I agreed to take his place. It's okay, isn't it?"

Jim planted his hands on his hips and looked him over. "You've been running hard lately. How do you feel?"

"Good. Real good." The Dexamyl he'd taken was hitting. His body felt a little off. Had to get by Jim. Wanted to be on his way. "Well? Is it okay?"

"How long will you be gone?"

"Should be back before dawn."

"It's all right this time, but next time, clear it with me before you agree."

Gene let out his breath. "Jim, I tried, but I couldn't find you. Never had any problems before, so I agreed. Marc is sick as a dog. I wasn't trying to go around you."

"I know," Jim said. "I just don't want you down again."

Gene nodded. The pills weren't setting too good, but he was committed. "No problem. Got to get to the brief. I've only got a few minutes."

Jim didn't move. "Gene, when you get back in, I want you to see the doctor."

At Gene's frown, he added, "Just for a checkup."

"Yes, sir! Thanks."

He started toward the briefing room. Jim and Johnny were on their way to the hootch, but when Gene stopped to adjust the bowie, he overheard Johnny say, "Something's not right with him.

He's been—" Gene missed the rest, as they walked out of hearing range. He shrugged, went on to the briefing room, and took his usual chair.

He was barely seated when Marc's PL, Devin Walker, announced, "Tonight's mission is to eliminate the province chief. Hard intel shows he's playing both sides and has interfered with several ops in the recent past."

So now he dies, Gene thought, and leaned forward, listening as Dev went over every detail at length—what to do at the objective, no friendly forces, no prisoners.

"Just get in and get out before anyone wakes up," Dev said. "Point man, radioman, and I will be the search element. Gene will be taking Marc's place in the security element. Gene," he said, pointing to an exact location on the chalkboard diagram, "I want you at this point so you can see most of the village, to take it under fire if need be. Freddy, you're here," he added, pointing at another location. "Understood?"

Gene nodded when Dev looked at him. Everything was pretty much SOP.

"Any questions?" The PL glanced around. None of the SEALs said anything. "Let's move out. Get on the boats and under way in five minutes."

Gene stood and opened the door.

When the squad reached the MSSCs, sampans were already tied down on top of the bows, and the boats were warmed up. When the last man had boarded, they pulled away, heading for the drop-off point.

During the ride, the only sounds Gene heard were the engines. No one moved, no one spoke. Not even Freddy Fanther, with his XM-203, sitting two men away from Dev. It was almost as though he were out there alone. Very alone—like each man was isolated inside the bubble of his own silence, his own thoughts.

The boats turned north and slowed to an idle, moving quietly into the enemy's backyard. The sound of their diesels softened even more. The word was passed.

"Get ready."

The MSSCs turned into the bank. The sampans were lowered gently into the water. The squad loaded into them for the long, slow trip upriver to their objective.

As they paddled north, they stayed on the east side of the river, using the tree shadows cast by the moonlight. Very quietly, they floated farther and farther into enemy territory. Like the others, Gene carefully lifted his paddle out of the water and gently placed it back in at each stroke, to avoid any splashing.

Just a nice smooth ride up the river, he thought. A moonlight cruise.

It was almost 0100 hours when they eased past a small village where everyone was fast asleep. In their silent passing, he could see the glow from the cooking fires, which also provided the villagers with light. The objective was about a mile farther on. With twenty to thirty minutes left until they reached the target, the boats glided to a halt.

Gene used the time to put on more green and black face paint, making sure to cover all visible skin—eyelids, ears, inside the ears, neck, hands. Huddled near to him, the six SEALs from Delta's squad did the same.

When they'd finished, the sampans continued to creep toward the village and the target.

Gene went over the details with every stroke of his paddle. They knew which hootch in the village—even knew the location inside the hootch—the province chief would be sleeping in, lying on a bamboo floor mat. Get in, get out. Short and sweet. Just make the hit. They were in a free kill zone. Everybody was enemy. While the search element was inside, he could say they were spotted, and then would be allowed to take the entire place under fire. Why not hit them all? They had the element of surprise, had the firepower. Since the target was on a river, they could scramble the Sea Wolves for support.

Come on, Gene, he told himself, you know you've got to stay with the plan. Even though it was a free kill zone, he couldn't lower himself to Colonel Nguyen's level. Couldn't kill just to kill—unless they had weapons in their hands. Not likely. There'd be kids in there, and it wasn't their war. But God, he ached to. Couldn't blow away enough of them to make up for Willie. He wanted to see blood run in floods.

The sampans pulled into the bank. The squad inserted. While the security element set security, the search team pulled the sampans onshore and hid them just inside the tree line.

Upriver, about three hundred meters away, Gene spotted a few of the hootches. From here, he thought, they would patrol, and come in from the jungle, behind the village. He lifted the cover from his watch. Almost 0200 hours. It would take about thirty minutes to an hour to sneak in and make the hit. And about thirty more, max, to quietly sneak back to the sampans. They'd need another hour to hook up with the waiting MSSCs. So they'd still have plenty of darkness—be long gone before any of the villagers woke to find their chief dead.

Dev gave the signal to move out. The squad dropped into file formation, with Gene in Marc's place.

It wasn't bad, moving through the jungle. The mud was not too deep, and the moon provided a little light so he could see, as he stepped carefully around and over the snaking tree roots, ducked vines, avoided the clutches of thick brush.

The steady hum of mosquitoes was a constant in the hot, wet night air as the silent squad patrolled closer to the outside perimeter of the village. They were using every possible shadow to cover their presence. The smell of human habitation began to taint the dark odor of the jungle.

Then they were there, at the edge of the clearing, halted by a signal from Dev. The layout of the hootches was just as described in the briefing, Gene saw.

At Dev's signal, the squad's security element took up position and moved in. Gene went in slowly, ensuring that each step forward was a silent one. His position would be more exposed than the others if a villager passed. He had to be in position not only to cover the village as a whole but to cut the target's hootch in half at a three-foot level should anyone awake.

Search and destroy wouldn't move in until security was set. He found a small wood pile and knelt, but found he was unable to see the right flank security. It was important that, from each security position, the men on his left and right sides could be seen so he could assist them as well. He moved more to the right side of the woodpile.

There, he thought, looking to the right. Freddy was in sight. He turned. Okay on the left side too. Both men were in position and ready to respond, in a split second, to any situation that might occur. As was he.

He caught shadows separating from darker ones and tensed. The search and destroy team was moving in. All three of them were bent over—crouched to provide a smaller target. They swept their weapons smoothly, steadily, back and forth across the area as they approached the entrance of the target's hootch. The radioman went down on one knee, looking outward, past Gene's and Freddy's security positions, ready to provide cover fire to their rears if needed.

Gene kept his breathing steady, a control on the adrenaline racing through his body. The hootch was covered on all four sides now. Each man's position was covered by at least two other men, one on the right and one on the left. He leaned forward just the slightest bit. The point and the PL were moving slowly into the dark doorway of the hootch. Once inside, the point man would make the hit while Dev set security for him. Anyone who woke before the task was completed would be eliminated by the PL.

Gene tried to swallow. He focused harder on the doorway. The point man would use a .22-caliber pistol with a Hush Puppy on it. Before firing, he'd look for an angle that would ensure the round would enter the brain, and not be deflected on hitting the skull. He listened intently, but heard nothing except insect sounds and his own heartbeat.

The point man and the PL exited the hootch.

Well done, Gene thought. Very damned well done. Less than two minutes had passed, but to him, slick with sweat, it had seemed like two hours.

The point and PL moved toward the jungle, and as they passed, the other members of the squad fell in behind them. In patrol formation, they disappeared into the dark of the jungle.

No one heard, Gene thought. No one knew that, in just a few hours, they'd find they needed a new chief. Smooth and silent. Exactly the way their ops were meant to be. Perfect. So far. He ducked under a branch. Vines slithered across one shoulder and the side of his neck. At least, he hoped they were vines. His stomach lurched. For a moment, his shoulders hunched, but he walked on, putting his concentration on making each step silent.

When they finally reached the sampans, it took less than a minute to get them back in the water. They boarded and started paddling out as silently as they'd paddled in.

Gene's thoughts were still with the hit. He knew what it must have been like inside the hootch. He'd executed the same kind of op himself. Go into the dark, he thought. Try to focus. Count the sleeping bodies of wife and children. Locate the target. Take the angle and squeeze the trigger. *Puff*. The round goes off. The body twitches slightly.

And, he thought, the people sleeping would be shocked when they awoke. They'd wonder how it happened. They'd seen nothing, heard nothing. He dipped his paddle carefully, watched it cut into the dark water with barely a ripple.

The only problem he'd had running that type of op had occurred when the target, like this one, had a wife and children. It had bothered him, imagining how the children would respond—their sorrow and hurt over a father dead. But he couldn't dwell on that, or it would chew him up inside. He had to focus on the need for the mission. The hit would save lives. Personal feelings had to be put aside.

Gene snapped out of reverie. They'd almost reached the MSSCs. The radioman made contact to let them know they were coming into the boats' position. If for some reason they couldn't have made radio contact, they'd have used blinking lights. They could not just paddle up to them without warning. The MSSCs would consider the squad enemy moving in and open up.

But things had gone well, gone as planned. Just as they did on most SEAL ops. And Freddy Fanther—skate that he was aboard Seafloat—hadn't made a wrong move out in the bush, he thought as he helped get the sampans aboard the boats so they could head home.

Sitting on one of the benches as they neared the Son Ku Lon, Gene realized how comfortable he'd become in the bush. It had become part of him, as it had, he guessed, for others who had been there before him and all who would follow—no matter what branch or unit. If they lived long enough.

When they reached the Son Ku Lon, the MSSCs opened their engines up to full speed. Gene asked the boat personnel next to him for a cigarette and lit up. He thought about the next op and wondered how long it would be until he'd be back out. He just needed to find out who'd be going. It would be at least twelve hours more before the pills wore off. Until then, he'd be wired.

He stood. The boats were flying down the river. The surface was like glass, with no chop. The air rushed past his face and through his hair. It felt good. It was still warm, still sticky, but somewhat cooler out on the water. Seafloat lay just ahead.

The boat pulled into the Float and docked. Gene strolled into the briefing room, with the rest of Delta, for their debriefing. That would be short and sweet too, he thought, just like the op. And yet, same as with the business-type sampan, he had a feeling of incompleteness. It was frustrating. He'd been hyped to kill and hadn't. Not one fucking round had he fired. Should be glad, but he wasn't.

The debriefing over, he went to the cleaning table and sprayed some WD-40 on the 60, then tiptoed to his rack. Inside the hootch, everyone slept. Brian was curled up on the floor, the old man fast asleep in Brian's rack.

Gene shook his head. Knowing the old man, he probably didn't fall asleep. Probably passed out. The old coot sure could put hard liquor down. No doubt Brian wanted to make the old man's last night the best possible. He sure did have a liking for Raggedy.

As quietly as possible, he took off his ammo belts and set them next to the 60. They'd stay there until he could find someone to go out with. The sun was starting to rise, and he could smell bacon and coffee.

He left the hootch and headed for the chow hall.

"Hey, Michaels," the cook yelled, "where you been? Haven't seen you in days."

"I'm still here, Cookie," Gene answered. "Been busy."

He picked up a tray. Cookie was one big man. Stood six foot eight and black as midnight.

"How do you want your eggs?"

"You mean you've got real eggs and not that powdered crap?" Cookie grinned. "Sure do."

"How about two over easy?"

It wasn't long before Cookie walked over and handed him a plate with four eggs on it. Fresh eggs were a real treat, and when they did get their hands on some, it was usually two to a person.

"Thanks." Gene looked down at the eggs and then up at the big cook. "You didn't have to do that."

"Don't mention it," Cookie said. He leaned forward, big hands resting on the table. "By the way, do you think you could get me a North Vietnamese flag to take home?"

Gene grinned. So that's what it was all about. "Good as done. I'll bring you one down myself." When they did bring flags back from an op, they sold them for forty or fifty bucks each in Binh Thuy. There were a couple in his locker. God, but bacon, eggs, and hot coffee smelled good. Worth a flag any day.

By the time he'd finished eating, people were standing in line outside, waiting for the chow hall to open. A new day, he thought, and wondered who he'd be going out with. The sooner, the better. He was ready.

CHAPTER TWENTY-ONE

LESS THAN FIVE HOURS later, Gene was back in the jungle carrying the 60 for Sean and his KCS patrol again. Just hours after returning, he filled in for a still-sick Marc on an overnight observation op. There'd been an encounter with some VC on their way out. He remembered cutting one of them in half with the 60, but not much more. When he'd gotten back from the second op, he'd popped some more pills and pulled an overnighter with his own squad—an interdiction. Then they'd booked, and after a brief firefight at the pickup point, arrived back at Seafloat both muddy and bloody.

Days and hours got all mixed up. Gene began to mark time by whether he needed some more pills, or how long he had until next Warning Order or Patrol Leader's Order. All that mattered was the next op and how many enemy had been eliminated during the one just finished. Willie's death cut deep. That he hadn't been with his friend on that last and final op was a torture. A lifetime of belief in God had died that day.

Karen's letters continued to be dropped unread into the foot-locker. They covered the Bible. Gene no longer even wanted to see it. The driving need to operate kept him careful around Jim, who thought he was sleeping between ops, and who thought he was eating when, in fact, he left most of his food untouched.

It was an effort to try and seem normal around the squad. In

SEAL training he'd learned to be impassive and to conceal emotion. He'd put that training to use many times, but never as rigidly as after Willie's death. With little food and no sleep, training and the desire to kill sustained him—and pills.

Hatred grew each time he put on green face. In the jungle, he killed any enemy holding a weapon that he could, so long as neither mission nor patrol was endangered. The record for silent kills was his. He ached to find Colonel Nguyen and watch him die. Johnny, at NILO, avoided him, knowing what he wanted and having no hard information to give.

In the hootch after one op, Alex showed him a snapshot just received from his mother. It was a photo taken shortly after SEAL graduation. None of them looked old enough to buy a beer. They hadn't been, and most of them still weren't. Later, while shaving, Gene had looked at himself and realized he'd aged ten years in the five and a half months since their arrival on Seafloat. The photo had depicted a boy's face, a huge smile. Now he shaved a lined face gone cold and hard, the dark eyes darkened further, reflecting death. His way of life. He wondered what he'd look like at the end of the next two weeks, when their six-month tour of duty was up. They'd be flying back to The World then. There wasn't much time left to find Nguyen.

Gene looked out over the black mass that was the jungle at night. Behind him, faint sounds of music came from the hootch. His fellow SEALs, over the past nine days, had been constantly busy, either on ops or drinking and playing cards, before going back out into the bush for yet another op. None had noticed that he hadn't slept. They knew he operated with anyone going out and were used to seeing him coming and going. Only two had sensed something amiss.

Leaning against the hootch having a cigarette a couple of nights earlier, he'd heard Tommy ask, "What's up with Gene?" and Roland had answered, "Nothing. He just loves to operate." Murmurs of agreement had come from the rest of the squad. Tommy had replied, "Oh, yeah?" and his tone let Gene know he'd got the answer he had expected, but wasn't comfortable with it.

Marc knew what was going on. Still, he'd kept his promise and said nothing. As the days passed, Gene was aware that the Eagle, though silent, was watching.

Moonlight reflected off the water. The Dexies were working. In a short time, their squad would be going out again. Just after midnight, they would be running a search and destroy mission to take out a weapons cache. Cruz had gotten the info on their hard target and had the okay from Jim to run the op. It would be Cruz's first time as their patrol leader.

And that was fine, Gene thought, running his thumb along the edges of Willie's cross. The squad had complete confidence in Cruz. They'd never question his abilities. He was a great operator. If shit hit the fan, Cruz would do what he had to do and would be mentally capable of handling anything thrown his way. He'd asked Jim to be his APO. Together, they were busy preparing for the early morning hit, planned to occur under cover of the darkness just before sunrise.

Intense, shaky, itchy to go, Gene studied the jungle and the river and waited. The Warning Order had gone down. The PLO was set for 0100 hours. The squad had prepared their equipment and, except for him, had gone to bed. Over the last seven days he'd allowed the pills to build up in his system, and before they wore off, he took more. He couldn't sleep. He waited, and paced Seafloat's deck when he couldn't stand still.

He scanned the river once again, then went back to the briefing room to study the map. Not the map of the combat area he'd be following Cruz into, but a map of the northeast. Colonel Nguyen's area. Impulsively he took Nguyen's shoulder patch out of his pocket, stuck it on the map with a black pushpin, and hung Willie's gold cross over it. Intently he studied all possible areas in which the colonel might be found, comparing intelligence reports in relation to the many sightings reported.

Sometime later, Jim and Cruz entered, to set up for the PLO. Before they could cross the room, Gene had put the shoulder patch and cross back in his pocket.

"Anything I can do, You-O?" he asked.

Cruz shook his head.

Gene left them, and went back to the hootch to get ready for the PLO and into combat gear and green face for the op. When he entered, the squad was getting dressed, donning their operating gear and painting their faces. The paint had become a weapon in and of itself. The sight of green faces streaked with black horrified the people of the Mekong Delta, keeping them in constant fear of those who wore it, and who always left dead and wounded behind.

The rest of the squad left for the PLO. Gene, hand on the light switch, looked around the hootch. In Delta's half, Marc and his fellow squad members slept. Their area was dark, the nets pulled down around their beds. That half of the hootch had an empty look. Almost all of them had their equipment packed and staged outside. In less than forty-eight hours, they'd be on their way back to the good old U.S.A.

In full combat gear, Gene turned off the light and started to leave the dark and silent hootch, then stopped. Walking soft, he went to the Eagle's rack. For a moment he stood and listened to the regular breathing that told him Marc was in deep sleep. His whisper was barely audible. "In case, my friend, I don't see you before you leave, thanks for your silence." They'd faced death together many times, seen the devil's face in the fiery hell, and walked out laughing with their weapons still smoking. "I'll miss you, Eagle. Take care. God be . . ."

Gene went silent. He couldn't finish the sentence. "Take care, my friend."

Silently he left the hootch.

When he reached the briefing room, Cruz stood at the front, ready to give his Patrol Leader's Order. Jim sat at the back of the room next to the chair Gene always took. They acknowledged each other with a look before giving Cruz their full attention.

"Tonight's mission," he began, "is to search and destroy a weapons cache located two rivers west of Twin Rivers." He pointed to the map and gave the exact coordinates of its location. "Intel," he continued, "has been received by interrogating POWs that came out of the area. Intel states that about twenty NVA remain.

"They've been staging the weapons to the west in an attempt to get them moved to the north. The weapons are under the seventh grave site on the left side of the graveyard."

Shit, Gene thought, and glanced at Jim, who grinned at him, then motioned toward Doc, who had suddenly sat straight up in his chair. Cruz continued.

"The enemy's camp is five hundred meters to the south and the west. Back here." He pointed to the location on the map.

Gene shifted the 60's position slightly, listening as Cruz went on to cover every detail, everyone's actions expected, and what to do under different conditions they might encounter. You-O, he thought, is standing tall up front. You'd never know it was his first PLO.

"No friendly forces," Cruz said. "There is air support and boat support if needed. They'll be standing by."

When he'd covered everything, he added, "Any questions?" and when there were none, he smiled and said, "Well, what are you sitting there for? Let's go kick ass and take names."

Outside, the squad jumped up and down again, to see if anything they wore rattled or came loose. Then they boarded the boats that would take them to their insertion point.

Gene checked his watch. It was 0215. Moving down the river made the night seem cool. Cool for Vietnam anyway, he thought. The sky was clear and star-studded.

Cruz passed the word. "We'll be heading down Twin Rivers in a few moments. Everybody stay down. Have your weapons ready. No noise."

Gene looked up. By watching the stars, he could see the change in direction to the left that the boats made. He couldn't help but wonder just how safe Twin Rivers would be. So many had died trying to get into the area. He stayed low and waited.

When they reached the fork that split the river into two, they took the one to the right. He thought of Raggedy for a second, whose village and the factory had been to the left. To his knowledge, this was the first time anyone had taken the river to the right. All other ops had either been blown to hell before that point or taken the left fork to try to find the weapons factory and then were hit.

Gene shifted position slightly to keep his legs and feet from going to sleep or cramping. So far, so good. He glanced around. Everybody was facing outward. Three to port and four to starboard, they were ready to rise from below the bulkheads and return fire instantly if they got hit.

The boat moved slowly down the steadily narrowing river. The banks were so close, the trees on each side were joined over the water.

"Get ready," Cruz whispered.

The boat turned into the west bank and stopped. One by one the SEALs inserted. They moved immediately into the concealing bush and set security until the boat moved back out.

Concealed in the foliage, Gene looked around and listened to the sounds of night. He took careful breaths, smelling the air, making sure no one was near, hoping no one saw them insert. Two finger-snaps caught his attention.

Cruz waved, signaling *move out*.

Gene watched Brian take point, moving on the compass bearing given during the PLO. With the rest, he dropped into file formation. Slowly, silently, they snaked through the heavy bush.

The clear night had brought out every bug. The air was so full of flying creatures, it was like walking through massed spiderwebs. Gene breathed slow and easy, trying hard not to inhale any of the tiny insects. Keep moving, he told himself. Just keep moving.

They rested about every hundred meters, listening, then moved on.

The terrain was a bitch to patrol through—a virgin area. Gene doubted that other humans had ever come into it. It was too hard to move. Passage was too slow to be of any use—except to SEALs. The enemy would never expect them to come this route.

Finally the jungle opened up a bit more, and the mud grew less deep. The patrol halted. Brian and Cruz disappeared into the bush ahead. When they returned, Cruz went to each man to say they'd reached their target. Back in position, he gave the sign to move in.

Gene stepped out of the jungle and into the graveyard. The left fork of the river flowed slowly by. Cruz and Brian had been right on the money. With all the weaving in and out they'd had to do to get there, they were right on the target. Lucky. In almost all the other ops, they'd hit the right place but had to shift one way or the other to move into the target area.

From fifteen grave sites away, Gene watched Brian, Cruz, and Roland at the seventh grave. They were using their knives to probe for possible mines that might have been laid to protect the weapons. Finding none, they began to remove earth from the grave. The one thing they didn't know was how deeply the weapons were buried.

Setting security, Gene was closest to the river, and to the south of their area, where he could look in the direction of the NVA camp. Nearby, Jim, Alex, and Doc, the rest of the squad's security element, also watched for anyone who might come in.

Gene waited, silent and unmoving, for the weapons to be unearthed. The digging was a painstaking process. Cruz and Brian, with Roland setting security next to them, were inserting their knives slowly, feeling for mines, then removing earth no deeper than the length of the blade, before probing again. The dirt was fairly soft, the grave only a few days old. There hadn't been time for the soil to settle and become hard-packed.

Cruz and Brian had dug down about two feet when a horrible, reeking stench filled Gene's nostrils. He cringed. Roland stood up, holding his hand over his face. Somebody gagged. Cruz and Brian lifted a decomposing body out of the grave.

Gene's fingers tightened around the 60. Even fifteen grave sites away, the smell was god-awful. He was grateful he wasn't on top of it. He'd have lost anything in his stomach. It felt as though he might anyway.

Cruz and Brian removed their sweatbands and tied them over their faces to aid their breathing, before continuing to dig.

They'd be breathing through their mouths, just as he was. It figured that the enemy would think anyone finding the body would give up. It was possible the weapons were under the body, just inches deeper.

After the two had dug down another foot, without finding a trace of the weapons, it was obvious to Gene that intel was wrong on the grave site. Inspecting all of them, to try to determine which one housed the weapons, would be fatal. You-O would realize that. The stench from the body contaminated the air. Anyone within a hundred yards could smell the rotting corpse. If the NVA smelled it, they'd investigate, knowing someone was looking for the weapons.

Cruz and Brian rolled the body back into the grave. Using their feet, they shoved in about a foot of dirt, to cover it up as fast as they could. Gene, trying not to gag, heard a chuckle. Crouched near the mound of dirt next to the grave, Roland was choking back laughter almost, but not quite, silently. Cruz and Brian were attempting to wipe off their hands with their headbands, at the same time gagging and trying to keep from puking their brains out. On the other side of Jim, Doc looked like he was about to have a fit.

Since the weapons hadn't been found, they had to take out those who'd hidden them, so nobody would be able to find the cache. If the weapons had been there, they'd have blown them up with C-4. Each of the squad carried some of the explosive. Put together and detonated, the C-4 would have blown the entire graveyard away. Now they'd use it on the NVA camp across the river. They had about two hours of darkness left to complete the second phase of their mission and be extracted.

At the river's edge, Cruz asked Gene if he'd seen anything at the graveyard while setting security toward the NVA's location.

"Damn," Gene whispered, instantly covering his mouth and nose. "You stink! Get away."

"Suck wind," Cruz whispered back. "You see anything?"

Gene, face covered, shook his head.

Cruz snapped his fingers softly and waved for a river crossing. Gene set security covering the left flank, and Doc took the right.

The river, about fifteen feet from bank to bank, was almost at low tide, but when Brian got about halfway, it was over his head. He started to sidestroke, holding his weapon in his right hand, parallel to the river's surface, ready to fire at anyone waiting for him on the far side.

Cruz passed the signal to inflate life jackets. Using them, everyone would be able to keep their heads abovewater.

Gene wondered just how deep it was going to be. With eight hundred rounds of ammo, five pounds of C-4, and the 60, there was no way he'd be able to stay above the surface.

Brian reached the far bank, disappeared into the bush, and finally returned to wave the rest of the squad over.

As each man entered the water, crossed, and got out, Gene was remembering a crossing in which he'd almost drowned. About the same size river, but the tide had been high. They'd inflated their life jackets then too, but just two feet in from the steep-banked side, he'd gone under. The jacket couldn't keep the combined weight of his person, plus the 60, the ammo belts, and his other gear, afloat.

Underwater, he had kicked off the bottom, but the riverbed was so soft he'd barely made it to the surface for air. As he had kicked off, he'd tilted his head back so his nose and mouth would break the surface of the water and allow him to suck in a quick breath. And it was real quick. Next to no time to suck in what air he could before the weight took him back underwater. Once on the bottom, he had thought he could walk across until he was able to reach the far side. Hell, he'd told himself, it was only fifteen feet.

He'd leaned forward and felt himself sinking into the soft mud. Then he started trying to run, but with each kick of his feet, the bottom gave way, and he'd move forward only inches. He increased his leg action, trying to run faster, but still the movement forward was only inches, and with the amount of exertion, he knew he was burning up a lot of oxygen.

He also knew the other members of the squad would not be concerned, because they were all very strong swimmers. They'd be looking for the enemy. He kept kicking at the bottom, and his chest began to pound, his body crying for air.

He didn't know how far he'd gotten, but he started to think about breaking off the belted ammo and letting it drop, as well as the 60, which weighed almost twenty-four pounds even after being cut down. He pushed the 60 to his back, letting it hang on its sling, continued to try to run, and, as a last resort, pulled at the water with both hands.

If he couldn't get air, he'd black out. There was no way of knowing just when he'd simply pass out and go limp. When it occurred during training, instructors jumped in, pulled people out, revived them. A very controlled situation. But in Vietnam nobody was standing by. He felt himself start to panic.

He broke off the first belt of ammo and let it drop, still kicking, hoping to reach the far side, to reach air. Reaching for the second belt, he felt the top of his head break the water's surface just before the point at which he knew he'd black out. Using the last ounce of air in his lungs, he pushed off the bottom and sucked air frantically when he broke the surface, before going back under. It was just enough that he knew he'd make it, that his head would be abovewater in a few more inches.

He had moved as fast as his legs could go, pulling with both hands, and had come up. For the first few breaths, he sucked hard, making enough noise to alert someone nearby. Realizing that, he controlled the sound, telling himself to be quiet, breathe slow. Finally he pulled himself out of the water on hands and knees and lay panting in the mud on the bank.

Jim was at his side in a moment. "What's wrong?"

Still breathing hard, getting air back into his body, he managed, "Too . . . too heavy. Couldn't stay . . . up."

"Stay there," Jim ordered, and went to get Doc.

In that short time, he was able to start raising his head but still couldn't pull himself up.

Doc began to talk softly to him. "Take slow deep breaths. In your nose, out your mouth. Come on, Gene. Slow down. In your nose, out your mouth." He patted Gene's back. "You'll be fine."

Eventually his breathing had slowed, life had come back to his body, and he had been able to sit up. It had taken fifteen minutes more before he'd recovered enough that the squad could move out.

Now, after seeing Brian's head go under, Gene knew he'd have to take a deep breath before that point in the river. He also knew it wasn't far across and that the tide was low. There would only be a few feet underwater before he'd be able to walk the rest of the way to shore. He couldn't let the past stop him from what was at hand. The rest had crossed. It was his turn.

Gene eased into the water. When he reached the point where he thought the rest of the squad had started kicking, he was ready to fill his lungs with air before going under. The water had risen to his mouth. He kept moving, but tilted his head back. The water covered his ears, leaving his mouth and nose above the surface. Get ready, he told himself. Get ready to breathe deep. But the riverbed sloped upward and in two steps the water level was at his shoulders.

You dummy, he thought. All that worry waiting for his turn had been for naught. He was taller than anyone in the squad. But it wasn't for naught, he realized. He'd confirmed what he'd learned in training. Never panic. Keep thinking. Stay in control.

Cruz signaled to move out. It had taken about ten minutes for the squad to cross. The enemy was a short distance away. Probably less than five hundred meters.

They moved south along the river, looking and listening as they got closer. Brian's hand went up.

Enemy in sight.

One lone man, Gene saw, standing on the riverbank in his undershorts, taking a leak.

Cruz used the starlight scope to better see the area ahead. With all the stars, the scope would be as good as seeing in daylight except everything looked green.

Cruz followed the man back to the camp. He returned to say there were two small hootches, with about ten men sleeping outside.

With daylight only an hour away, they moved into the jungle to approach the camp from the rear. If any enemy tried to run, they could only run to the river. And if they did, Gene thought, the squad could pick them off like ducks.

In position, he peered through the foliage at the sleeping NVAs. AK-47s lay on the ground beside them. The two hootches were about five feet apart. He glanced around. The rest of the SEALs were on line, about ten feet apart.

Cruz would initiate firing. When he opened up, they'd do the same, and run straight through the camp, hitting the enemy fast and hard. With surprise on the squad's side, the NVAs shouldn't even get a round off in return. Gene lifted the 60 slightly, ready to slaughter all of them.

In the silence, Roland made radio contact, using three squelch breaks, to alert the boats to stand by. When the crews heard the gunfire, they'd come up the river, to the target area, and extract the squad.

Cruz lifted his weapon. He fired, and the entire squad opened up fully automatic.

Gene concentrated on taking both hootches under fire, as did Jim and Roland. If there were ten men outside, ten more must be inside, so they fired low to be sure they hit anybody sleeping on the floors.

For thirty seconds, they stood fast, putting out almost fifteen hundred rounds along the ground and in the hootches.

"Move in," Cruz yelled.

Staying on line to ensure none of the squad members were caught in their own lines of fire, they moved out fast. Some of the enemy tried to get up and grab their AK-47s, but were blown down in the devastating volume of fire.

Gene ran past the hootches, pouring rounds through his entire area. Jim, also past them, paused to send up pop flares. The whole area lit.

"Cease fire!" Cruz ordered, and Gene took up the call. "Cease fire!" The boats would be on their way to pick them up.

Ten bodies lay on the ground. Ten more lifeless forms were inside the hootches. Total firing time had been no more than two minutes, Gene estimated, and almost six thousand rounds had been expended.

"He has a gun!" Brian yelled, and at the same instant, opened up on a wounded NVA.

Gene whirled with the rest of the squad. In unison, they fired in the direction of Brian's fire. The body jerked on the ground, the rounds ripping it apart.

"Make sure they're all dead," Cruz yelled out. "Jim, Roland! Frag the hootches!"

Running, Jim and Roland pulled pins, and as they threw the fragmentation grenades, they shouted, "Grenade!" and the SEALs hit the deck.

Gene heard the explosions ripping through the hootches and shrapnel whizzing overhead as it tore through the palm frond walls.

"Burn them," Cruz ordered.

Taking out MK-13 Day/Night flares, Roland and Jim lit the flare end and set the dry hootches afire.

Getting to his feet, Gene realized that they'd killed twenty NVA in two minutes, and with them, the secret of the weapons' location. Though he was grimly pleased that a few more had died in revenge for Willie, he regretted the weapons remained hidden.

Maybe, he thought, half listening to Roland on the radio with the boats, they'd stay in their grave for centuries. An image of the eerie fort they'd found came to mind, and he shivered, turned away, and walked with the rest of the squad to the riverbank.

It was full daylight by the time they docked at Seafloat. Once debriefing was over, the squad went to chow. Standing in line behind Cruz, Gene said, "You-O, you did a good job, buddy. Really a good op. Way to go."

"Thanks. If I'd known how good it feels to plan and run one, I would have led ops long ago. Now it's too late, damn it. We'll be going back to The World in ten days." He grinned. "Hell, I just might come back."

Gene stared. Ten days? Ten days before leaving for The World?

He felt a heaviness inside. They could be dead in ten minutes. Ten days was the same as forever. He took his tray and sat down to eat, wondering how long luck and good planning could hold up. Willie'd had three days to go.

On the way to the cleaning table, he passed Marc and Freddy Fanther carrying a footlocker to the helicopter pad.

"How you doing, bro?" Marc asked.

Gene looked into the pale blue eyes. "Okay, Eagle. And you?"

"Better each minute that passes. Big bash tonight. Last party. You better be there," he yelled back. "You go out on an op tonight, we go to war."

"You got it. I'll be there."

Cleaning the 60, he could still smell the decomposing body stink on Cruz and Brian and tried to stay upwind from them. They'd have no problem getting to be the first ones to scrub down. He went to hang the 60 from his rack before stripping down and waiting his turn at the rain barrel.

Feeling jittery, he decided to have a cigarette. He went back inside, got one, and some matches, and returned to rejoin the line outside and light up. He put the cigarette in his mouth, took out a match and struck it. He smelled burning sulfur, but the match wasn't lit. There at the tip of his right index finger was the flame. He raised his finger to light the cigarette, and drew, but got no smoke. He threw the match away and lit another one. Again, he saw his finger flame and touched it to the end of his cigarette. The smoke refused to light.

Jim, standing nearby, yelled, "Doc!" and pointed at Gene, who tried a third time to light the cigarette with his fingertip. They went to him.

"What's wrong, Gene?" Jim asked.

"Can't light my cigarette," he said. "See?" He touched his finger to the tip and drew on it. "The damned thing won't light." Naked, he stood staring at it.

Doc took his arm. "Come on."

He pulled away. "Wait a minute. I want a smoke."

"Okay," said Doc. "Here. Let me light it for you."

Gene handed the cigarette over, not remembering that Doc didn't smoke, would never so much as let a cigarette touch his lips. But that morning, dripping wet and covered with soap, he did.

"Here you go," Doc said, handing the lit cigarette to Gene.

Jim, still wet, towel draped around his waist, took Gene's arm. "Come on, Gene. Let's go inside."

Near the door, with Doc on Gene's other side, Jim saw Cruz and yelled to him, "Go get the doctor and get back down here."

Cruz, one leg in his swim trunks and one leg out, looked up at Jim. "What's up?"

"Damm it," Jim barked, "I said get the doctor! Now!"

Cruz, hopping toward the door, managed to get his other leg in the trunks and took off at a run yelling, "Out of the way!" at people blocking his path.

Gene sat on Jim's rack behind the plywood partition. The doctor looked at him and asked again, "What's wrong?"

"His pulse is 148," Doc said, holding Gene's wrist.

"Move over," the doctor said to Doc.

Gene waved his other hand. "What's you doing here, Doctor?" he asked. "Want some coffee?" He offered the doctor his pack of cigarettes. "Be careful," he warned. "It's hot."

After checking Gene's vital signs, the doctor told Jim, "He's on something. Let's get him down to sick bay. Hold onto him."

Silently the rest of the squad watched as he was led out.

In sick bay, the doctor asked, "What have you taken?"

"Nothing."

"Gene," Doc asked, "what kind of drugs have you taken?"

Gene shoved him away. "What the hell are you talking about? You know I don't do drugs. What's wrong? Why am I here?" Fear rose, and confusion. He tried to get up. "Let me out of here!"

Jim and Doc held him.

"Take it easy," Jim said. "Something's wrong and we've got to find out what you've taken."

Gene shook his head. "Nothing. Really. I don't do dope."

"We know, but something is wrong. Just take it easy."

"Okay. Guys, let go. I'm okay. Go ahead, Doctor." He looked quickly from side to side. "Can I have a smoke?"

"Sure," the doctor said. "Give him one."

Doc started to light one. Gene pulled it away. "Give me that! I'll light my own cigarette. You don't smoke anyway." He lit the cigarette and began to puff on it, while Jim told the doctor what they'd seen.

"You take any Dexamyl?" the doctor asked Gene.

"Yes, but only two."

"How long ago?"

"Just before going out."

The doctor looked at Jim, who said, "An hour or so after midnight."

"Have you been taking them long?"

Gene shook his head. "No. Just before going out on an op."

"He's been going out quite a lot since you released him," Jim said.

"When was the last time you got a good night's sleep, Gene?" the doctor asked.

Gene drew on his cigarette and didn't reply.

Jim's eyes narrowed. "Doc," he said, "go over to Johnny's and check the op reports."

While Doc was gone, Gene sat silently, not protesting as the doctor continued to examine him under Jim's watchful gaze.

In a short time, Doc returned and took Jim over to the side of the room. "He probably hasn't slept for ten days. If he's gotten any sleep at all, it wasn't much. He's been in the bush day and night."

Jim relayed the information to the doctor, who then turned to Gene.

"You'll be okay. You've worn yourself out. You hallucinated there for a short while from taking the Dexamyls. I'm going to give you a shot," he said, "that will counter the drug, and you'll be able to sleep."

"Then I'm okay? I can still go back out?"

"Yes, but not until you get some rest. You'll be fine, but don't take any more pills."

Gene nodded. He felt fine, but he'd do whatever it took to please the doctor. Whatever it took to continue to operate.

As he started to get up, Doc moved to help.

"I don't know what kept him going," the doctor told Jim. "No sleep in ten days. Even on Dexamyl he should have shown the effects before this. What's driving him?"

"I don't know," Jim answered. "I'll try and find out. When I do, I'll have a talk with him."

The doctor sighed. "He'll be coming down hard in a few hours. I guarantee he'll sleep. I'll stop by tomorrow just to check."

Meanwhile, Doc, itchy with the dried soap he hadn't had time to rinse off, marched a naked Gene back to the hootch. As they went, he delivered a fiery lecture about drug-taking, sleep deprivation, and absolute stupidity.

Gene ignored him, wondering which squad would be operating when the sun went down.

CHAPTER TWENTY-TWO

DARKNESS FELL EARLY ON Seafloat. Gene's last op lay three days in the past, as did the Eagle's party, and Delta Platoon's early morning departure for the trip back to The World.

By party time, Gene had been asleep for hours, knocked out by whatever the doctor had given him at the end of his sleepless, drugged, ten-day vendetta of revenge for Willie.

He'd come awake an inch at a time, fighting back to consciousness while trying to make sense of the voices around him, to separate them out. The squad . . . some of them were talking about him.

"—should have fucking noticed that he—"

"Can't watch every goddam body, Doc."

"—were here too. All of us. Nobody put it together, he was operating every fuckin' minute of—"

"Right on, Brian, but still—"

"No damned excuse. My bastard brain must've been half dead. He was in no damned condition. Could've been fuckin' killed or got somebody else killed, Cruz."

"But nobody *was*. And they never have been. Not if he's on the op."

"Fuckin'-A right, Cruz, and look how many he was out on, the last week or more. Day and night, man."

"Come in all bloody, covered with mud—"

"And smellin' like shit—"

"Talk about shit, we going to chow or not?"

And Gene drifted back into sleep until just before midnight when he woke again. He pulled on his jeans and went quietly outside, drawn to the west edge of the helo pad.

Since Willie's death he'd spent many lonely nights looking downriver trying to make sense of it all. Behind him voices floated in the darkness, the normal goings-on of men who'd separated from their families to fight for God and country. He could hear yelling and laughter, the rattle of empty beer cans, the mixture of music—all coming softly, disembodied, through the night.

Hours of sleep, he thought. Three days of oblivion, with no ops, no chance to get to the colonel and take revenge. He hated that fucking Nguyen. He'd just blow him up, or slice his fucking neck clear through his spine if he ever got the chance.

He looked down the Son Ku Lon at the jungle clutching the riverbanks. Its vast blackness seemed to reach out to the edge of the earth like a black hole that sucked all life from those who drew near. Those who dared to venture in might never be heard of again.

Scary. He stared at it. What was he doing here—all of them doing here? He was twenty years old. By law, a man, but inside, lots of times, he felt like he was still a boy. He'd never be a boy again. He used the 60 and the Bowie too well, too often. Not much left of innocence. That was for sure. Not after being thrown into this world of black and white, life and death.

He stared at the jungle. How many thousands had ventured in there to die? And if they lived to come out, how had they survived, going from playing street ball and dreaming of girls to the battle-fields of Vietnam, where the playing fields were covered with bodies, blood and bones, killing and being killed?

Maybe it was hating, like he hated the colonel, that saved them, got them through and out. He shuddered. A feeling came over him that maybe he'd gotten too close. Maybe he couldn't reverse his heading into the mouth of triple-canopied death.

All his life he'd been raised to believe in God and country. And his country had taken him from his mother—who had taught him to love all life—and transformed him into a killing machine, an assassin, a grim reaper for death. Him and Willie. God's will?

Gene closed his eyes for a moment against the memory of Willie always being there, when he and the squad came in from the bush. Watching and waiting, to see if he was safe. And then the god-damned colonel killed him. He killed him.

Gene spun and went back to the hootch.

Doc, Cruz, Brian, Roland, and Jim were playing cards. Drunk on their asses, he saw. Forty or fifty empty beer cans and a couple of empty liquor bottles lay on the floor around them.

Jim tried to stand, but couldn't. "Sit in," he said, and fell backward on an empty bunk. The rest burst into laughter watching him trying to recover.

Gene shook his head. "No thanks, Jim."

"Aw, come on. We're going home in seven days." He laughed. "It's over. Let's party."

"I can't. I'm just not up for it."

"Okay then, at least have a couple of beers with us."

Before Gene could reply, Cruz staggered through the doorway carrying a case of beer and an unopened bottle of Jack Daniels.

"Gene," he yelled, "how the hell are you? Here," he added, shoving the bottle into Gene's hands, "open it."

He opened it, watching as Cruz opened the case, and passed out beers. He started to set the bottle on the card table.

"Hold on," Brian ordered. "You opened it. The first drink is yours."

"Hoo-Ya!" the rest yelled, in unison.

"No, really, guys. The beer's fine."

Jim, holding onto the upper bunk to stand, called, "Come 'ere." Gene went to him.

"Closer," Jim said, turning his back to the others.

Gene moved in until their arms touched.

Jim rested his head on Gene's shoulder, and whispered, "Listen to me, you asshole. It's over. We're going home. I'm not blind. We've been together for a long time. I know you're hurting. I've seen you age overnight. I've seen you change ever since . . ."

Gene stood, stiff, staring at the plywood wall ahead of him.

"Ever since . . ."

"I know, Jim. Ever since Willie." It hurt to say his name aloud.

"Okay, then. It's an order!" Jim said, loudly. He picked up the bottle.

Gene took the bottle. "Here's to you, Jim." He lifted the bottle high. "And to you guys."

As it touched his lips, Doc started to sing, "Here's to Gene, he's true blue. He's a wino through and through. He's a wino so they say. If you don't go to heaven, you'll go the other way. So drink, chug-a-lug—" and the rest of the squad joined in. "chug-a-lug, chug-a-lug . . ."

The way they'd all survived so far, Gene thought. Drink 'til they passed out. The Eagle had passed out on his last night too. One minute those startling blue eyes had been looking at him, and the next they'd closed, and the Eagle had toppled over. At least he'd got out alive. Not like Willie. He swallowed half the bottle before stopping for air.

"Hoo-Ya!" they yelled, and he passed the bottle to Brian.

"Thanks, guys. Enjoy." He picked up a six-pack and the beer Cruz had given him. "I'll take these and leave you party animals alone."

Outside, the rain came down hard. He couldn't see the river-banks through the downpour and the dark. Opening the single can of beer, he walked slowly around the perimeter of Seafloat, passing sentries on guard duty.

Watching for Charlie trying to swim in and blow us all to hell, Gene thought, tossing the empty can, and starting on the six-pack. He was starting to feel the effects of the Jack Daniels, so he headed back to the helo pad, knowing he'd be left alone there.

How could he forget, he wondered, when he reached his private spot. All the booze in the world couldn't erase the scars, and he wondered if anything could take away the kind of pain he'd come to feel.

He downed the beer, opened another, and drank it nonstop.

Seven days left, and Jim had said they were shutting down. No more ops. He couldn't keep his promise to Willie. Time had run out. There was nothing more he could do to stop Nguyen's car-nage. No more ops.

He finished another beer and threw it overboard. The pouring rain covered the sound of its splash into the river. He tipped his head back to take the first drink of a newly opened can, closing his eyes against the rain, and told himself he'd be back. He could make another tour. If he played his cards right, he could be back within three or four weeks for another six months.

And then, he thought, crushing the can in his hand, he'd be able to hunt the colonel down. And when he found him, Nguyen would wish he were dead. He would wish the KCSs had him.

He finished the last of the beers sitting down, leaning against sandbags. The rain washed over him like an endless warm shower. His eyes closed, and he dreamed.

He was in a strange place, in an unfamiliar hootch. Smiling at him, Colonel Nguyen sat tied in a chair. There were voices outside.

"Stop!"

That sounds like Willie, he thought, but that can't be. Willie's dead.

"Gene, stop it."

That is Willie! He ran to the door, and looked out. Nothing. No Willie, nobody around. Just darkness and silence. He turned back, to see the colonel still sitting there, wearing a big smile and chuckling occasionally.

"You sonufabitch! At last we meet."

"Stop!"

He whirled to find Tong standing behind him. Tears streamed down his face and fell on the dirt floor. He was covered with his wife's blood.

The colonel laughed. "You stupid Americans. You cannot win this war. You send boys to do a man's job. Stupid Americans. You care too much for people like him." He nodded toward Tong.

Gene turned to find Tong gone, and swung back to the colonel. Brian and Cruz stood on each side of him. The colonel's hands were free, and the chair had disappeared.

"Gene," Brian said, "Jim said Colonel Nguyen has been found guilty as charged, by a KCS kangaroo court. He's waiting for you to bring him outside to be executed."

The sound of a drumroll filled the room. Gene wiped sweat from his eyes. When he looked up, he and the colonel were alone.

"It's time," said the colonel, "if you have the guts." His eyes were black and cold. "Are you willing to die?"

The door flew open. A dozen of the colonel's men entered.

"Well, you American pig, I'll let you live if you go now. If not,

I'll kill you where you stand, then cut you up into a thousand pieces, and spread your body over the Mekong Delta."

He saw the colonel's men were heavily armed, some holding long knives. The colonel was smiling.

"Okay. Let's take a walk in hell!" Gene yelled. He ran at Nguyen, kicked him squarely in the chest, heard the thud, and watched him crash into the wall.

The colonel came back fast, hitting Gene twice in the face. He felt blood trickle from his nose. For an instant, he glimpsed Tong's family and Willie watching, before a kick from the colonel sent him backward. Gasping for air, he tried to stand. The colonel jump-kicked again, hitting him in the ribs.

Gene rolled, and felt another kick in his side. Fighting to catch his breath, he heard the colonel laughing.

"Time to die, American pig," he yelled, and swung his foot again.

Gene reached to the bottom of his guts to gain the strength needed to stop that kick. Twisting and pushing the colonel away, he regained his feet; spun, and landed three roundhouse kicks to the colonel's head. With each impact, blood spattered.

The colonel staggered backward.

Nguyen understood they were in a fight to the death, and came at him. With all the force he could muster, he threw a punch aimed at Gene's face.

Gene blocked, wrapping his arm around Nguyen's, pinning his left arm in his own armpit, then snapping the arm upward, breaking the elbow joint backward.

The break was loud, Nguyen's scream louder. The colonel fell to his knees screaming, "Kill me, kill me! I'm a warrior. Let me die like a warrior."

Gene looked down at him. "I'd grant your wish and kill you quickly if you were a warrior, but you're nothing more than a sick animal. You torture and murder little girls, you rape and kill innocent women just for fun. No, you'll not die yet."

There came a knock on the door. Gene opened it to find Tong's small daughters covered in dried blood. The four-year-old held out her fist, opened it, and inside was Willie's cross.

Gene reached in his pocket where the cross had stayed since Willie's death, but it was gone. The girls disappeared.

"Gene. Hey, Gene. Wake up buddy. You sleep here all night?"

"Where am I? Where is . . ." His head hurt. "Man, what a nightmare. I guess I passed out." He sat, held his head, and heard the Sea Wolf pilot walk away, saying something about chow time.

Stiffly, Gene got to his feet. The morning sun was rising. Its warmth felt good. Still wet from the rain, he headed to the hootch for dry clothes, and from there to the chow hall.

Nothing being served looked appetizing. Carrying two slices of bread and a cup of coffee, he joined Roland and Cruz.

"Where'd you split to last night?" Cruz asked.

Gene yawned. "Went down to the helo pad. Guess I passed out." He shook his head. "Had this nightmare. Seemed so real."

"Let's go."

He turned to see Brian and Doc.

"Jim and Johnny want us all in the briefing room."

Cruz frowned, surprised. "We going out?"

"No way," Roland said. "We're shut down. After last night's drunk, nobody can go out in the bush."

Gene took a last bite of bread, and stood up to walk out with them. "Wait one, guys. I need a refill."

They waited, then left together.

"Why the meeting?" asked Brian, and then answered himself. "Maybe it's just a debrief before returning to The World."

"Or maybe," Roland said, "it's the first step of being deprogrammed before getting back to civilization."

Doc scratched at his mustache. "Hell, man, who knows? Let's just get it over with."

"And party," Cruz said.

"Sounds good to me," Brian answered.

"You guys are crazy," Gene said. "I don't want to see another beer until I hit the States."

They rounded the corner to see two men from Tommy Blade's platoon, armed and standing guard over the briefing room.

Doc blurted, "Oh, shit! We're going out! I know it!"

Behind him, Gene paused just long enough to look down the Son Ku Lon and into the jungle, shrouded in shadows and waiting. He followed Doc through the door.

CHAPTER TWENTY-THREE

GENE FOLLOWED BRIAN, CRUZ, and Doc into the briefing room and took his usual chair next to the door. Up front, Jim and Johnny were studying the maps. As they settled down, Johnny took a few steps toward center front, looked around, and said, "You guys all look like shit."

Doc grabbed his head. "Not so loud. My skull is going to explode."

Johnny, tall and straight, his uniform so clean and well pressed he looked like a Ken doll, smiled slightly. "I'm sure you're all aware that you'll be going home in six days, counting today."

In the silence, Gene noticed Roland's shoulders hunch just the slightest, as though he were about to be hit.

"And that Jim's given you orders to shut down operations.

"However," Johnny continued, "I've just received information on a big operation. It's been confirmed by three sources."

Gene sat up a little straighter in his chair. Johnny was turning his class ring around and around on his finger with his thumb like he always did when he was uncomfortable.

"We must act within six hours from now to ensure the success of the mission. I felt you people should have first choice—if you want to go out one last time." He drew a breath. "If not, I'll give it to Tommy Blade's squad. No matter what you decide, this information cannot leave the room. The choice is strictly yours."

Brian and Cruz glanced at each other, then back at Gene. Doc stared straight ahead, scratching his mustache.

"Your squad," Johnny said, "has one of the highest, if not the highest, success rates on all operations, in spite of the fact that over ninety-eight percent of them have included heavy combat."

"It's gonna be a dick-dragger," Doc muttered.

"I want you all to know that it's not going to be a cakewalk. In fact, it may be costly. The odds will be against you, and you'll be on your own during most of the op."

Nothing new there, Gene thought.

"You'll be up against a numerically superior force."

Gene shifted in his chair. Get on with it, Johnny, he thought. Let's hear it.

"Gentlemen," Johnny said, his voice solemn, "we have a hard target. We've located Colonel Nguyen."

A low pulse began to throb in his throat. Momentarily Gene closed his eyes, tipped his head back.

"The mission will be to capture, or eliminate, Colonel Nguyen. But preferably the former. We badly need to interrogate him. If there's *any* way to take him alive, do it."

Gene opened his eyes to find the squad turning again to look at him, then turning quickly away. It was a damned miracle. They'd found the bastard. He sucked in a deep breath in an attempt to quiet his insides.

"Man, this is fucked up." Doc was almost yelling. "We've only got six days left."

Jim moved forward to stand next to Johnny. "Guys," he said, "we've done our job well. I'm proud of each and every one of you and proud to have served with you." He shook his head. "But I can't tell you what to do. You assholes never listen to me anyway."

Laughter broke the tension.

Jim laughed with them, then sobered. "This mission is strictly voluntary. No one will think less of you if you don't go. I want to remind you that this is classified Top Secret. Discuss it with no one. Alternates from other squads will be selected for those of you that stay behind. Information will be issued on a need-to-know basis." He paused for a moment, then added, "I want you all to leave and think about it. You've got thirty minutes to let me know your decision. Gentlemen, you are dismissed."

Gene stood up and opened the door, but was the last out. For the first time since Willie's death, he found himself struggling to keep from laughing aloud in triumph. They had him. The fucking colonel was theirs at last. In front of him, Doc stomped away, talking to himself.

"No fucking way! Not this time. No, sir! No fucking way. I'm staying home. I'm gonna get drunk, dammit!"

It was funny as hell, but the fact that Doc had resorted to using the most basic cussing was a sure sign he was really upset. The rest, Gene noticed, were quiet. There was no indication, no way to know, who'd be going and who, other than Doc, would be staying. No matter who went or who stayed, he'd be going. Capture, hell. Nguyen would pay for Willie. That promise would, by God, be kept or he wouldn't be coming back with the squad.

He spent the next thirty minutes deciding just how the colonel would die.

In the hootch around him, the rest of the squad sat or lay on their racks, looking around. They were trying to see who would or would not be going by means of eye contact.

"You guys are fucking crazy," Doc announced.

Brian sat up. "For what?"

"I'm sorry," Doc said, "but no way. No fuckin' way." He went to the icebox, pulled out a beer, chugged it, then threw the empty can across the aisle. "No fuckin' way," he repeated, and went to get another.

Gene, getting into combat gear, heard but ignored him. He'd kept his operating equipment ready, hoping for the day to come when they'd go after Nguyen.

The word was passed for the squad to return to the briefing room. Gene, leaving the 60, its ammo, and the explosives behind, strapped on his bowie knife. With Willie's cross and Nguyen's shoulder patch safe in his pocket, he headed for the briefing.

When everybody was settled, Jim again took center floor.

"As I stated before, no one will think any less of you if you decide to stay home. You've all done your time. You've all earned your spot in American history and kept the legend of SEAL Team alive. So those of you who are not going may leave at this time, but remember, remain silent on this operation."

Doc stood. "I'm sorry, guys. I've nothing left." He walked out.

Nobody else moved.

Gene felt what he knew they all felt. They hadn't ever gone out without Doc to take care of them. And they'd all, always, made it back safe. Maybe this time—

"The rest of you are sure?"

Again, nobody moved.

"Johnny," Jim said, "bring in the other corpsman from Tommy's squad."

The briefing room door flew open and banged against the wall. In came Doc.

"Fuck it," he said.

The squad stared, unbelieving.

Gene shot to his feet. "Doc, you don't have to do this. It's okay. It really is."

"I followed you all into hell," Doc said. "I'll follow you out. So let's get it on." He stomped to his chair and sat down.

As one, the SEALs yelled, "Hoo-Ya!"

Tears stung Gene's eyes. He blinked, swallowed, and drew a long, steadying breath.

Jim grinned. "All right. Like Doc says, let's get it on."

He went through the Warning Order, detailing to each of them their position, weapons, and amount of explosive they'd carry. "The objective is one hundred thirty miles north of Seafloat," he said. "There will be no friendly forces until dawn, and they'll be approximately half a mile due east of the target. Colonel Nguyen's force is known to be five thousand plus."

"Oh, shit," said Doc.

For sure, thought Gene. Five thousand to seven. Now, those were odds.

"Excuse me, sir," Doc called out.

Jim looked at him, eyebrows raised in question.

"Can I change my mind?"

The squad broke into laughter as Jim slowly shook his head.

Jim concluded the Warning Order and told them to be ready in two hours for the PLO. They'd board the boats and leave immediately afterward—as always.

There was little talk as they left the briefing room. The squad was getting ready, mentally, for what appeared to be their most challenging op. Gene saw only grim expressions as they passed him at the door.

The odds had hit home. There'd be no room for errors. They'd gone up against big odds before—fifty to one was usual. With the element of surprise they'd always come home safe. But five thousand to seven . . . They had to be perfect. Even the slightest noise, the slightest reflection, smell, mistake—anything could take away the element of surprise, and there would be nobody coming home to Seafloat alive.

Sitting on his bunk, Gene watched, studying each man, every movement, every physical emotion, faces, eyes, and voices. They all knew one another's fears and secrets, and how far each could be pushed before striking back.

They were doing as he had done—going through a psychological change while they prepared to go into battle. It was akin to psyching up for a big football game, but the intensity was far greater. Here, now, they had to face their fear of combat, of seeing themselves in the enemy's position. Dead. Face blown off, half a chest gone, guts, arms, legs, sprawled on the ground.

Nothing about it ever changed. After every dick-dragger, once safe back at base, he'd visualized himself—instead of Charlie— dead. Sitting on his bunk, he caressed the 60. Fear. Nobody could imagine real fear unless they'd come close to death. The lump in the chest—it hurt—breathing accelerated, the heart pumped harder, adrenaline pounded through every vein.

They had to direct that adrenaline flow—not at the fear, but at the mission. It had to be directed to their senses—their eyes and ears, and to sound, touch, and smell. By the time each of them had gone through his own psyching-out period, he'd become a warrior who feared nothing. Neither life nor death mattered. Only the mission had meaning. They'd feel no pain. If they got shot, no biggie. If blood wasn't pouring out, they didn't think about it. They just fought, just kept going, because if they stopped, they'd surely die.

Gene watched as Doc painted his face green and striped it with black. In combat, if they were shot up bad, bleeding heavy, and Doc couldn't get to them, like on the Mighty Mo, they'd treat themselves, bandage the bleeders, pick up their weapons, and continue to fight. They'd never give up.

He remembered Tommy saying that the only way to kill a SEAL was to "shoot him in the head, then shoot him in the head again, because if you don't, and there's the smallest spark of life in him, he'll find a way to reach up and take you with him."

"You-O," Brian said, "I know I owe you for the Jack Daniel's."

Gene jumped off the bunk. They had another hour left before the PLO. His equipment was ready. All he needed to do was strap the ammo belts on, secure grenades to the bowie's belt, and sling the 60. He opened his footlocker, moved the stack of unopened letters from Karen, took out a pad of paper and a pen, and left the hootch.

Alone at the edge of the helo pad, he wrote home:

My Dearest Darling, I had this feeling come over me. I've never felt it before. I'll be going back out into the bush in an hour and I don't think I will be coming home this time. I'm sorry I haven't written for so long. There has just been a lot going on with me. My heart aches, but today the ache will be no more. I wanted to let you know that I really love you. I will till the end of time. You made me whole. I'm sorry I wasn't able to see you carrying our unborn child. Tell our child that Daddy loves the both of you, and I'll be watching over you from heaven. I only wish I could have held our baby, and held and kissed you one last time. Remember only the good things. How we laughed, touched, loved. Raise our child to hold his head high, to love all life. Pray not for my safety. Pray for my soul. I love you. Gene. X X O O.

He addressed the envelope, then inserted the letter and sealed it. He tucked it inside his shirt, next to his heart. The SEALs would bring his body back. They'd see the letter reached her.

Back at the hootch, he finished mounting out his gear. Only Doc was there. The rest had gone. Silent, they walked over together.

Security was doubled outside the briefing room.

When they entered, the others turned to watch until they were in their chairs. Jim stood at the front.

From the back of the room, Brian announced, "Everyone present. We are secured." He sat down.

Jim looked at each of them, then called Johnny over.

Sprawled in his chair, the 60 lying on his lap, Gene listened as Johnny went over the intel—where it came from, how old it was. There was a small problem. The target area had not been cleared. The province chief had refused any U.S. op within a ten-square-mile radius of their objective.

He must know, Gene surmised, who or what was in there, or there wouldn't be a problem. No matter. The Vietnamese politicians often played both sides. What the chief didn't know wouldn't hurt him. There'd be no intelligence leaking out that would get the squad hurt.

Jim went through the PLO, his confidence in his plan and in the squad obvious. He laid out the details. He was going to run a major diversion. There would be a phony Army insertion. Twenty-one Chinook helos would land half a mile to the east, coming in with three waves of seven each.

"We've arranged," he said, "for twelve helo gunships, and two fixed-wing planes with twenty-millimeter cannons to fly cover for the Army helos. They'll return fire as Charlie moves in to confront what won't be there. Tomorrow. At first light."

He took a careful drag on his cigarette, not disturbing the lengthening ash. "If it works, every NVA will be pulled away from our hard target. Intel has it that, no matter what happens, six NVA always remain with our target. We have to be in position before first light. When the helos draw fire, the gunships will open up. We'll wait ten minutes, then we will take out the six bodyguards and capture, if possible, Colonel Nguyen. If not, eliminate him."

The ash fell to the floor. Jim took a final drag, then stubbed the cigarette out.

"We won't have longer than ten minutes to complete the mission before Charlie realizes there are no ground troops and swarms back to protect the colonel. Our two Sea Wolves will be hovering in the west, less than five minutes away, to come in for extraction."

In the silent room, Jim covered every detail: frequency, call signs, emergency action, and every move each man would be making.

Gene felt the energy the squad emitted. The very air seemed charged.

Jim paused. "Are there any questions?"

Doc stood.

"Yes, Doc?"

"Just . . . standing up."

There were grins and low chuckles from the squad. Jim checked his watch, looked up, and said, "It's 1500 hours. Let's go kick some ass."

Chairs screeched against the wooden floor.

Gene waited until the room was empty, then walked over to Johnny, who was erasing the chalkboards and removing maps. He pulled his letter to Karen out of his shirt. "Johnny?"

He turned. "Yeah?"

"No questions," Gene said. "Just mail this if anything goes wrong."

CHAPTER TWENTY-FOUR

WITH THE LETTER TO Karen safe in Johnny's hands, Gene caught up with the squad. They were boarding the lone Medium SEAL Support Craft that had been standing by. He went aboard.

"Jim," said Cruz, "can we have Gene say a prayer before we pull out?"

Gene's stomach felt as if its bottom had fallen out. Nobody'd ever made such a request. Not these guys. Especially not You-O. He was so stunned, he couldn't open his mouth.

He grabbed a quick look at the rest of the squad. In full combat gear, weapons everywhere, faces painted, they could have stepped right out of a nightmare.

"Maybe," he said, "it would be better if each man said a silent prayer."

River water lapped against the side of the boat.

Cruz shifted his weight. "We'd like you to lead us in our prayer. Some of us . . . don't know how to pray."

He tried to swallow. Couldn't. Many a time they'd kidded him about praying. Once, when he'd been sitting and reading his Bible, You-O'd walked over to ask if he was reading a fuck-book, then if it was a shit-kicker.

Brian, behind Cruz, stood. "Gene, this is our last op. We think your prayers have kept us safe."

It didn't matter what he believed now. It was what they believed. "Bow your heads," he said, and for the first time ever, he saw them do it. Even the four boat support people.

"Dear Heavenly Father," he prayed, "we all come to You in prayer. Please guide and protect us this day. Bless our loved ones at home. Amen." If there was a hell, he was probably going there now, feeling the way he did, and had since Willie.

"Move out," Jim ordered.

He watched the boat crew cast off. They were heading to an objective that some of them might not return from. The ride would take about two and a half hours. They had to insert at dusk because the tide was going out, and if the boat wasn't headed back before dark, it would be grounded until high tide again.

The MSSC skimmed the water's surface as it flew down and up rivers, and through fast, hard banks around turns. Gene sat silently, watching the other SEALs fiddle with their equipment. Every one of them was pumped to the max, he thought, ready to kill anything in their way.

The boat coxswain turned. "You guys look like you come from hell."

Roland stared at him and, voice quiet, said, "Yeah. You're right. We've been there before, and now we're going back."

The coxswain looked away and never said another word.

Gene ran his fingers over the 60, thankful for the breeze that came with the boat's movement. It made the heat seem not quite so bad.

Jim peeled the cover off his watch face to check the time. Then he looked around and checked the map.

Gene knew he was keeping a close eye on timing and direction—same as he'd do if he were running the op. And, like the rest of them, Jim would be waiting to respond to any ambush they might run into while, at the same time, running over every detail of the op in his head.

Gene tightened his headband, fought the urge to wipe the sweat off his face for fear of losing face paint, and scratched the itch next to his crotch through the tough fabric of his Levi's 501s. Jim flexed his shoulders, and Gene wondered if he'd ever sewn up his Levi's after the time Doc cut them open. He grinned to himself, remembering, heard a sound that turned out to be Doc shifting position, and sobered.

He didn't need to psyche himself up. Hatred did that. All he wanted to do was get his hands on Nguyen. Prisoner, hell. Come morning, the colonel died. Fast, slow, it didn't matter now. Only that he died. Images from the nightmare flickered through his mind. It had seemed so real.

"Ten minutes," Jim said very quietly. "Get ready."

As one, the squad got up and moved to the front of the boat.

Gene touched the 60, the bowie, and his ammo unconsciously. They had to get off fast and fade into the jungle. There would be no radio contact until daybreak, and no support. Once off the boat, they were isolated for the next twelve hours or so. Five thousand NVA, he thought, almost tasting the number. Five thousand to seven.

The MSSC slowed to an idle, then swung to the starboard side.

Silent, Jim pointed. Go!

Within seconds they were off the boat and about twenty meters into the bush.

Jim, arm lifted, moved his finger in a circle. They rallied to him and circled, waiting for the boat to head home, while they froze in place, looking and listening. Within a minute the MSSC was out of hearing range.

Sundown in ten to fifteen minutes, Gene thought. Damned blood-sucking mosquitoes were coming out. He could hear them hum.

It was dark when Jim, going to each man, whispered to him, "Keep your eyes and ears open. Moving out in five minutes."

In the PLO, he'd said they had a good chance of running into an enemy patrol or even a company base camp. The closer they got, the higher the chance.

Snap!

Jim. They were heading out.

In file formation, the never-ending mud sucking at his feet, vines and God-knew-what brushing his face, Gene headed into the jungle. He figured they wouldn't run into anyone until they were at least halfway to the objective. But still, they'd better be ready.

Their pace was good. They had to cover a lot of ground early on, because the closer they got, the slower they had to go to move in, silent and close. The night sky was clear, with a three-quarter moon, and studded with stars. The moon gave them some light and made traveling easier, but it was harder to conceal themselves. He could keep Roland in sight, ahead of him, with no problem.

An hour and a half later, Jim signaled a break, and they sat down in place. Each of them kept watch over a designated area.

In the total silence, Gene felt the sweat running down his face and body. He wasn't tired, just hot. He found nothing unnatural in the sounds around him, and there was no smell of the fish oil that signaled an enemy presence.

After ten minutes, Jim, going from man to man, whispered, "Picking up pace. Close up."

They'd been keeping six to ten feet apart, but now they'd close to three or four feet. He pulled Willie's cross out of his pocket, looked first at it, then up through the trees to the stars. Then he looped the chain around his neck and tucked the cross inside, where his sweat-soaked shirt would keep it stuck to his skin. If the SEALs wore dog tags, he couldn't have worn the cross. Couldn't take chances with metal next to metal.

Jim signaled *move out*.

In a slow run, they darted in and out of the shadows of trees and bushes. Fast, silent, deadly.

To Gene, who was just behind Roland, Jim, and Brian, it looked as if they were passing through the jungle on a current of night wind. Just slightly glimpsed, the three dark forms appeared and disappeared without sound.

They were making good time, covering a lot of ground, but mud was clinging to his boots, adding weight to every step. After a long time, his muscles began to ache. Sweat poured, and his eyes stung.

Another hour passed before Jim called a break.

Gene's clothes were as wet as if it had rained. He sat, a little winded, heart beating more rapidly. Nearby the squad rested, shadows within shadows, but all at full alert, every sense working at its fullest, every sound analyzed within a split second to determine whether they'd been detected. Ready to kill.

Sitting, Gene studied the night as memories flashed—the R&R Center, explosions, claymores going off in the chase that followed, running for their lives. They'd been lucky to reach safety. Especially with so many enemy yelling, screaming, shooting, trying to stop them. And after the claymores, the sounds of the enemy's dying—the cries. Yet they had kept coming. Yeah, they'd been lucky that night. And God knew none of them would ever forget the sight of that eerie fort. But this time they wouldn't have the darkness to hide in. This time it would be bright morning, and they faced over five times the enemy force.

He let his breath out slowly, almost a sigh. If anything went wrong, if the helos were late, they'd never see the sun set.

Jim snapped his fingers, and they were moving again.

The mind's funny-awesome, Gene thought. Takes everything in, analyzes the sounds—movement, insects, reptiles, birds. They had to spot the enemy before the NVA spotted them, and not make contact if the mission was to be completed. If they got into a firefight, the element of surprise would be lost, and no one—no one—would get close enough again for a long time. It had taken over six weeks and thousands of man-hours to locate Nguyen.

He dodged a branch and heard water running nearby. It was a creek. Small. Too small for sampans.

SpecWar Headquarters Saigon had given top priority to this mission. Gene wasn't the only one who wanted the colonel, but he was the one who'd get him. Finally he felt at ease with himself. It wouldn't be long until he could make things right, and keep his promise to Willie.

He sent a mental message ahead to Nguyen: We're coming for you.

He snapped back. The patrol was slowing down—back to their normal speed. He needed a break. The 60 had grown heavy, and a good four inches of mud had built up on his boots again. His leg muscles were trembling, trying to adjust to the slower pace. He snapped his fingers, halted the patrol, and sent the break sign, first to the men in front, then to the men at the rear.

Jim came down to see who had called the break and to make sure someone hadn't been hurt.

When he approached, Gene signaled that he'd stopped the patrol.

"You okay?" Jim whispered after moving in close.

"Just tired. Need five minutes."

Jim nodded okay and returned to his position just in front of Roland.

Looking back, Gene saw Cruz leaning against a tree, catching his wind and scanning the brush and trees around him for movement.

Relax, he told himself. Slow, deep breaths. In your nose, out your mouth. Relax.

At the sound of Jim's fingersnap, the squad moved out again.

They must have passed the halfway point by now, Gene thought, tilting his head to avoid a vine. Small patrols would be combing the area, split up into company size and spread around the colonel's perimeter. He was headquarters for all of the NVA's operations in the Delta region.

The squad moved progressively slower as they closed on the colonel's location.

Gene could feel his energy level rise, the adrenaline coursing through his body. They had to be ready in case they were hit, to cut loose with everything they had and then run like hell. Outright book! One slight metallic click, a cough, or the least human sound could bring Nguyen's battalion crashing down on them.

Ahead of him, Jim's fist went up. The patrol halted, and Gene watched Jim go forward to where Brian should be, at point.

Minutes passed. Two . . . three . . . And Jim returned. Hand signals came back. Visual contact had been made. Detour northwest. As indicated in the PLO, they'd keep the base camp to their right as they circled it. Jim had believed enemy patrols would be farther into the bush, and not just inside their own perimeter. The fastest and safest way for the squad would be to travel between the NVA patrols and Nguyen's base camp.

Silently the SEALs, dark shadowy forms, moved left.

Now Gene could see the glow from the campfires, dim radiations through the tangled and dense jungle. He could hear them talking, but was too far away to distinguish individual words.

Jim signaled to Brian, fifty meters deeper.

Just a little too close, Gene thought.

Crack!

Branch broke. He froze. Came from just in front of him. Had

anybody heard? Sweat rolled down his face and stung in his eyes. He wet his lips and tasted salt. Quiet. Not a sound.

They moved out, heading northeast, the camp now to their right rear. What they wanted now was more distance between them and Nguyen's headquarters.

Listening to the sounds of the camp as they left, Gene took mental notes on its possible size, its location, how far away the squad would be come morning, and which way the NVA would come from to confront the planned diversion. The camp, he estimated, was some five hundred meters behind the squad now.

Again, Jim's raised fist stopped them dead in their tracks.

Roland passed the signal back to him. Enemy patrol. The squad tracked them by their distance and direction.

Gene passed the signal to Cruz, behind him. Then, as Brian, Jim, and Roland had, he slowly turned his body to face left, and lifted the 60. You-O would signal Alex, who would signal Doc at rear security.

Gene strained to see. He could hear them now, but still couldn't see. No, wait . . . there! Shit! First spotted up front, some twenty to thirty meters away, they were now at about fifteen meters. Silhouettes. Had on helmets. NVA. Not Viet Cong. AK-47s. Moving back toward camp. They must be coming off patrol.

Don't move, he commanded his body.

Now, at ten meters, the enemy was weaving separately through the area. Their weapons appeared to be at the ready. None of them talking, none smoking.

Don't move, he commanded himself. Don't breathe. Think black. Become the jungle. He willed himself into invisibility, willed the patrol to pass.

Crack!

He chilled, every hair standing, then realized that this time the sound, though again from in front of the squad, came from farther away.

The NVA patrol stopped short, looked left, and headed that way, toward the sound's location. Once they were out of sight, the SEALs moved on.

Flexing his shoulders under the weight of the bandoliers of ammo, Gene let out a long, slow breath. A little too close for comfort. The objective couldn't be much farther. They didn't have but a few hours left to get there and get set. They'd busted their asses just to get as far as they had.

Roland, a shadowy, dark form, seemed to drift out of the dark place ahead and into another one. Gene followed him.

Damn. So close, yet so far until dawn. Keep moving, he told himself. Nguyen's out there . . . The phrase ran through his mind continually. The closer they got, the more his hatred built, the more frequent the images of Willie in the body bag.

Jim stopped the patrol.

Looking hard, Gene could just make out the small flickers of dying campfires in the distance. He shivered. This was it. They'd made it.

Moving very slowly, the squad started out again, aware of every detail of their surroundings. It grew easy to see the small lean-tos sheltering the sleeping enemy. They were dark forms against the glow of burning embers. But it was the majority of men, hidden in the shadows behind bushes or just sacked out on the ground, who concerned him. If any of the squad stumbled on one of the sleepers, it would be over in the blink of an eye. The SEALs would die, like the soldiers at that eerie fort on the way to the NVA's R&R Center. Strange how that fort kept coming to mind. Spooky.

They were northwest of the area, keeping it on their right, just as they had with the base camp earlier. It was slow going and time ticked away. Seeing the fires ahead left no doubt in Gene's mind that they were at the target area. The intel for the op had been extremely accurate, thank Christ. Now, if the location of the colonel's hootch and the communications hootch was equally accurate . . . Time was getting critical.

They were still heading northwest. The targets were northeast of their location, and the camp area was too large to detour around. They'd have to move through it, as planned in case that scenario arose.

Seconds later, the squad changed direction. They were going straight through.

Moving with great caution so as not to disturb the sleeping enemy, the squad ghosted through the center of the camp. All weapons were trained on the sprawled men lying on the ground under the lean-tos.

The 60's weight, and the nine hundred belted rounds, cut into Gene's shoulders. No time to think about what-ifs—it was too late. He had to think light, like a feather drifting on a cool summer's night. He moved smoothly and silently, weaving ever so carefully through.

Ahead, twelve hootches dotted a six-hundred-square-meter clearing. They skirted around its edge, using the shadows and dark jungle foliage.

Fifty minutes more, and the shit would hit the fan. Not far now, Gene thought, his attention focused on two hootches set apart, about twenty meters from the north side of the clearing's edge. They needed to get around to them, without any enemy waking. It was a real quiet area. With their patrols out on the far perimeter, and the base camp at least three-quarters of a mile away, the enemy must feel damned safe here. There weren't even any roving guards. He moved into another shadow.

It was too perfect. Maybe knowing he had the province chief on the take, and that the chief would keep out all military action, the colonel had let his guard down. Gene breathed carefully, controlling even that, as he set each foot down.

But maybe information on their op had leaked out, and they were moving deeper and deeper into a death trap. He cut off the thought.

Almost directly behind the two hootches, the squad slowed down, then stopped to look and listen for movement. Any movement at all.

Gene caught Jim's signal to disappear and become one with the earth. As one, the squad eased their bodies into the heavy brush and were gone from sight.

All they could do now, Gene thought, was wait. Wait to see if the diversion would work. Would Nguyen stay behind? Would the helos be on time? If they were late by five minutes, it would be day, and they'd surely be detected. They had nowhere to run, and limited ammo. If it hit the fan, they'd never see tomorrow, but they'd take as many NVA with them as they could. Even Doc.

He stared at the two hootches. The man he hated so much lay peacefully sleeping inside one of them. He concentrated, sending a silent message that he was there, and wondered if the colonel could hear him talking in his dreams. Today, Nguyen would meet his maker.

From his position, Gene could make out the rest of the squad. Except for Roland, they were all facing the hootches. Roland faced to their rear and guarded their backs.

Minutes ticked past. Only a few remained until the choppers were due. He listened intently and finally heard the very faint hum, not of insects, but of rotor blades. Lots of them.

Be still, Gene warned himself. Be still. The helos were coming closer and closer. And louder. He heard movement around the hootches and talking. Then thirty to forty NVA ran for cover in the jungle's edge. There was movement behind the squad's position. If they weren't well concealed, he thought, they had seconds to live.

The helos came in from the south and aimed for the landing zone, flying high so they'd be seen. As the first wave of seven peeled down, Gene thrilled with pride. Gunships broke formation and circled the landing choppers. Perfect to the second. At the same instant, dawn broke on the horizon.

Orders were being given, and enemy troops surrounded them. Five thousand to seven . . .

The gunships opened up. It sounded like World War III had erupted half a mile away. The NVA hit it, running toward the landing zone. Man, Gene thought, look at them all. It was still too dark to make out more than forms running to the east, but there were a lot of them. Making a helluva noise yelling. The choppers were drawing heavy fire.

He focused on the hootches, where armed men were standing, and hoped the squad stayed undetected for the next ten minutes. One man ran toward another, who was standing alone, off to the side of the first hootch. The standing man yelled at the runner when he stopped, slapped his face, and pointed toward the landing zone. The runner took off.

And Gene suddenly realized the solitary man had to be Nguyen. It's you, he thought. It's you! He sized the enemy up. Nguyen was taller than most Vietnamese—five ten or five eleven, maybe 170 pounds. His muscles were the long, hard, ropy kind, his movements smooth and fast. As a former Vietnamese SEAL, he was no doubt a black belt in tae kwon do. He'd smacked that guy like a striking snake. Just *wham!*

Head tipped downward so the whites of his eyes didn't show, Gene studied Nguyen and felt the slow burn of his hatred fueling the desire for Nguyen's neck in his hands. No matter what training the murderous bastard had, he could take him, if he ever got his hands on him.

The OV-10s opened up with their 20mm cannons and all hell broke loose half a mile away.

It was deafening with the heavy automatic weapons, explosions, the gunfire, and yelling to the left, but there was no movement around them.

Click . . . click.

At the fingersnaps, he turned his head to see Jim's signal.

Slowly, slowly, he left the concealing jungle, hoping no NVA were behind them while they crept out. Every man in the squad knew what his next steps would be as they all moved in on the objective. He smiled to himself. Their hard target. His. And he thought, Colonel, you're mine. They were going to pull it off.

Jim signaled Roland to make contact with their Sea Wolves. Without hesitation, Roland switched his radio on, and at the same time Jim waved the squad forward. They had less than ten minutes to make the hit and get out.

Brian and Jim ran toward the hootch on the left, leaving Roland to cover the rear and make the contact with the Wolves for the squad's pickup and extraction. Doc, You-O, and Alex were to take out the communications hootch, while Gene had orders to deliver heavy fire at any resistance from either hootch.

As they sprinted the thirty meters to the backs of the hootches, four of the six guards were visible, as was Brian's target, the colonel, still standing apart from the others.

Amazingly, their attention drawn toward the sounds of gunfire, none of the enemy saw or heard the SEALs coming. Gene hadn't believed they'd be able to cover the thirty meters without having to open up. They had. Without signals, as if they'd rehearsed it, the squad stepped out simultaneously from behind the hootches and opened up on the bodyguards.

Nguyen ran, and Brian took off in pursuit.

"Fuck!"

Gene spun, saw Doc on the ground, and cut loose on the communications hootch, ripping it to shreds with the 60.

Doc got to his feet.

"You okay?" Gene called.

"Yeah."

"Set security," Jim yelled. "Roland, get the Wolves in here. Now! We need them. Now!"

Brian shouted, "I've got him! He tried to duck into a tunnel."

The squad set security in a circle, fifteen meters away from Jim, in the center. Brian was yelling at Nguyen to move, trying to drag the colonel to Jim's location.

"Gene," Jim yelled, "help Brian. Roland, get over here with the radio. Where are the Wolves?"

"On their way."

"How far out?"

"Five minutes," Gene heard, running to assist Brian. But when he came face-to-face with Nguyen, he shook with a sudden fury. Once they'd made their move on the hootches, he'd momentarily forgotten about killing the colonel, caught up in the execution of tactics. Now he went cold.

Brian was struggling to handcuff the colonel. Without thought, Gene hit Nguyen harder than he'd ever hit anything or anyone. The blow lifted Nguyen off the ground and rocked him back three feet.

With the colonel lying dazed on the ground, Gene stood over him, shifted the 60, and reached for his bowie.

"Gene, don't!"

He twisted away from Brian's grip on his arm and looked him in the eyes. "Stand off."

"Jim," Brian yelled, "get over here!"

The bowie hissed from its sheath. Gene knelt over Nguyen, grabbed a handful of his hair, and lifted his head to expose his throat. A single sweep of his blade, and Nguyen's head would be severed from his neck.

He stared into the colonel's dark eyes. "You sonofabitch."

Nguyen hissed at him. *"Dau-mau-mee!"*

Gene brought the blade down and stopped it, barely breaking the skin at the side of Nguyen's neck. He held it there.

"Gene!" Jim yelled.

"Wolves," Roland shouted, "four minutes out."

A gentle slice across the neck with the bowie would cut the carotid artery. Bloody death in less than a minute. He felt a hand on his shoulder.

"*Gene.*"

"Don't worry, Jim," he said, not breaking eye contact with Nguyen. But don't think I wouldn't like to. He grabbed a handful of the colonel's black hair, jerked him to his feet, and half-shoved, half threw him at Brian, three feet away.

"Get that fucker tied up, and gag him," Jim ordered. "Quick. We're out of here."

"Wolves coming in three," Roland yelled.

Gene turned just in time to see the Wolves appear far out, over the treetops. They were coming in low from the west, to extract them.

The squad had moved to encircle Brian and the now docile Nguyen and secure their position for extraction. Gunfire and rocket explosions filled the morning air. Brian, gripping Nguyen's arm, was shifting his weight so he could throw his prisoner down to handcuff him.

"Fuck you!" Nguyen, in a burst of motion flipped Brian to the ground and snatched the K-bar knife from his H-harness before any of the squad could move. He took a few fast steps backward, putting him a good eight feet from Brian.

Almost instantly back on his feet, Brian swung his Stoner up and aimed. By then, the entire squad had Nguyen in their weapons' sights.

"Come on, you fucking American pigs!" Nguyen yelled, brandishing the knife. "I'm not going back alive!"

"Drop the knife," Jim ordered.

"*Dau-mau-mee,*" Nguyen replied. "Come and get it."

Gene ached to trigger the 60. But their orders were to capture the colonel if at all possible, and he seemed to know it.

"Wolves," Roland shouted, "two minutes out."

"Drop the fucking knife," Jim yelled at Nguyen, "or we'll blow you away."

"Do it!" Nguyen yelled back. "You American assholes are

weak. You die easy, like Willie, like the Green Beret officer, like the French. This is our country. You'll never defeat us."

Jim spoke to Brian, standing just to his right. "Take him out."

"No!" Gene shouted. "No! Wait! Jim, he knew Willie's name! He has an informant back at the Float!"

"Wolves, one minute out," Roland yelled. "What do I tell them?"

"Nothing," Jim yelled back. "Let them come in. You got this, Gene?"

"Yes, sir. I can take him alive."

Gene handed Jim the 60, pulled the bandoliered ammunition off over his head, and dropped the belts to the ground.

Nguyen, poised and waiting, wore a half-smile.

Gene walked slowly to within three feet of him.

"If Gene gets into trouble," Jim commanded, "blow the fucker's head off."

Gene moved closer, and Nguyen slashed out with Brian's razor-sharp knife, missing—but not by much. As they circled each other, Nguyen slashed out twice more, but was blocked each time. Then, suddenly, he charged, in an attempt to stab.

Gene grabbed Nguyen's arm as he thrust the blade toward his stomach, and twisted it while stepping forward and under, flipping the colonel to the ground. Controlling Nguyen's arm, he used a wristlock until the knife fell from the colonel's grip. When he reached down to retrieve the K-bar, Nguyen kicked him in the head. He lost his grip on the colonel's arm, and suddenly they were in a wrestling match. The other SEALs closed in to club Nguyen into submission, but suddenly firing erupted close by.

"Contact! Contact!" Cruz yelled, and Gene heard him open fire, just as Nguyen went for his eyes. Now it really was one-on-one.

"On line with Cruz!" Jim yelled to the squad."

As Gene and Nguyen fought, the rest of the SEALs opened up, trying to drive the enemy back into the jungle's edge. Forces from the camp they had passed had heard the firing and were moving in to assist Nguyen's troops. They had started to run right into the clearing when Cruz spotted them.

"Roland," Jim shouted, "radio the Wolves to pull out. It's a hot LZ!"

Overhead, the helos were thirty to forty feet from the deck when they got the call, and quickly pulled up.

Gene and Nguyen were in hand-to-hand combat, and Gene found fighting with Nguyen like doing battle with a wild animal. His twists and lunges were powerful, and he was incredibly fast. In addition, Gene was handicapped by his Levi's and jungle boots. Nguyen had landed several hand-strikes, and Gene had a bloody nose and a gash above his left eye.

The sound of the firefight filled the air, and Gene recognized the sound of his own 60, just as Nguyen twisted loose and jumped back. He was almost smiling when Gene landed his first blow. His snap kick to Nguyen's midsection sent the colonel back four feet.

"How do you know Willie's name?" Gene asked as they circled each other, trying to find an opening for their next move.

"You Americans think we're stupid," Nguyen said. "We have men everywhere. I even know who you are now."

He bolted forward with lightning speed, landing another blow to Gene's jaw, and followed it with a kick to his stomach. When Gene doubled over, Nguyen came up with a knee to his head, sending him backward to the ground.

The squad had stopped the enemy from coming into the clearing, but were still receiving heavy fire from the jungle's edge. There was no way of knowing how many enemy there were, nor whether they had radio contact with Nguyen's other forces.

"Roland," Jim called, glancing back at Gene and Nguyen, "have the Wolves lay down some rockets into their position, slow them down enough so we can get Nguyen secured.

Doc, Alex, Cruz—maintain fire! Roland, over here with me to call in and direct the Wolves' rocket strike. Brian, get back there and help Gene," Jim yelled. "Kill that fucker if you have to."

Nguyen, winded, was standing over Gene. "You are Michaels," he said triumphantly. "I have heard that you have searched for me a long time." He moved in again, fast.

Gene rose to one knee and landed a powerful blow to Nguyen's sternum, stopping him in his tracks.

As the colonel sucked for air, Gene got to his feet and saw Brian sighting his Stoner.

"No!" Gene screamed. "No! He's mine! I've got him!" He wiped his bloody face with his sleeve, clearing his left eye so he could see.

"Gene," Brian shouted back, "Jim said to kill him."

"Goddammit, Brian, just get the Wolves in here. I'll take him."

Nguyen laughed. "Your time has run out. You stupid Americans. My troops surround you. You SEALs are nothing. You are little children to us. Toy soldiers."

Gene heard only the words "little children," and in the purple haze of rage that engulfed him he saw only Tong's small daughters, dead in the burned-out village.

"Fuck you, you sonofabitch! You're going back to hang!"

He went after Nguyen in a fury of kicks and blows that Nguyen no longer could block.

Now hurt, the colonel still fought, landing several more blows to Gene's face and body. But the purple haze had turned on, and Gene no longer felt pain.

He dropped to the ground, and with a swift motion swept the colonel's legs from under him. As Nguyen hit the ground, Gene followed with a heel to his chest. Nguyen buckled, his head lifting. Gene landed a smashing blow to the head, and Nguyen lay motionless. It was over.

Brian knelt, rolled Nguyen on his face, then handcuffed and gagged him.

"Wolves in for a hot extraction!" Jim yelled. "Get ready to move!"

The squad ran to surround them. Gene was bent over, breathing hard, and Brian was standing guard over Nguyen.

The Wolves came in fast. Gene sucked up a lungful of air, and with all the strength he had left, jerked Nguyen's limp body up, threw him over his shoulder, and carried him to the helo. At the doorway, he threw him inside, then climbed slowly in, himself, followed by Jim, Roland, and Brian.

Cruz, Alex, and Doc boarded the second helo, and seconds later they were lifting off.

Jim stared at him. "Jesus, Gene. You okay?"

Gene grinned, slowly getting to his knees. "Yes, sir. Couldn't be better." Nguyen was just coming around. He had a shocked expression, as though he couldn't believe he was secured in their helicopter.

His smile gone, Gene reached in his pocket. He pulled out the epaulet he'd found in Tong's wife's hand and threw it in the colonel's face. "Here's your badge of honor, you sonofabitch. May you burn in hell." Then he took his usual seat in the doorway and went silent, staring down at the jungle below.

Behind him, Jim got on the radio. "Mission accomplished," he said. "We have a package coming in." He turned to Brian and Roland. "You two make sure nobody says a word about Nguyen or the possibility of an informant on Seafloat."

"What's going to happen to Nguyen?" Brian asked.

"He won't be given to the South Vietnamese. He'll be interrogated by U.S. only. If the informant gets wind of his capture, he may split before he can be identified. When we touch down there'll be a helo waiting. Brian and I will transfer him immediately. No one will even see him."

Gene, sitting in the doorway, saw that the sun was barely up. The diversion had broken contact, and all forces were heading back to their bases.

"Jim," Brian yelled, over the noise of the helo's engines, "I'm sorry, man. I never thought he'd try to escape."

Gene turned around. From the look on Brian's face, he was really pissed at himself.

"Don't worry about it," Jim yelled back. "I didn't expect it either. His only chance to survive was to make a break and attempt to reach the tree line."

"Yeah," Brian said, "but look at Gene. He's a bloody mess!"

"His choice," Jim said, and they all laughed.

"Great fight, though," Gene said. "Admit it."

"Hoo-Ya!" they yelled.

Brian burst out laughing. "Great fight, all right, but the best is yet to come."

Gene looked around. "What do you mean, the best is yet to come?"

"When we land, who do you think is gonna be waiting?"

"Who?"

"Hah!" Roland laughed. "I know—Doc!"

Gene cringed. "Oh, man. Do I look that bad?"

"Worse," Jim said, and they laughed again.

Well, Gene consoled himself, the diversion had worked, and with Nguyen all trussed up on the floor a few feet away, they'd sure as hell achieved their objective. Once the colonel had given them the intel, he'd be tried by his own people, and they'd hang him for sure. Payback time, for all his crimes . . . and for Willie. Let Doc do his worst. It was time to celebrate. He leaned against the door frame and relaxed.

CHAPTER TWENTY-FIVE

EXCITEMENT RAN HIGH WITH the guys. The sounds of their voices filled the helo as they flew back to Seafloat.

"Man, we did it—Jim, good op, you bad-ass—did you see how many there were? The dumb shits, did they bite the big one—I can't believe we walked through the center of them—and Gene, what a fight—"

He couldn't see who was saying what, but he knew their voices. Below, the dark green of the jungle seemed to stretch away forever. It undulated, like the sea, and like it, concealed for all their secrets beneath its surface.

"You okay, Gene?"

"Yeah."

"Good. You did good," Jim said. "I knew what you planned, what was running through your brain. Marc Kenau told me before he went home."

His fingers tightened around the 60. Treetops flowed away below.

"I knew, though, you'd do what was right. Didn't say anything because it was something you had to do by yourself if you were to survive." Jim rested his hand on Gene's shoulder. "It's over. Let it go."

He looked at his lieutenant and felt the burn of unshed tears. "Yeah, it's over, but it still hurts."

Jim squeezed his shoulder. "Just hang in there. The hurt will go away—in time."

It was over now. Really over. And here they were, ready to go back to The World. Nobody'd had to go on the op, yet they all had, knowing at the outset it would be the hardest, most dangerous situation they'd faced, and the largest number they'd gone against. They'd all believed that not all of them would make it back.

"—walked right through the middle of their damned camp!" somebody said behind him.

Yeah, he thought, a perfect op. The squad had drawn fire, but achieved their mission objective, and they were going home. The diversion forces, though—they'd taken a massive number of enemy rounds. Nobody knew their status yet.

"Hey, Gene!" Cruz yelled. "You still have the magic. Still nobody ever greased or bad hurt with you along."

He turned around, just in time to hear Alex's reply.

"You forget the prayer you asked for when we started out?"

Cruz, startled, stared at him.

The rest of the squad shot looks at one another.

"Gene," Jim said, "you have one of thanks for us?"

He sighed, resigned to following through, and bowed his head. "Dear Lord, thank You for protecting us. Thank You for the justice done this day. Amen."

"Amen," they chorused, and grinned. "Hoo-Ya!"

Gene just shook his head.

Johnny was waiting when the Wolves landed at Seafloat, and congratulated Jim, the first one off, then shook hands with the rest of the squad as they debarked. "Well done," he repeated, "well done."

"Debrief in an hour," Jim said on the way to their hootch. "Get some chow, change, and I'll see you at the briefing room."

"You sure?" Doc questioned. "We can relax now and party? No more going out?"

"You got it, Doc. It's party time."

They yelled as one. "Hoo-Ya!"

Doc wasn't satisfied. "You wouldn't bullshit me, would you, sir?"

"No, Doc. Not you, buddy. You can pack tonight and sit on the helo pads for the next four and a half days if you want." Jim grinned. "We're done. We're going home."

Johnny started to walk away.

"Just a minute," Jim called. "Let's debrief now."

"What about chow?" Roland asked.

"Don't worry," Jim said. "Everyone in the hootch. You-O, get beers." He grinned. "Put them on Johnny's tab. He's buying."

Gene felt the urge of habit, wanted to get the 60 cleaned, have her ready. Just in case. But he waited while Cruz passed out beer. A six-pack each. Around him, tabs started to pop.

"Just a minute, guys," Jim said. "The debrief first."

They gathered around him.

"Was it dark out there?"

"Yeah," they answered.

"Was there mud?"

"Yeah."

Looking at them, Gene could tell by their expressions that they, like him, were wondering what the hell Jim was doing.

"Did you see any enemy forces?"

Then it dawned on him. Who the hell cared about this last debrief? Jim was just going through the steps.

"Well," he asked again, "did you see any enemy forces?"

Jim held his can of beer up. The squad did the same.

"Did Gene beat the shit out of Nguyen?"

"Hoo-Ya!" they yelled, and chugged their beers.

"Well," Jim said, "I guess we're done, then. Anybody want to drink with me?"

Gene carried his beer to his rack. There was a letter on his pillow. He picked it up, turned it over. Sealed, but no address. Just "Gene Michaels" written on the front. He shoved it in his back pocket and headed for the door.

"Gene," Jim called, "aren't you going to party?"

"Got something to do," he answered. "Won't take long." He went over to the helo pads. Tommy's squad was getting ready to go out.

He'd wanted a few moments alone, but with all the activity, he decided to wait until dark. He went back to the hootch. Just inside the door, Johnny stopped him.

"Here," he said, handing back the unopened letter to Karen. "Can't tell you how glad I am I won't have to send this."

"No gladder than I am," Gene answered, stuffing the letter in the back pocket of his jeans with the other one. "But thanks a lot."

"And this just came in for you." Johnny smiled and handed over a folded sheet of paper.

Gene opened it. The first word he saw was in big, bold letters: *Congratulations!* The next words stunned him. *You are the proud father of a baby girl. 6 pounds, 3 ounces. Born 0337 September 20, 1970. Both your wife and daughter are doing well.*

"Hoo-Ya!" he yelled at the top of his voice.

The squad went heads-up.

"What the hell?" said Cruz.

Gene felt like his grin would split his cheeks, but he couldn't stop it. "A daddy! Karen! Baby girl! A daddy!" He was so overwhelmed that he couldn't get a complete sentence out. "Hoo-Ya!"

"Hoo-Ya, Gene!" they yelled back.

He turned to Johnny. "Thank you! Thank you so very much."

"You're very damned welcome," Johnny said, laughing. "See ya." He waved and headed back to the NILO office.

"Let's go swimming," Roland yelled, and the SEALs started stripping.

In minutes, Gene was the only one of the squad left on Seafloat. He jumped on the sandbags, then vaulted on the roof. From ten feet above the water, he yelled, "Hoo-Ya!" leapt outward and up, executing a one-and-a-half forward flip. Lordy, the water felt good.

All around him the river was alive with laughter, grab-assing, dunking, and splashing of the squad. Above them, onlookers from Seafloat's crew were stopping to watch before going about their work.

Lot of jealousy and resentment up there, Gene thought. Everybody not in SEAL Team worked regular hours, either on Seafloat or ashore, building the Solid Anchor airstrip. They put in lots of eighteen-hour days. Yet they seldom saw the SEALs work. When they were on Seafloat, the SEALs drank and played endless card games or slept—and some went out at night.

He dove, a long, smooth glide underwater, and came up just in time to see the helos take off with Tommy's squad aboard. He floated, watching. Flying low and building speed, they passed just overhead, and he saw Tommy sitting in the doorway, yelling down, "Hoo-Ya!"

God bless and be with you, he thought, then realized He had, just as a hand hit the top of his head. Before he could respond, Cruz shoved him underwater.

When boats started coming in to dock a while later, the squad had to put an end to the swim. Climbing back aboard Seafloat, Gene realized the impromptu river antics had been one of the best experiences he'd had in a long, long time. They'd had a real blast. The war had aged their faces, but inside, the boys were still alive. He toweled dry, glowing, then settled down atop his rack to write Karen.

> *Congratulations, sweetheart! It's hard to believe that I'm a daddy. Does she look like you? Does she have hair? What color are her eyes? I can't wait to see her for the first time.*
>
> *How are you feeling? I wish I could have been there to help you through it all. I was hoping I'd make it back in time, but I guess she couldn't wait. I love you both so very much. I'll be home in less than a week, and we'll be a family again.*
>
> *This has been one of the greatest days of my life. Not only did I find out that I'm a daddy, I also realized that after six months of fighting, we've made a difference here. No matter what the news media says or the protesters say on the street, this is a just war. It's not a political war for us, it's a war to preserve life. I know I've never told you what we do, or anything about my operations, but today we captured a very cruel, ruthless person. Because we did, I know that at least for today, there are old men, women, and children who will be able to sleep in peace tonight. The cruel person will be replaced in a few days, but until then, maybe, just maybe, the villagers can smile again. I'm proud this day.*
>
> *War changes people, my love, on both sides. I have changed as well. Some things for the better, some not. To save a life is so gratifying. Especially if it's a child's. I can't explain it now, in this letter. Maybe when I get home.*
>
> *Take care, my love. Hugs and kisses to you both. God bless and take care of you. Love, Daddy.*

"Chow's on, guys. How about a break?" he said when the letter was in the mailbag.

Jim threw in his cards and ended the game. "Sounds good."

Over two dozen people were in line when they reached the chow hall, and something smelled mighty good.

You-O, in front, passed the word back. "Hamburgers and pizza."

The squad was the last to leave the tables. By then, Gene had gone back for seconds and then thirds. He was so full, he thought his stomach would burst, but he'd enjoyed every bite.

Back at the hootch, the movie crew was hanging the bed-sheet screen. In an hour, dark would fall.

"Let's get back to the card game," Doc said.

Gene stopped inside the door. "Count me out for a little while."

They went off, and he climbed up to sit on his rack and gather the unopened letters from home to read. Good to be back, he thought, reading through the stack. Things sound good at home. Karen's doctor was satisfied her pregnancy was going well, she'd painted a crib for the baby, their name had risen nearly to the top on the waiting list for Navy housing, the other church members prayed for him too . . . He wanted to go home so bad he ached.

He came, finally, to the envelope bearing only his name. Opening it, not knowing who'd sent it, he felt a little strange, a little nervous. He unfolded the single page and read.

To my brother: I'm writing this for Willie too. You meant a lot to him. You meant a lot to all of us. We may have kidded you about your Bible and praying, but you showed us there was Someone looking over us. I know you're in pain and I know if Willie could be with me to write this, these would have been his words too:

Hung my head over, hung my head low
Saw my God waiting, waiting for me.
He entered my life once but I went astray
Then asked for forgiveness and came back his way.

P.S. I hope this eases your pain, my brother.

Gene read the signature, Eagle, through a blur of tears. He'd left him a poem, after all. Hadn't forgotten. He read it again. Willie in heaven—the Eagle remembered, cared—believed. But he . . .

Outside, night had fallen. The guys were still playing cards, the movie was on. Gene dropped to the floor from his top bunk and headed once more for the helo pad, needing to be alone. The sky was full of stars, the tide going out to sea. And, finally, he was surrounded by silence.

Jim was right. It was over and somehow he felt at peace about Willie. There was nothing more he could do except remember him with love. Reaching into his pocket, he pulled out the cross. He looked at it lying in his palm for a long time, then raised it to his lips and kissed it.

"Good-bye, my friend," he whispered. "Rest in peace."

He saw its shine for a second, in the moonlight, before it disappeared into the river, into the outgoing tide.

Lifting his head, he drew in a breath, smelling the fresh coolness of the night air, the green of the jungle. A couple more days and he'd be going home, back to Karen and life and laughter, and it truly would be over. He laughed suddenly, filled with anticipation, before jumping off the pad and heading back to the hootch to join the rest of the squad in celebration.

Walking into a burst of laughter, he asked, "Guys, got a seat open?"

"Sure do," Doc said. "You've got all the money." He giggled.

Man, he thought, Doc is wasted. He looked around. And so was Jim. Brian, Alex, and Roland were feeling no pain but still going strong. You-O was out like a light, lying on the floor still holding an open can of beer. Gene laughed again. He loved these guys, and they were all going home. They'd survived. He sat down and put in his ante.

Before the first hand was over, Jim lurched to his feet.

"Excuse me," he said, clapped his hand over his mouth, and ran outside.

Holding his cards in the surprised silence of Jim's quick exit, he heard a noise that sounded like somebody blurting "ralph," and then another and another.

At the table, they started to laugh, and were interrupted by yet another "ralph!" Then came silence. They waited, grinning.

The door swung open. Jim came in, wiping his mouth. "Move over," he said, "and give me a beer."

An hour later, he passed out, facedown on the table, sending poker chips everywhere.

"That's it," said Doc. "Let's call it a night."

While Doc and Roland flopped Jim in his sack, he and Brian did the same with You-O. Alex, too far gone to help, just watched, then staggered to his own bunk.

When morning came, Gene woke well rested. For the first time since Willie's death, he'd slept like a baby. No tossing, no night sweats. He felt so good, he woke the rest up for chow and as they dressed, told them the practical joke he had planned. Up and feeling good, they caused a ruckus.

"Shut up out there," came Jim's voice from behind the plywood partition, just before he appeared around the corner, holding his head and moaning. "What time is it?"

"Chow time and hot coffee," they chorused on their way out the door.

Gene knew Jim wouldn't give a damn about eating, but the thought of hot black coffee would bring him to the chow hall.

By the time the squad had their plates filled and got seated, Jim walked in.

Looks like hell, Gene thought. Sick and hung over. He watched as Jim got a cup of coffee. Holding it in both hands, sipping it slowly, he walked over to the table and took a seat.

"Good morning, sir!" Doc yelled.

"Not so loud, you asshole. My head is going to explode."

Gene stood. "Guys?"

The rest of the squad reached under the table, pulled cans of beer from between their feet, and lifted them to eye level. As one, they pulled the tabs. There came the sounds of popping followed by the smell of beer.

Jim paled, started to say, "You assho—," slapped a hand over his mouth, and ran out the door.

"Hold it!" Brian said. "Shut up a minute."

They quieted.

"Ralph!" they heard. Then, "Oh, shit! Ralph! Ralph!" and they howled, holding their sides, laughing until tears came.

They'd started to calm down when Jim walked past the open

door and yelled in, "Assholes!" and they burst into laughter again.

Once chow was finished, they strolled back to the hootch to begin packing. Two and a half days left on Seafloat before they'd fly out to Binh Thuy, then on to Saigon for two days and finally home to the U.S.

As Gene went through his gear, getting it ready to pack, he realized he was hearing a lot of air traffic overhead. He looked up from his footlocker to see the rest of the squad listening as well. Without a word, they left the hootch to see what was happening.

The Army was flying in, by helicopter, 105mm cannons, placing them on the south bank. As the squad watched, Johnny and Tommy joined them.

"When did you get back?" Gene asked.

"Around four this morning," Tommy said.

"Good op?"

"Not this time. We set up an ambush, but the intel wasn't good enough. Nobody crossed."

"Hey, Johnny," Cruz said, "what's going on with the 105s?"

"Bringing in a South Vietnamese artillery company to help protect Solid Anchor," Johnny answered.

He was turning his class ring round and round on his finger, Gene noticed with a growing feeling of dread.

"We're getting reports of enemy buildup, and threats to hit the airstrip five days from now," Johnny added.

That's three days after we leave, Gene thought. Hope we're gone and they don't hit the strip early.

It was almost dusk before the helicopters had finished bringing in twenty-five 105s and the company of South Vietnamese, who set up camp around the artillery.

At evening chow, Jim had recovered enough to join the squad. Relaxed, sitting around a table full of emptied plates, they were content.

"What's the movie tonight?" Gene asked.

"*True Grit*," Jim said.

"Sounds good to me." He glanced around at the rest. "Let's get set up and watch the show, then after, how about a card game?"

"Yeah," Brian said.

Agreed, they all left to get ready.

Beer and insect repellent . . . all they needed for movie night,

Gene thought as they stood just inside the hootch doorway, shooting the breeze, waiting for the film to begin. But he stiffened when Johnny walked in, and he saw the look on his face.

"Where's Jim?" he asked.

"Inside," Gene said, pointing into the hootch toward the plywood partition. Can't be, he thought. Just can't.

Johnny went in, and Gene could hear the murmur of their voices, but not individual words.

"Movie in ten minutes," somebody called outside.

As they started out the door, Johnny and Jim came out from behind the partition.

"Wait a minute, guys," Jim said. "Johnny needs some help."

CHAPTER TWENTY-SIX

THE ENTIRE SQUAD FROZE in place, staring at the two officers.

"He needs three volunteers to go out tomorrow," Jim finished.

Amid the instantaneous moans and groans, Doc spoke up.

"No fuckin' way! I'm packed and ready to go home. I'm not about to unpack."

"Doc," Jim interjected, "you're safe. No corpsman needed this time."

Gene took a deep, resigned breath. "Who's going?"

Johnny answered. "Tommy, and Tommy's OIC-John. We need three others."

"It's a simple op," Jim said. "Just fly in and pick up an old man or woman to bring back for interrogation."

"We have eight hundred South Vietnamese Marines we're going to send in, to confront the large troop buildup before they hit Solid Anchor," said Johnny. "We'll pound them first with the 105s. Before that, you'd just fly in and fly out. There will be other teams in the same area, doing the same thing. We want to locate their stronghold before we hit them with the 105s, then send in the South Vietnamese Marines to kick ass."

There was silence while they thought about it.

Gene studied the floor. Jim thought it would be a KISS. Didn't always turn out that way, though, and he had a baby daughter now. Hadn't even seen her yet, or held her. If he went, he might never. But, God, if the op worked according to plan, lots of people that would be dying would live instead—including the Seabees at Solid Anchor.

"What the hell," Gene said finally, "I'll go, Johnny."

"So will I," Brian said.

"Okay. Can I lead the op? Act as patrol leader?" Cruz looked at the two, waiting for an answer.

They looked at each other. Jim spoke first. "Okay by us."

"No problem," Gene agreed, and Brian nodded.

"I'll go check with Tommy and John," Jim said. "If they agree, you're PL."

Five minutes later, he was back. "They agreed."

Cruz called for a Warning Order at 0400 hours, Johnny thanked them, and they headed out to watch the movie.

Afterward, Gene, Brian, and Cruz spent some time getting weapons and equipment ready. One more time, tomorrow, Gene thought, hanging the 60 back in its sling, and we'll have one and a half days left until we leave. He climbed into his bunk.

Cruz had a hard time waking him.

"Gene . . . hey, Gene . . . it's time."

He sat up, fighting his way to consciousness, rubbing his eyes.

Cruz went off to wake Brian as Gene dropped to the floor and reached for his jeans.

When Brian was dressed, they walked together to the briefing room and entered to find it full of people.

Six five-man teams listened as Johnny went over the op.

"Just get in, grab a warm body, and get out," he said. "No contact. Get in and get out."

Then he released the six squads to their patrol leaders.

Cruz took over Gene's group and went over the op in detail. "Brian, point man. Myself, PL. Tommy, radioman. Gene, assistant patrol leader. Lieutenant John, rear security." He took a breath. "Everyone, take your basic equipment load."

Gene concentrated as Cruz went over the map, showing them the location into which they'd be going.

"It's a small fishing village," he said, "with three or four hootches. The other five teams will be within a thousand meters, so be careful if we have to open up."

And they'd better damned well be careful too, thought Gene. Real careful.

"Four teams will be leaving within the hour, by boats or sampan," Cruz said. "We'll be inserted by helo at pre-dawn, and so will Group Six. Flying time to the objective is one and a half minutes."

Another slide down the line through midair. Gene shifted in the chair, hoping there wouldn't be a reception committee waiting to grease them in the village below.

Cruz went on, covering every detail, even though the op was to be a hit-and-run. "We'll only be on the ground for a few minutes," he said. "Grab the first villager you see, and split. Be ready at 0515 on the helo pads."

Back at the hootch, Gene belted on the eight hundred rounds that he'd already linked together. Then, impulsively, he decided to take an additional seven hundred rounds. Since they wouldn't be patrolling in, the extra weight wouldn't matter. When they flew out of the village, he could open up, and fire the 60 for the last time. The extra rounds added a good six to eight inches around his body.

Boy, he thought, the belts were really heavy. But that was okay. Back on board, after the op, he could burn the ammo up, just for fun. He'd never been able to do that before.

Cruz walked in. "Let's do it," he said, and then did a doubletake. "Christ! You got a war going we don't know about?"

Gene explained what he had in mind.

"Well, hell," Cruz said. "Why not?"

The five of them walked together to the waiting Sea Wolves.

"Don't you wish all our ops had been this easy?" Brian commented, climbing aboard.

"We ain't back yet," Tommy growled.

The sun was almost due to rise when the chopper lifted off for the one-and-a-half-minute flight.

Above the noise of the rotor blades, Cruz yelled, "Okay, guys, get in, get out. Take no chances."

The helo descended. They jumped out, slid down the line, and landed in the middle of a small rice paddy. Three hootches sat about sixty meters away. Dropping into file formation, they had started to move quickly toward them when, about thirty meters in front, a woman stepped out from a clump of brush.

She carried a small baby, Gene saw, wrapped in a blanket. He stared intently. The baby, he thought. Something's wrong with the baby.

The woman called out, motioning them to come.

Gene froze. Something was wrong with the whole damned thing. Shit! Women always hid or ran when they came in. Always. She was calling them to her! Then it hit him—the baby's forehead was shiny and white! It was a doll!

He scanned the area—fast. Movement. Bushes to the left.

"Ambush left!" he yelled, and opened the 60 up.

In an instant the entire squad came on line, firing. Bodies jerked erect, and some fell, dead or wounded, out of the brush. The squad faced the rest, hit them hard, and firing nonstop, moved toward the enemy position.

"Kill the woman," Cruz yelled. They spun. She had disappeared—baby and all.

There was a yell from Brian. "Ambush, right!"

Gene and Cruz spun and fired right, driving the enemy from concealment.

"Tommy!" Cruz yelled. "Get the Wolves in here. John, stay with Tommy!"

From the rice paddy, Tommy yelled back, "Reports coming in! Teams Two, Four, and Six getting hit!"

The 60 sang, and with Brian and Cruz firing beside him, they drove more enemy forces out of ambush and into the open. Even as they blew them away, Gene realized they were surrounded. The squad had dropped dead into the center of an enemy camp.

"Team One's been hit," Tommy yelled. "Enemy pulling back, contact broken. Enemy's coming our way!"

It was like a turkey shoot. There were enemy targets everywhere he looked. "Cruz," he yelled, "look out!" About six feet ahead of him, Cruz was firing left, and couldn't see the machine-gun post turning on him. Gene opened up.

Cruz turned, saw, and turned back to see the 60's tracers pass just a foot from his body. Two enemy soldiers fell, taking some of the bushes down with them, and exposing their .51-caliber machine gun.

As the three of them forced the NVA back, Tommy and John relayed radio messages. "Got to get out," Tommy yelled. "The NVA are all coming into this location. We've got combat to our rears!"

"Have the Wolves keep their heads down!" Cruz yelled back, and Gene knew the Wolves couldn't use their rockets for fear of hitting one of the other teams. They were making fake runs to keep the enemy busy.

The 60 blazed. He, Brian, and Cruz had to keep the enemy backed up—keep the area clear so the Wolves could land to pick them up. They'd shoot one NVA, and as he fell, the others would jump up and try to run away, only to be hit themselves.

They had to get out. The NVA was swarming the area.

"Pick up what you can on the way back," Cruz shouted. "Tommy, call the Wolves in!"

Bodies lay everywhere, bleeding among weapons, ammo cans, bushes . . .

They grabbed three ammo boxes from one hootch—they couldn't be ammo, Gene thought; they were too light—and ran for the drop zone. Around them, gunsmoke whirled and rice flattened in the wind as the Wolves set down.

"Gene," Cruz yelled, "get ready. "You're first!"

It was SOP for the 60 to be first on. Gene took in the situation. Tommy, John, Brian, and Cruz were turned toward the left rear of the Wolf.

"Come on," Tommy yelled, "they're coming through the bushes!"

Half on, he discovered he couldn't get a clear shot, with the 60, without hitting the helo's tail blade.

Jumping off, he ran the fifteen meters to where Brian and Cruz stood fast, returning enemy fire. Rounds were striking and erupting the paddy water all around them. Gene let the 60 sing.

Never letting up on the trigger, he yelled, "Get out of here! Get on the chopper. I'll cover you. Dammit, get!" And when they didn't instantly leave, he screamed, "Go, dammit! I'll keep their heads down."

The 60's barrel glowed red. Rifling in the barrel was burning out. He ran backward, firing, hearing voices yelling, "Let's go! Let's go!"

Gene was five meters from the door. The enemy was trying to maneuver. He stopped, reloaded, and opened up again.

Brian and Cruz were aboard, and the pilot was yelling, "We're hit!"

"Take off," Gene yelled back. This was it. He wouldn't be going home. "They're coming in! Take off! I'll hold them down!" The 60 roared. "Go! Go!" he screamed, and the Wolf lifted behind him.

With the Wolf eight feet above the ground, the 60 blazing, melting in his hands, Gene leapt, hooked his left arm over a skid, clutched the front of his cami shirt in a death grip, and the helo took off. Hanging under the helo, he fired down at the enemy, who were trying to run underneath and bring the Wolf to ground.

Above him, Brian was on his belly in the doorway, reaching down and trying to grab him, but he couldn't reach far enough.

"Can't get enough speed to clear the trees," the pilot yelled. "Hold on!"

Gene held. Arm hooked over the skid, cami shirt clenched in one fist, the 60 in the other, he held on.

The helo climbed almost straight up, trying to clear the triple canopy. Gene was terrified. They weren't going to make it. Dangling from the skid below, he was going to be ripped off against the trees.

For a moment, the helo seemed to stall. Then it spun 180 degrees around, and they were heading down, and back over the enemy position. Gene managed to throw one leg over the skid just as they skimmed again over the NVA. The enemy fired up, and Gene, hanging on below, fired back.

By the time they'd crossed the enemy zone, the chopper had picked up enough speed to clear the tree line.

Above him, Cruz lay flat beside Brian, who reached down and took the 60 from Gene. The white-hot barrel sizzled against his arm and fried the skin, even as he threw it back and away.

Cruz grabbed Gene's shirt, then Brian took hold. Together, they pulled Gene inside.

Brian had a burn that was four inches long and two wide, starting at his wrist. He whipped off his headband and wrapped it around the wound.

Gasping for breath, Gene asked, "Are you okay, Brian?"

"Yeah. How about you?"

He nodded. "I'm okay."

"Look at that!" Cruz yelled.

Gene looked. Off to the side, just above the trees, he saw Seafloat's American flag, flying straight out and full. Tears flooded his eyes, and he blinked rapidly, then wiped them away as best he could, filled with thankfulness at the sudden, beautiful sight of it.

They'd been scared to death. The op that was to have been so easy had turned out the most dangerous ever. They should have died in that rice paddy. They almost had.

The helo made its approach and landed on Seafloat.

When they got off, both Seafloat's doctor and Doc were there waiting. So were people with stretchers, and people waiting to take care of them. The op had been aired over Seafloat's PA system, and everybody on it had heard the pitched battle.

When they saw the squad was not only all safe but nobody even wounded, the crowd began to applaud, and as the squad made its way through them, the applause grew louder. People patted them on the back as they passed, and Gene heard a man say, as he stepped clear, "Those are some bad motherfuckers."

They stopped at NILO with the strangely lightweight ammo cans.

"Here, Johnny," Gene said. "Some documents."

Standing beside Johnny, Jim asked, "Are you all okay? Anyone hurt?"

"Brian got burned on the 60's barrel. Doc's got him." Gene said, "And Jim, we need a drink. A stiff drink."

At the hootch, Cruz broke out a bottle of Jack Daniel's. They passed it around, each taking a big swig.

"Jim," Gene asked, "how about the other teams?"

"They're all coming back in. No one hit."

They stared at him.

"Well," Gene said, "we found them."

Doc scratched at his mustache. "No shit, you found them. Listening to you guys over the PA scared the hell out of me." He jumped up and started walking around. "All I could see was you guys all shot up. And everybody was waiting, if not to help, to see the blood. Nobody thought you'd come back in one piece." He walked around faster. "You could hear the gunfight as the radio messages came in. You ever scare me like that again, and I'll shoot you!" Hands on hips, he glared at them, eyes glittering with tears.

"No sweat," Brian said, his voice soft. "We had the charm with us. Gene's still got the luck."

The metal bed frame was cool in his palm. He looked down at his feet. Canvas jungle boots against a steel floor. Was it luck? Or was it really Him? What, for Christ's sake, had kept them alive out there? Alive with rounds coming in from all sides. He reached for the bottle.

They finished it, and still shaky, started on six-packs of beer.

All the ammo he'd wrapped around his body was gone. He counted the remaining rounds left on the 60's belt. Forty-seven. He'd used 1,453 rounds that day—and it hadn't been for fun. He sucked in his breath, then let it out slowly.

After a while, they went outside and cleaned their gear, then stowed it in their footlockers, ready to fly home. After several hours, the 60 was cool again. Taking it apart, he'd seen the barrel was shot, as was the operating rod, the spring, and the firing pin. Looking at the pieces, he wondered if it would have fired even one more round.

There was a bullet hole in the forward hand grip. He touched it, ran his fingers over it. How it had gone through without hitting his arm, he would never understand.

The squad walked to chow together, their fear numbed by booze.

He looked up as Tommy came over.

Standing tall, Tommy turned to Cruz. "You did a great job out there as PL, kid." He shook his hand before looking down at Gene and holding his hand out again. "If you hadn't jumped back out with your 60, I don't think we'd have gotten off the ground. You kept them down long enough to get out." He paused, then added, "The chopper took a hundred and thirty-one rounds. It's a miracle we're here."

He shook Brian's hand. "You three did some ass-kicking. John and I only got one magazine each off, into the first ambush site." He walked away, leaving them looking after him.

To have Tommy, a legend in the teams, compliment them, was a real honor. There was a moment's silence before they grinned at one another.

"Well, guys," Johnny said as he and Jim sat down at the table, "want to know the outcome of today's little op?"

Gene shot him a dark look. "I'd rather forget it, but okay. Let's hear."

"The ammo cans you brought back had more documents and maps than have ever before been captured. You found what we were after." Johnny smiled.

Gene stared at him. "Excuse me, sir, but the next time you have a simple op, keep your mouth shut, sir. There is no such thing as a simple op."

Johnny nodded. "You've got it."

"Total op time," Jim said, "was ten minutes. Three minutes air time, one and a half minutes each way. Seven minutes on the ground."

"Ten minutes," Brian repeated, wonder in his voice. "Ten minutes . . ."

"Yes," Johnny said. "You landed in the middle—the very center—of the 89th Artillery Company from the T-10 NVA Battalion. Today's the first time they've ever lost in combat. During your seven-minute visit, you killed twenty-two and wounded forty-seven. With more intel coming in, those figures could climb."

Their "Hoo-Ya!" deafened the room.

"So," Cruz asked, "it was a success?"

"Oh, yes." Johnny grinned. "Very much so. Again, thanks a lot. You guys did a great job."

Back at the hootch, after chow, things were quiet. Doc, Alex, Roland, and Jim wanted to party. Brian, Cruz, and Gene were still shaken. They'd never come so close to dying.

"Never," Brian said. "Never. Not even on the Mighty Mo."

Gene left the hootch. He wanted to go over to the KCS camp and see Truk before leaving Seafloat. He respected Truk more than any other Vietnamese he'd met or fought beside, and this would be his only chance to say good-bye.

He got a Whaler and headed for shore, thinking of all the firefights Truk had survived during the six months Gene's platoon had been on Seafloat. He wondered just how many more Truk had experienced through all his years. Not only was he a courageous man, Truk was also a loyal, truthful man who loved life. He was dedicated to his wife, Chou Li, and was a compassionate father to his children.

Gene landed, walked into the KCS camp, and a half dozen children ran up yelling, "Michaels, Michaels!" They wrapped their arms around his legs.

"Where's Truk?" he asked.

"With Momma-san," the oldest answered.

Gene went to the hootch doorway and yelled, "Truk! Truk, you old fart. Get out here."

Truk limped out of the door, still pulling his pants up.

Gene laughed. "Sorry if I got you at a bad time, my old friend."

Truk smiled. "No problem. Chou Li heard your voice. She say to take my time. She wait for my return."

"Glad you're still going strong. Be careful, wise one. You'll have another baby soon."

"I hope so, my friend. Children are most sacred to us. Through our children, we live forever."

"I know," Gene said. "Did you hear I'm a Papa-san now?"

Truk nodded. "Yes. I happy for you. You make good for your child. You good man. Now, you too will live forever. You have many baby-san. They will carry on all you do."

"I'm leaving tomorrow."

"Yes. My heart is sad. You know our people." Truk nodded to himself. "I also happy for you. You brave man. Much fighting for our people. You kill boo-koo Viet Cong, many Communist. Yet your heart sorrows, and you cry for our losses. I will miss you, Gene Michaels."

"And I, you, Chief. I hope the war ends soon, my friend, for all of us. The children are the ones who are losing. I'll be glad to hear them laugh freely again."

Truk patted one of his sons. "They will miss you."

"Truk . . ." Gene made his decision. "Truk, when I first came over, I planned on making only one tour here. I'm no longer planning that. I have about eighteen months left to serve. I want to return. I just don't know how to tell Karen—my wife—or if she'll understand. Your freedom is worth fighting for."

Truk hitched up his pants. "I will wait for you. Now you say good-bye to Chou Li."

Gene could not refuse. He had been their dinner guest many a night. He followed Truk inside.

Chou Li was standing, a sheet wrapped around her waist. She wrapped her arms around Gene's waist, her eyes filled with tears, and squeezed tight.

He hugged her, kissed her on the forehead, then turned to Truk. "You keep your ass down while I'm gone. Leave the fighting to the young men, and keep your village together."

Outside, as he walked to the Whaler, Truk's children ran beside him, asking to be swung around. He hugged each one, then pushed the Whaler off the bank to head back. "Sleep peaceful tonight," he called to them, "and dream of magical things. For tonight, you're safe."

He went to bed early, thinking that when he woke up, he'd have only one more night on Seafloat. The ops were truly over. He closed his eyes, hoping to dream of green fields, wild flowers, family picnics under big oak trees, and children singing.

In the morning, he woke from a nightmare—sappers floating down the Son Ku Lon, Seafloat going up high-order in explosions and flames, the squad dead, blood everywhere, and he longed to begin the trip back to The World.

The last day flew by. Everything seemed to pick up speed. Jim pulled him aside in the late afternoon.

"Congratulations," he said, and shook his hand.

"What for?"

"You were put in, and have been accepted, for Combat Military Advisory status. When we get home, you'll go through SEAL Advanced Training for SEAL Military Advisors."

Gene was speechless. People needed four to six tours before they could get into SAT. It was the elite of the elite. "You're kidding!"

"Nope," Jim said, shaking his head. "And I'll be going through it with you. Now, let's go get something to eat."

After evening chow, the squad went to the movie. *True Grit* again. When it ended, they played a last game of poker and hit their racks at two in the morning. The choppers were due in at 0600 to fly them out.

It was 0530 hours when Johnny woke them. "Everybody up. Time to hit it, guys. Your birds are waiting."

Without a word, they rose, dressed, and carried their footlockers to the helo pads. An Army chopper would carry the lockers. Sea Wolves would carry the SEALs.

They were warming up their engines when the time came to say good-bye to Johnny. "I'll take you out for dinner forty-five days from now, when you get home," Gene promised. He turned then to Tommy, standing a little apart.

"What can I say? You taught me well. It was an honor to have been at your side in combat." He studied Tommy's face a moment. His seventh tour . . . "Take care, my friend, my teacher. God be with you." He took a step back, stood tall, and saluted.

Without a word, Tommy came to attention and snapped one back in return.

The salute told Gene, the way no words could, that Tommy was proud of him. Prouder than even a father could be, because Tommy knew what they'd each endured.

He turned and ran to the waiting helicopter. Jim was right behind him.

"Got everyone?" he asked.

"Head count," Doc yelled.

Each man sounded off.

"Let's go," Jim called to the pilots, and gave a thumbs-up signal.

The Wolves lifted off and circled for the last time. They were headed north, first to Binh Thuy, then Saigon, then The World.

Five thousand feet below, Vietnam, with its bloody miles of death hidden, was beautiful with the thousands of rivers, the rice paddies, the jungle. There were rainstorms off in the distance.

Sitting in the doorway, legs dangling, the jungle rolled away behind him, and Gene watched Seafloat disappear. The last thing he could see was the American flag flying above the triple-canopy jungle.

Three weeks after returning to the United States, Gene Michaels, in a full dress uniform, was ceremoniously awarded the Bronze Star and the Silver Star medals, and two Vietnamese Crosses of Gallantry, to become one of the nation's highest decorated SEALs. Five months later, he began his second tour in Vietnam.